Buyers Beware

Critical Caribbean Studies

Series Editors: Yolanda Martínez-San Miguel,
Carter Mathes, and Kathleen López

Focused particularly in the twentieth and twenty-first centuries, although attentive to the context of earlier eras, this series encourages interdisciplinary approaches and methods and is open to scholarship in a variety of areas, including anthropology, cultural studies, diaspora and transnational studies, environmental studies, gender and sexuality studies, history, and sociology. The series pays particular attention to the four main research clusters of Critical Caribbean Studies at Rutgers University, where the coeditors serve as members of the executive board: Caribbean Critical Studies Theory and the Disciplines; Archipelagic Studies and Creolization; Caribbean Aesthetics, Poetics, and Politics; and Caribbean Colonialities.

For a list of all the titles in the series, please see the last page of the book.

Buyers Beware

Insurgency and Consumption in Caribbean Popular Culture

PATRICIA JOAN SAUNDERS

Rutgers University Press
New Brunswick, Camden, and Newark, New Jersey, and London

Library of Congress Cataloging-in-Publication Data

Names: Saunders, Patricia Joan, 1968– author.
Title: Buyers beware: insurgency and consumption in Caribbean popular culture / Patricia Joan Saunders.
Description: New Brunswick, New Jersey: Rutgers University Press, [2022] | Series: Critical Caribbean studies | Includes bibliographical references and index.
Identifiers: LCCN 2021038289 | ISBN 9780813571225 (paperback) | ISBN 9780813571232 (hardcover) | ISBN 9780813571249 (pdf) | ISBN 9781978805927 (mobi) | ISBN 9780813572864 (epub)
Subjects: LCSH: Consumption (Economics)—Social aspects—Caribbean Area. | Consumers—Caribbean Area. | Popular culture—Caribbean Area. | Caribbean Area—Civilization.
Classification: LCC HC151.Z9 C6263 2022 | DDC 339.4/7—dc23
LC record available at https://lccn.loc.gov/2021038289

A British Cataloging-in-Publication record for this book is available from the British Library.

The poems "Brief Lives" and "Meditations on Yellow" by Olive Senior, from *Gardening in the Tropics* (Toronto: McClelland & Stewart, 1994), are used with permission of the author.

∞ The paper used in this publication meets the requirements of the American National Standard for Information Sciences—Permanence of Paper for Printed Library Materials, ANSI Z39.48-1992.

www.rutgersuniversitypress.org

Manufactured in the United States of America

For my mother, Shirley Blackman

For her sisters, Marva Benjamin, Beulah LaCroix, Cynthia Jones, and Rose Blackman

For their mother, Linda Inez Blackman

And, for their great-grand-daughter and granddaughter, Imani Hope Inez Saunders

Contents

	Introduction: Between the Devil and the Deep Blue Sea—Situating Caribbean Pop Culture Globally	1
1	Is Not Everything Good to Eat, Good to Talk: Sexual Economy and Dancehall Music in the Global Marketplace	23
2	Buyers Beware, Hoodwinking on the Rise: Epistemologies of Consumption in "Sistah Lit"	47
3	"Who's on Top?": Power, Pleasure, and the Politics of Taste	70
4	"Fashion ova Style": The Art of Self-Fashioning in Jamaican Pop Culture	93
5	"Outta Order" or "Outta Door?": Caribbean Women Performing Power, Politics, and Sexuality	124
6	Gardening in the Garrisons: (Un)Visibility in Contemporary Caribbean Art	144
	Conclusion: "Puuulll Uuuuuuup"	174
	Acknowledgments	189
	Notes	195
	Bibliography	205
	Index	215

Buyers Beware

Introduction

Between the Devil and the Deep Blue Sea—Situating Caribbean Pop Culture Globally

Buyers Beware: Insurgency and Consumption in Caribbean Popular Culture emphasizes the need for caution in the unpredictable terrain of consumer culture in the Caribbean region, particularly at this historical moment. It also critically examines what practices of consumption mean for Caribbean citizens across a range of classed, gendered, racial, cultural, regional, and international spaces. For upper-middle-class Black (and, in Jamaica, brown) Caribbean citizens, consumption often manifests through weekend trips to Miami and New York to shop for designer clothes, wedding gowns, and other luxury goods like handbags, shoes, and luxury experiences. Admission to exclusive clubs, parties, and restaurants not typically frequented by members of the general public has the added attraction of yielding future gains through networking with potential clients and business associates. Being in the right place with the "right" people places a premium value on these exclusive events at home and abroad. Premier cultural events like Fashion Week in New York and Art Basel in Miami provide localized spaces for participants and observers to display their wealth and cultural capital while rubbing shoulders with or, at least getting a glimpse of, the ultrawealthy classes that they aspire to join someday. In these instances, admission to exclusive parties hosted by VIPs or luxury brands elevates the social value of consumers who strategically use social media to solidify their status as emerging consumers among their peers at home and abroad.

Working-class consumers, like the women (known as informal commercial importers or ICIs) who purchase clothing, shoes, and fashion accessories to sell on their return home, see traveling to Miami and New York as a business trip that can improve their circumstances. In other words, the trips in and of themselves have value to the extent that they translate into goods for sale to other working-class and working-poor people. In these communities of (largely) Afro-Caribbean women from Trinidad, Guyana, Jamaica, and Haiti, who move back and forth between Miami, New York, Washington, DC, and Venezuela (before the economic instability that now plagues the country), their consumption is a means to an end, not an end within itself (Ulysse 2008). They travel to different cosmopolitan centers to buy goods in bulk—usually cosmetics, "knockoff" designer shoes and clothes, underwear, hair for weaves, and handbags. Once back home, they sell these items in small stalls in city centers and through mobile operations that cater to office complexes and other businesses whose employees sometimes place orders in advance. Other ICIs sell their purchases to vendors, who then sell their goods on the sidewalks in the busy city centers. These businesswomen cater to eager consumers who may have the means to purchase store-bought items but are intent on saving money to be invested in other, more obvious markers of conspicuous consumption like jewelry, home appliances, digital technology, and cars. For the consumers who patronize these informal commercial workers, cultural experiences are still a critical part of their consumer practices. However, those experiences are of the more local "exclusive" variety and include events such as private fetes held by sports personalities during Carnival, Crop Over, or other holidays, particularly in Trinidad, Jamaica, and Barbados. Money and personal connections are the primary keys to entry to these fetes, which reinforce the perception that participants in these events socialize with "exclusive" communities on a regular basis.

Conversely, the lack of money precludes economically disadvantaged communities from participating in cultural events like Crop Over and Carnival in Trinidad and Tobago. During the 2019 Carnival season, many of the more popular mid-sized and larger band costumes range in price from $3,000TT to $7,100TT (approximately US$500–$1,130). These prices are typically for Carnival Monday and Tuesday costumes but do not include Jouvay band costumes. As a friend from Jamaica who played mas this year commented on Facebook, "It's perfectly possible to play Jouvay and play mas on Monday and Tuesday with $4,000 TT. You just not going to a single fete."[1] His comment highlights the extent to which even the most ardently nationalist rituals and festivals are now customized to provide exclusive experiences for those whose desires and budgets can accommodate their costs. Small independent bands, like Vulgar Fraction, have emerged in response to the aggressive commodification of Trinidad and Tobago Carnival. The Belmont-based group operates out of Granderson Lab, a dynamic creative space developed by a small group of self-described "arts instigators"—Sean Leonard, Chris Cozier, and Nicholas Laughlin, founders of

Alice Yard.[2] Vulgar Fraction's Carnival experience is priced much lower than those of larger bands because it relies on the creative labor of band members and the use of everyday materials that cost less than the beads and feathers typically used in great quantities in Carnival costumes. For those who want the full experience of Carnival replete with top-shelf liquor, access to the well-heeled and well-positioned members of Trinidadian society, and a safe environment within which to enjoy all these perks, the price tag can run between $15,000 TT and $20,000 TT (between US$2,200 and $3,000).

In diasporic Caribbean communities in the North, consumption takes on another equally complex manifestation, particularly in the Carnival traditions of New Orleans where "everyone wants to be seen in acts of conspicuous consumption and expenditures" (Roach 1996, 206). These rituals of consumption are integral to identity formation and can also reveal the underbelly of institutional and structural inequity when money is scarce to nonexistent. To appreciate the power of consumption as a means of articulating social and political identity, one has to take seriously how the most economically dispossessed shape, participate in, and complicate our notions of consumer culture and indeed the "value" of culture in these communities. In both New Orleans and Trinidad and Tobago, the two-day ritual of Carnival is first and foremost about the ephemeral nature of life and the chance to live out and perform selves that participants may otherwise never realize. By Ash Wednesday costumes are discarded or destroyed because they will not be reused for the next Carnival season. To the viewer, this ritual of destruction may appear to be a manifestation of frivolity, a wasteful expenditure for people with so little disposable income. However, the judgment implicit in the language of value speaks to the desire of Carnival performers and participants to escape the quotidian demands of a life shaped by structural inequities. As Joseph Roach notes, the destruction of the costume is necessary for the renewal of the performer, and the debt for this renewal is not exacted in dollars and cents but rather in "sweat blood" (206). The costume itself is the means through which performers can shed the oppressive weight of inequity they endure throughout the year. In this respect, the suits that Mardi Gras Indians wear share a political ideology and metaphysical grounding with several of the traditional costumes in Caribbean Carnival celebrations, such as the dragon, fancy sailors, blue devils, midnight robbers, jab-jabs, and the fancy Indians. Interestingly, these traditional costumes now stand in stark opposition to the commodification of Carnival in the Caribbean region, in large part because they tend to lack the glitter and festivity of most of those worn on Carnival Tuesday. In fact, most of these costumes harken back to Carnival's historical routes/roots in slave societies in the Americas.

This connection to a slave past is arguably one of the reasons these masquerades and costumes have been relegated to the margins of contemporary Carnival celebrations in countries like Trinidad and Tobago. It is not that these costumes are resistant to commodification but rather that this aspect of Carnival and performance does not appeal as widely to the experience being sold to tourists visiting New Orleans and the Caribbean region. Earl Lovelace's novel *The Dragon Can't Dance* ([1979] 1988) succinctly maps the political and social trajectory of the relationships among traditions of resistance in poor Black urban communities that preserve Carnival traditions (stick fighting, dragon dancing, blue devils, steel bands), Trinidadian middle-class citizens, and the government/corporate interests that have now come to define Carnival in the global context. As the desire for less confrontational and contentious masquerades in Carnival grew from the corporate sector, those who "bowed" to these desires were rewarded with sponsorships for their bands. This shift, according to many critics, forecast the decline and near-total marginalization of traditional masquerade and the rise of "pretty mas" in Carnival, which was designed to attract foreign investors and tourists.

As with Carnival, the evolution of cricket in the West Indies has reflected the polarizing nature of debates about cultural traditions and cultural commodification. To a greater degree than other cultural institutions, cricket changed to reflect the emergence of a uniquely West Indian regional identity. However, West Indies cricket did not resemble the mimicry often attributed to formerly colonized subjects in adapting colonial institutions to suit their needs. The West Indies style (refashioning) of the game forced the British themselves to redefine how the game was played and, more importantly, what cricket symbolized. The West Indies team changed the style of bowling to a fast-paced approach, which left players for England with bruised egos and bodies when they were brave enough to stand in the crease to receive the rapid balls. West Indian bowlers were criticized for vulgarizing the art form with their more "aggressive," "undisciplined" style of play; their fast-paced style of bowling left English players bemoaning the loss of the sport's refined nature. In the end, however, in an effort to regain their eminence in the sport, England changed their style of play and indeed their whole approach to the sport because there was no turning back once the West Indies cricket team took hold of and dominated the sport for nearly twenty years. In short, their refashioning of the sport did not reflect the gentlemanly, polite, respectable (Victorian) values that were the standards by which the British measured all who played cricket. The responses by West Indian fans during the test matches also drew criticism because of the carnivalesque atmosphere. British cricket officials perceived that their "high-brow" cultural institution had been significantly diminished by this refashioning by West Indian consumers (i.e., players and fans alike). The struggle between what many in Trinidad consider the scourge of consumerism in Carnival and the traditional masquerade that for hundreds of years had been the country's social conscience was replicated in the sport's evolution, as drastic acts of "self-fashioning" produced a new brand of cricket in the West Indies and eventually globally. The push and pull between these two cultural institutions are symptomatic of contrasting and at times contradictory ideologies that have shaped debates and critical dialogues about the impact of consumer culture on popular culture in the Caribbean in the twentieth century.

Offering a third space for critical inquiries about the practices of consumption in (and of) Caribbean popular culture, this project begins by posing a different set of questions to guide our consideration of the possibilities that free markets have created for new constituencies of consumers. If we envision Caribbean popular culture as a local space engaged in struggles for (and access to) the same goods, services, and experiences as their international counterparts, how might this complicate our readings of consumption in (and of) the Caribbean? This analysis focuses on Jamaica, Haiti, and Trinidad, paying particular attention to how these Caribbean countries figure into and are informed by popular representations from Britain, Canada and the United States; it also examines the different ways the Caribbean is produced internally. Moving beyond earlier analyses of these representations, this book considers the various ways these representations have been consumed, recycled, and revised to benefit Caribbean subjects who do not have the same bargaining power as other consumers around the globe but are invested in the practice nonetheless.

The admonition in the book title is directed at a particular brand of cultural consumption that relies on romantic notions about the item or experience being purchased. It is also intended to evoke a sense of caution and, in some cases, apprehension in local and international consumers about their notions of cultural "authenticity" when purchasing Caribbean cultural items and experiences. Quite naturally, in a global market where knockoffs or counterfeit products now command a large part of consumers' budgets, and vacations to far-flung, war-torn regions of the world are now a form of cultural capital, the desire for authenticity is stronger than ever. These desires undoubtedly create considerable anxiety for producers and consumers alike, while also having a tremendous impact (in positive and negative ways) on local and global markets. The power of counterfeit goods to destabilize the balance of fiscal power in the global marketplace drastically shifts how consumer goods are deployed as a counterbalance to a (real or imagined) "lack" in the Caribbean—lack of resources, access, power, authority, and ultimately control. Yet, this shift in fiscal opportunity is not sufficient to destabilize the power of more traditional constructions of the famed blue waters and white sandy beaches of typical destinations like Negril, Ocho Rios, and Montego Bay—all of which signify loudly in discourses of excess that have historically framed the natural landscapes of the Caribbean. Arguably, constructions of exotic pleasure zones have effectively reinscribed stereotypes of the region as a tropical paradise, on the one hand, and as a place where lawlessness prevails, on the other. Romantic notions about tourist safety are founded on the belief that, in the rare instances that laws exist, they are there to protect the tourists from the "natives." Even the way we have come to understand citizens who reside in the Caribbean is shaped profoundly by the marketing of the region as an exotic paradise. Popular representations often feature residents who function as "extras" in a tourist's fantasy. Although this is certainly an oversimplification of the negotiations that take place between tourists and Caribbean citizens, I analyze performance as one critical mode of engaging the complexities of these exchanges, and it frames much of my work here. I am also interested in the conventions and iconography used to produce "the Caribbean," particularly the wide range of cultural texts that go beyond the typical representations. In fact, in response to the increasing significance placed on "authentic" cultural experiences in travel and tourism, this book considers the extent to which unsanctioned expressions and performances of Caribbeanness now shape how people consume, engage, and experience the region to an even greater degree than tourist brochures once did.

Given these shifts in consumer practices and desires, *Buyers Beware* asks whether we might better understand the Caribbean as a social and political space through practices of consumption at home and abroad. What makes the Caribbean region so desirable yet so anxiety producing? How is the Caribbean deployed as a trope for Blackness that is at once hyper-visualized and simultaneously erased or recognizable only through images that tourists have consumed via media marketing? Iconic male figures like Bob Marley, Sidney Poitier, and Usain Bolt have given way to another generation of iconic pop culture figures, such as Rihanna, Nicki Minaj, and Winston Duke, all of whom have emblazoned the creative talent of the region into the global popular imagination. Socially and politically, the Caribbean region is also the site of contradictory impulses embodied in its tremendous pride in Haiti, as the first free Black nation state in the Western Hemisphere, and its, at times, indifferent attitude toward Haiti's natural and national disasters. This book takes as its critical focus the extra, the excesses that occur away from the glaring lights of tourism brochures, while still demanding the curiosity and attention of visitors and citizens alike. With increased access to online technology, local artists, audiences, and citizens are now capable of interrupting mainstream representations with their own versions and productions of Caribbeanness. Leaving behind many of the often visited and thus sanctioned cultural texts, this book examines these critical categories as they appear in "less respectable" segments of popular culture that proudly jettison any aspirations toward middle-class respectability. Such popular cultural performances are invested in the practice of consuming as the primary mode of exercising power, authority, respect, and, ultimately, humanity in communities where these avenues of citizenship have been foreclosed. Recently, these cultural products and performances have burst onto the global marketplace, becoming what I call "insurgent cultural representations" of the Caribbean that previously would not have risen to prominence. I argue that many of these forms of cultural expression call into question the legitimacy of highbrow and what Belinda Edmondson (2009) describes as national "middlebrow" culture as the medium that speaks for the masses. *Buyers Beware* asks readers to treat these "common," "lowbrow" (con)texts with the same critical attention they would pay to dominant mass cultural representations of the region, so they can read them against the grain. We begin by considering how their "pulp" characteristics—their emphasis on contemporary fashion, music, sex, fast food, and television—are instructive for the ways in which race, class, gender, sexuality, and national politics are constructed, performed, interpreted, disseminated, and consumed both within the Caribbean and beyond the region's borders. In other words, rather than deploying popular forms of consumption as the arenas in which these battles are simply contested, I engage popular cultural forms as the discourse of analysis to interpret race, gender, and sexuality in the Caribbean.

In *An Eye for the Tropics* (2006), Krista Thompson examines the critical role that nineteenth-century visual culture played in shaping the picturesque tradition of photography in the Caribbean region. She explores how photography developed in such a way that the Caribbean would eventually be produced specifically for consumption in the post-emancipation era. Her work is of singular importance for my understanding of the role of visual culture in how Caribbean people see, perform, and (re)produce their selves for consumption at home and abroad. Thompson's analysis of the concomitant growth of tourism and the fruit industry in the United States is particularly important because of the role photography played in grooming the aesthetic palates of people who purchased postcards and photographs that conjoined "exotic fruits" and "exotic bodies" in the popular imagination. However, she is careful to warn her audience that the subjects of these photographic images also found ways to disrupt the hegemony of the photographic gaze. It is with this caution that I aim to embed my critique of how popular cultural modes of expression borrow from and revise some of the stereotypical representations of the region to formulate what Thompson (2006, 255) refers to as "alternate image worlds."

The critiques made by cultural critics like Thompson are valuable because she points out that the "cautionary" aspects of consumer culture are not always enacted in explicit gestures but are sometimes rendered through subtle bodily gestures and everyday practices like eating, drinking, entertainment, fashion, the "look" (or gaze), and last, but not least, sex. Although there is no doubt that the history of desire for the Caribbean has shaped many contemporary consumption practices and desires in Caribbean, I argue that dominant modes of representing Black sexuality in mass culture are constantly being challenged through unscripted (and even perverse) trends that occur in the local scenes of popular cultural performances. These unscripted occasions are, more often than not, deployed in very strategic, even contradictory ways that subvert the hegemonic power structures that have historically limited Caribbean subjects to the category of the "consumed" (i.e., prey) or, in the worst-case scenario, as bottom feeders.

Material culture is now one of the most critical sites of intersection between consumption and power across a range of modes of cultural production. These intersections are invaluable for interpreting the political aims, anxieties, values, and desires that inform how subjects exercise their power as consumers and citizens. Much has been written about the extent to which the Caribbean region has been imagined in ways that satisfy the desires of those for whom this part of the world has primarily served as a supplier of labor and luxury items, including sugar, bananas, cocoa, rum, and slaves. Since independence in the Caribbean region, demand for many of these luxury items has declined, and vacation experiences have emerged as another commodity, one that provides a valuable means of accumulating forms of (cultural) capital based on travels "off the beaten path" and walks on the "wild side." One of the major selling points of these adventures is the comfort and reassurance that the "natives" are not only safe and friendly but are also happy to accommodate visitors in any way possible. These adventures have a long-standing history in the Caribbean and have changed as the demographics of the global, desiring subjects have changed. Black and white women have begun to avail themselves of the "forbidden" fruits once reserved for their male counterparts. Forays into the "lower regions" are an emerging performance of power through consumption that is part of the new upward (and outward) mobility of female consumers in the global marketplace.

The "lower regions" refers both to the geographical landscapes under consideration, those "exotic" regions of the world where the people who inhabit them are available and interested in being consumed, and to representations traditionally defined as "lowbrow" in canons of cultural production. The preoccupations with governing sex and sexuality in Caribbean popular culture constitute an effort to preserve the morality of the poor and working class, particularly because sexual desires are, according to the nationalist narrative, susceptible to corruption by foreigners. Although middle-class consumers comprise the constituency with the resources to consume and, in so doing, shape how they inhabit and perform their own Caribbeanness, they consume in the same spaces where the working poor perform their own aspirations as consumers. Edmondson has coined the phrase "Caribbean middlebrow" to describe how culture works to validate certain constructions of race, color, sexuality, and gender—all of which go a long way toward framing the discourses of respectability that have remained one of the last vestiges of the Jamaica's colonial Victorian past. However, the term "middlebrow," like the equally problematic "lowbrow," carries with it a range of problems. Edmondson (2009, 10) reminds us of the precarious nature of the concept of "middlebrow" in the Caribbean:

> Lifted from American Cultural studies, it suggests a confluence of economic and cultural status, or that consumers of middlebrow culture are, in fact, middle class. This definition may well work for the United States, with its consumer culture and large middle-class population with easy access to middlebrow "goods" like cheap novels. It works less well in the Caribbean, where poverty is endemic, and buying a book, however cheap, may mean not buying something else. Although middlebrow literature is largely read by

> middle-class readers, I want to emphasize that what people read reflects not just who they are (in terms of socioeconomic status) but who they wish to be. This concept is what I call aspirational status. So middlebrow literature reflects the validation of class status, yes, but it may also reflect the desire for higher class status—or the reconciliation of middle-class and working-class status.

Edmondson's analysis of the problematic nature of terminology when thinking through class and its connections to Caribbean culture are particularly astute, especially in the case of Jamaica. What and who represent the middle classes in Jamaica have changed drastically with the rise of new information technologies that now provide unparalleled access in ways that were unimaginable twenty years ago. Information technology has also tremendously influenced entertainment, which, in turn, has blurred the lines between what Edmonson (2009, 10) calls "aspirational culture" (the desire for social mobility and standing) and "authenticating culture" (the desire to connect)—albeit problematically—with working-class culture.

Although the economic gulf between the working poor and the middle classes in countries like Jamaica and Haiti is growing wider and wider and increasingly starker in the twenty-first century, the gap separating middlebrow and lowbrow culture is shrinking. This is due, in large part, to a desire to authenticate cultural identities through participation in various modes of cultural expression typically associated with the working poor. If markers such as literacy, education, and adherence to community values and rituals once distinguished the middle classes from the working poor, these same markers, now applied to popular culture literacy, have become the yardstick for the working poor to measure the cultural authenticity of the middle classes—but in relation to locations and traditions once considered "vulgar." Cultural traditions that began as modes of resistance to colonial and postcolonial oppression or as the release valve needed for poor people to express themselves, their joys, and their sufferings have become some of the most sought-after cultural commodities and experiences for locals (particularly those from the middle classes) and tourists alike.

By examining the everyday practices of consumption of popular culture, we can highlight the ubiquity of certain consumer goods and practices that have come to define the parameters of interpretation and experience for consumers of and in the Caribbean. This analysis is a departure from earlier debates about consumer culture and its relationship to popular culture and the "masses" in Caribbean studies. There was a tendency in these debates to overemphasize the hegemonic impact of consumer culture in shaping the desires of consumers in "underdeveloped" locations, while underestimating the complex negotiations and performances at work in popular culture. Two prevailing institutional perspectives framed these debates: one that situates Caribbean consumers as mimicking, unconscious buyers and another that positions Caribbean consumers and cultural institutions as easily falling prey to external, predatory, foreign-desiring subjects and trends. Cultural critics like Gerard Aching, Shalini Puri, and Stefano Harney have sought to articulate the truly complex nature of these polarizing notions of culture in the Caribbean by arguing that creolizing, douglarizing, and other modes of cultural adaptation and refashioning of the most canonical of colonial and contemporary traditions more astutely reflect the reality of cultural production and consumption in the Caribbean region.[3]

Is Not Everything Good to Eat, Good to Talk: Sexual Economy and Dancehall Music in the Global Marketplace

Chapter 1 looks at Jamaican dancehall music, particularly song lyrics by popular artists such as Buju Banton, Spragga Benz, and Bounty Killer, to consider why this cultural product emerges as one of the most representative commodities of Caribbeanness abroad. Unlike reggae music, dancehall has always had a deeply ambivalent relationship to its audiences abroad—in large part because of the sentiments expressed reflect the social and political climate from which the genre emerged. Dancehall music is a troubling and yet productive terrain for considering how consumption practices rooted/routed through economic policies abroad shape the way people in the Caribbean imagine and perform their cultural identity at home and abroad. I argue that dancehall music is one of the insurgent modes of mobility within the region that, from its inception, was positioned as an oppositional force to the way the region was historically imagined as consumable culture. Why, for example, have the palate (for food, fruit, and sex) and bodily adornment (clothing, fashion, tattoos) become such integral modes of expressing not only cultural authenticity but also nationalist politics for working-class consumers? Dancehall music is a wonderfully ambivalent and complex mode of cultural expression because, despite its reputation as a mode of "cultural slackness" (for pleasure, mostly sexual but at times violent and certainly consumed with commodity fetishism), it is also an invaluable barometer for the social and political climate in Jamaica. For these reasons, cultural critics are often at odds about how to interpret what Natasha Barnes (2006, 90) calls "the consumptive pleasures" that occupy the interstices of commodification in popular cultural expression. When we examine the breadth of political and social issues addressed in dancehall music, we are left with as many questions as answers. How do dancehall lyrics shift in focus and content when women, whose labor has historically been undervalued, are the major consumers and producers in the new global economy? What kinds of social and political anxieties emerge from shifts in the flow of consumption, not simply from South to North, but also between (and within) the Caribbean nation-states of the Global South? How are gender and sexual relationships affected by the influx of women as fiscally empowered, sexually desiring subjects in consumer and popular culture? How is masculinity imagined and performed differently through practices of consumption given the gender shifts in the marketplace? How do the terms of engagement in the marketplace change when communities, which were once imagined as dietary supplements by desiring global consumers in the North, enter the marketplace as desiring subjects with equally voracious appetites rooted in local (rather than global) desires?

In *Cultural Conundrums* (2006), Natasha Barnes argues that cultural institutions were once intimately tied to the nationalist agendas of middle-class, international state powers with the authority (and means) to devour or, at the very least, transform the wants and desires of local consumers to reflect those of the nation-state. However, subjects inevitably created spaces within systems of control where, as Barnes's analysis of utopic and dystopic popular cultural institutions reveals, popular culture can function in unpredictable and even contradictory ways. Rather than focusing on the forms of culture themselves, *Buyers Beware* concentrates on instances in which these popular incursions occur through different modalities of consumption. Instead of only paying attention to the homophobic lyrics in dancehall, I propose that we also consider the overwhelming economic anxieties around consumption of various sorts (sexual, fashion, culinary, leisure) that emerged in dancehall music during the implementation of economic policies driven by structural adjustment programs (SAPs). Popular songs from the 1980s to the late 1990s reflect social anxieties not only about the state of the economy and labor restructuring but also about the seeming decline in the moral values of the society. As women gained greater power as consumers and laborers, there was an increased effort to police female sexuality. More specifically, my critique focuses on moments when popular cultural texts express the desire to "devour" the government and international consumers, particularly through violence and trickery, and usurp the government's authority precisely because of its inability to provide the poor with access to commodities such as respect, which they so desperately desire. Despite its intangibility, as Deborah Thomas's *Exceptional Violence* (2011, 143) astutely argues, the immutable value and currency of "respect" (not to be confused with respectability) in the global marketplace cannot be underestimated in the social imaginary of Jamaica (see chapter 1). To be sure, respect is accorded a high position on the dietary pyramid due in large part to its close relationship to having the ability to feed one's family and self, rather than being fed on.[4] At the same time that anxieties about being consumed by desiring consumers are having an undeniable impact on cultural production in Jamaica, there is a curious cultural phenomenon emerging in other metropolitan spaces, one born from the same anxieties circulating in the Caribbean region.

Buyers Beware, Hoodwinking on the Rise: Epistemologies of Consumption in "Sistah Lit"

Chapter 2 focuses on several "sistah lit" (U.S. Black chick lit) novels to examine the extent to which stereotypical constructions of the Caribbean region and its citizens are now being widely appropriated as a kind of camouflage that enables performers and other artists to launch contemporary acts of "urban marronage," or subversive escape. These acts include "hoodwinking," or con artistry and are based in a tradition of trickery or "anancyism," that is central to Caribbean folk culture.[5] Anxieties about Caribbean men descending to the "lower regions" of sexuality are expressed as newly compromising positions that put women "on top" socially, economically, and sexually. In these narratives, women not only hold the economic power in relationships with men but also become predatory consumers who search for their "prey" sexually. The twentieth-century voyagers are Black and white women who have, with the same shifts in economic markets, achieved economic security and independence to varying degrees and are now free to explore exotic places and experiences once reserved for men. One of the most recent (and most unusual) instances of "hoodwinking" in the arena of popular culture is the fairytale romance represented in Terry McMillan's best-selling novel, *How Stella Got Her Groove Back*, its cinematic adaptation directed by Kevin Rodney Sullivan, and McMillan's ex-husband Jonathan Plummer's subsequent pop novel, *Balancing Act*. In McMillan's novel, as in the film, the fictional character Stella is an autobiographical composite of McMillan. When taken together, these texts chronicle a romantic dream turned social nightmare as fiction evolved into a real-life drama when McMillan, an American tourist and consumer, discovers that Plummer, the Jamaican subject/object of her affection, is not what was advertised; namely, a romantic, loving, heterosexual Jamaican man. When McMillan first meets Plummer, she falls in love with him despite, or possibly because, he is twenty-three years her junior. The couple manage to navigate the complexities of maintaining a long-distance romance until Winston (played by Taye Diggs in the film) eventually moves to the United States to live with Stella. This romantic narrative goes off the tracks when Plummer comes out to McMillan seven years into their marriage, and the two take their divorce battle into the court of public opinion. My critique of this scandal pays specific attention to the rare occasions when popular culture runs up against its political and interpretive limitations during exchanges between citizens/consumers and other actors in the forum of public opinion and experience. These occasions, I argue, provide us with rare, complicated glimpses of the unimagined consequences of the perverse conditions of modernity that seem unlikely and, at times, surreal. I evoke the concept of "perverse modernities" here in the same vein as Jack Halberstam and Lisa Lowe, referring explicitly to the complex, unpredictable, constitutive relationships among sexuality, desire, race, class, and gender.[6]

The "terms of engagement" for Caribbean consumers are slightly different from the terms offered to those who historically controlled the circuits of consumption and the resources that enable citizens to participate in the global economy. However, as new markets and systems of dissemination are expanding, there is both an increased flow of goods and services and a decrease in the state's ability to control and ensure the authenticity of brands and, for that matter, experiences. Popular culture is one of the most widely disseminated commodities, with music, fashion, films, and pulp fiction (especially romances) accounting for large market shares in global cultural industries. The idea of popular culture as the great "equalizer" across different communities has gained traction because of the increased availability of cultural commodities through rapidly changing technologies of dissemination, particularly via informal economies that thrive worldwide. These new modes of accessibility come with tremendous benefits, but they also increase the likelihood of counterfeit commodities and goods reaching consumers whose desires for and in the Caribbean often exceed their economic capacities. In these sociocultural business transactions, prior (historical) experience between sellers and buyers can (over)determine the level of customer satisfaction. Many of the stereotypical constructions of Caribbeanness, perfected in colonial discourses and visual regimes, are reappearing in contemporary pop culture representations of "first" encounters between Caribbean consumers and other global consumers (especially Americans) who are also eager to get the "best deal" possible. At the same time, however, there is always the underlying threat of anancyism that has long been integral to post-emancipation survival in the Caribbean region. What is commonly referred to as "playing dead to catch corbeau [vulture] alive" in Trinidad and Tobago is called being a "jinnal or ginnal" in Jamaican parlance, and each country has its own cultural designation for these performers who, like the Anancy spider, have made an art of the "con."

"Who's on Top?": Power, Pleasure, and the Politics of Taste

Following in the same tradition of anancyism and the art of the "con," chapter 3 explores how this tradition of survival manifests itself in the works of the Haitian Canadian author Dany Laferrière. Many of the protagonists who populate Laferrière's works, although rich, are manipulated by people we would usually think of as economically disadvantaged: in the Haiti that Laferrière creates, traditional hierarchies of power and mobility are unreliable at best and treacherous at worst. Poorer, less fiscally powerful consumers seeking to gain monetary/social advantage utilize other forms of wealth: youth, beauty, and sex, just to name a few. Much of his fiction is preoccupied with consumption of varying kinds, but he pays particular attention to the consumption of food and Black bodies for pleasure and sexual satisfaction. His writing provokes us to wonder what kind of "inside information" is provided by sexual intimacy and how this information is decoded, disseminated, and valued as cultural capital in the global marketplace. Put another way, Laferrière meticulously explores "cultures of taste" and "cultures of desire" among seemingly disempowered communities, particularly among poor women and children.

In McMillan and Plummer's romance (both real and imagined), heterosexuality is a masquerade donned by queer men to leverage their power as desirable, Black masculine subjects. Laferrière asks us to consider how young girls might deploy sexuality in a similar way, not simply for gain but also for self-gratification.

His protagonists are teenagers who are unafraid to explore their sexuality in openly unabashed and often dangerous ways. More often than not, these tendencies land them in dangerously compromised economic and social circumstances. For the protagonists of *Dining with the Dictator*, many of these social circumstances—far from being obstacles that limit access to traditional pathways for social improvement—become fertile opportunities for acts of what Mimi Sheller (2012, 17) refers to as the everyday politics of "inter-embodiments," which allow subjects to make erotic agency a viable means to resist different forms of exploitation. Once again, I return to the palates that emerge from "cultures of taste" in the Caribbean region to consider the kinds of anxieties and ambitions revealed by culinary, cultural, and sexual fetishes and, for that matter, mask. Some of the questions Laferrière invites us to engage include the following: What are the impacts of popular cultural texts that effectively naturalize visual discourses of excess, hypersexuality, consumer insatiability, and violence in countries like Haiti? By extension, how do these visual and discursive regimes frame our understanding, interactions, and consumption in areas of the world designated as "underdeveloped," "First World," or "Third World?" Do we interpret and experience our sexual and social activities in these parts of the world differently because of these designations?

Dining with the Dictator and *Heading South* and Laurent Cantet's film adaptation (by the same title) give consumers another entry point into the complex landscape of Caribbean pop culture. All pop culture texts require a good amount of cultural translation because the very idea of what is "popular" relies on an ambiguous slate of iconography, social and political locations, and demographics. Cultural translations shape our understandings of everything, including the names of fruits (carambola, jimbilin, and five fingers), the language used to situate ethnic identities (red, Spanish, and creole), and dance in the region (jook, wine, and dagger). In this regard then, translation is not limited to texts written in another language than English but encompasses these Caribbean texts and so much more. As such, we engage with the different versions of the texts on their own terms, but with an eye toward their valence in different nationalist contexts. Our interpretations of these cultural texts are informed by the location of production and the cultural milieu within which they circulate and signify. The work of translation, therefore, is not always aimed at cultural or even linguistic representation; it can also short-circuit our interpretive efforts. The translations of Laferrière's novels and their film adaptations provide us with a unique opportunity to consider the extent to which translation can effectively obfuscate the circuits of consumption.

The race and gender dynamics in Laferrière's works encourage readers and viewers to consider whether the roles performed by those being consumed and those doing the consuming have shifted, particularly among tourists and those in the Caribbean. Any critique of the Caribbean as a "paradise" or a "tourists' playground" needs to engage in a larger analysis of the intimacies that join pleasure and power in narratives of desire, sexual freedom, love, and transactional sex, and there are few Caribbean writers whose body of work is so thoroughly consumed with these issues as Laferrière. His novels and films consider the close intimacies of sexuality (broadly configured), desire, and the complexities of how power is exercised through sex. His work obliterates the lines that have traditionally separated these experiences, thereby allowing sexuality and desire to bleed into one another such that we must consider the possibility of reading beyond our traditional paradigms for consuming representations of Black youth culture and of female sexuality. The complex exchanges among tourists, locals, and visitors in Laferrière's novels have given rise to what I refer to as a range of "fair trade" practices exercised by citizens "from below"—below the belt, below the radar, and beneath the noses of consumers who have come to Haiti to extract resources and services (which include sex and other forms of labor). In these instances, what we commonly consider fair and even trade is very much open for debate and even requires moments of perverse redefinition to recuperate political and social agency for young, poor Caribbean subjects. The complex cartography of exchanges between consumers in Laferrière's novels reminds us that practices of consumption are never limited to a two-way exchange between the producer and the consumer. There are always a number of circuits of consumer practices that have overwhelming impacts, not only on what culture is produced but also on how the systems of production can be corrupted to form different mechanisms of survival for some of the most compromised Black bodies in the global marketplace.

"Fashion ova Style": The Art of Self-Fashioning in Jamaican Pop Culture

Chapter 4 examines the transformative qualities of "racial queering" through one of the dancehall icons with Caribbean routes/roots: Vybz Kartel (Adidja Palmer). Kartel's verbal affinity for and countless homages to female genitalia have earned him the title of the "pum-pum laureate" of Jamaican dancehall music. My analysis of Kartel's music and his body modification is aimed at exploring why, quite unlike his contemporaries, he has been equally as public about his penchant for "pum-pum," his love of ink, and his practice of skin bleaching. This newfound affinity for the "lower regions" of women suggests a lyrical turn away from the anxieties expressed by earlier dancehall artists; however, this is actually not the case. Instead, Kartel's lyrical turn reflects an effort to reestablish the order of things in the dancehall in discursive style but certainly not in terms of fashion, as his skin bleaching makes "clear." Arguably, these modes of cultural expression could not be more incongruent with dancehall culture, but somehow he has managed them (literally and figuratively) in such a way that they have allowed him to corner a fashion market with unparalleled, albeit problematic, success. This consumption is unapologetically sexual in ways that reflect the explicitness of dancehall music but is unequivocally unlike dancehall in its embrace of oral sex as part of a culinary menu for many of hip-hop's most "hardcore" rappers. To be sure, hip-hop has always been consumed with commodity fetishism, but the emergence of these (and other) queer performances of racial and sexual identity is a good reason to pause for critical consideration. Or is this a return to more "palatable" signs of Blackness that can be easily exchanged globally under the guise of style, fashion, or both?

Vybz Kartel's promotional bleaching campaign was a precursor to another modality of body modification that, I suggest, was an effort to reinscribe his Blackness in a manner that he truly controlled. Shortly after the outcry began in response to his bleaching, Kartel launched his line of bleaching crème. In this regard, his body modification campaign was a layered act of reinscribing, or refashioning, himself to tell a story different from what his dark skin foreclosed. This practice has its parallels, curiously enough, in professional sports, particularly in the National Basketball Association where Black bodies are rigorously scripted into a sameness that may be profitable to the league but also denies individuals one of the most basic avenues of expressing themselves and their identities. The explosion of body art in the NBA occurred shortly after the NBA instituted its rigid dress code; many argue that it was imposed in response to Allen Iverson's infamous press conferences, which featured his braided hair, fur coats, an occasional do-rag, baseball caps promoting other professional sports and teams, and almost always a respectable amount of bling. Most often, the baseball caps were chosen to fit with the rest of his sartorial style. Iverson has commented numerous times in interviews that his style of dress was not chosen to flout the norms of what was acceptable: he was simply dressing the way successful people in his neighborhood and community dressed. Whether or not players' body art was in direct response to the NBA dress code is less important than how they and performers use bodily adornment as a way of performing their selves publicly while laboring in commodified contexts that make them hypervisible and invisible at the same time. Kartel's assertion that this skin "is a living breathing canvas" speaks to his awareness of how Black "flesh" has always animated the aesthetic of refashioning the self. Furthermore, Kartel and many other artists and entertainers are increasingly undertaking insurgent modes of embodied resistance.

In this regard, this performative aspect of dancehall music and performance is not unlike the body of work emerging by contemporary Caribbean artists who are also critically engaged in conversation through their representations of the dancehall space. Caribbean art typically was concerned with representations of respectability and an aesthetic that sought to romanticize "folk culture." However, many artists, particularly those born just after independence and disillusioned with its unfulfilled promises, have turned to developing a new registry within which to articulate their own vernacular iconography. Artists like Leasho Johnson are using similar insurgent modes of representation to engage both with the decline of late capitalism in the Caribbean region and the dehumanizing impacts of the economic experiments that were part of globalization. Johnson's choices of media, content, and form not only reflect concerns about the erosion of social and cultural institutions and movements but also draw unambiguous links between the colonialism and globalization in the region. His deployment of colonial iconography that once represented the "exotica" of the region is set against or rather in relation to contemporary iconic products, phrases, dances, and the tools of the trade in dancehall culture. His use of public space for some of these installations is particularly important because it cuts to the heart of critical questions about what Krista Thompson (2006, 289) describes as the "intrinsically linked circuits of consumption that interlock modernity and tropicalization on the islands [and] how these processes are inextricably linked to the selling of the islands' touristic image." Johnson's public installations and his repurposing of iconic objects effectively create insurgent representation that make these well-known images and products seem ambiguous and out of place to viewers.

"Outta Order" or "Outta Road": Caribbean Women Performing Power, Politics, and Sexuality

Chapter 5 explores the variety of ways these social and political locations are being transformed through sexual, social, and gendered performances into potential modes of challenging institutional power structures and their overwhelming impact on disenfranchised citizens. I want to push the envelope on discourses of performativity by considering the song lyrics and stage performances of one of Jamaica's most prominent female dancehall deejays, the indomitable Lady Saw (Marion Hall). I examine Saw's lyrics, particularly those she performs in "diasporic" locations, such as Miami where Jamaicans make up, after Haitians, one of the largest Caribbean immigrant populations. I analyze one of her performances on stage at Bayside Park as part of Sting, which is an annual concert/competition among dancehall deejays. My discussions in earlier chapters consider how Caribbeanness is constructed largely in the discursive and performative realms of everyday life. Here, my analysis turns to Lady Saw's performance on stage, her use of costume and bodily gestures as a means of "outing" herself as an artist whose very presence in the genre represents the embodiment of dancehall culture as a queer cultural space. I compare Lady Saw's stage performances to the rise of what can only be described as queer performance within Jamaican dancehall culture. My use of the term "queer" in this context is intended to signal a reference to sexuality but not solely, or even primarily, to homosexual or lesbian sexuality. As Nadia Ellis suggests, the term is particularly useful in the context of Caribbean popular culture because with (and through) it we can "generate a conversation about whether and how queer can be queered in relation to Caribbean studies" so that the term does "not in any simple way mean gay, lesbian, bisexual, homosexual, or any of the categorical terms we use to define people's sexuality. To be sure, I don't mean to exclude those categories from view. But I mean, perhaps, to supplement or modify them" (Ellis, 2011, 11–12). This deconstruction of the term "queer" is very useful for thinking about Lady Saw's performance of Black female sexuality, particularly the political economy of sexuality for Jamaican women in a tourist-driven, economically depressed social environment. I analyze how these performances in "farign," (the Jamaican patois term for abroad) create opportunities for deeply sexual and political modes of resistance through the genre often identified as "slackness" and through a performative language that has historically been misogynistic.

Lady Saw's stage performances are legendary and not simply because of her songs. They are almost always an education in the intricacies of performing the sexual self socially, politically, and culturally. Furthermore, her music is also concerned with what it means to perform these sexual identities within the music industry as a Black female diasporic subject. Very few female dancehall artists have embodied such a wide range of performance personas throughout their careers as Lady Saw. Arguably, she raised the bar among female deejays in dancehall through her constant variations of "femininity." These personas ranged from the sultry queen of the throne to the leather-clad dominatrix seemingly well equipped to distribute the appropriate punishment to anyone who steps out of line. Yet several of her performances include moments of "outing" many of the misogynistic discourses and practices that obfuscate women's agency as performers in the dancehall. Lady Saw's ability to make very private moments, those that are typically shared among women (about women's health, what they desire sexually from men, who they are attracted to and why), part of her public performances has, I argue, created critical spaces for other dancehall artists to be equally sexually suggestive while advocating for political agency in the midst of their "slackness."

Spice, another very prominent female dancehall artist in Jamaica, recently released a song titled "Black Hypocrisy" that condemned colorism in the country and its long-standing power to determine opportunities for young women with dark skin. But it was her appearance on social media platforms and a few weeks later on the U.S. television show *Love and Hip Hop Atlanta* with skin that appeared to be bleached that really shook up the cast and its viewers. Whereas colorism has been a part of Black American culture, it has rarely been the topic of discussion on reality television, and the fact that the show's only Jamaican cast member decided to raise the issue in such a public, performative fashion raised eyebrows and tempers. Her costars reacted defensively, castigating her for buying into discourses of self-hatred that promote altering skin color, hair texture, and other physical characteristics to get ahead professionally. Spice effectively borrowed a page from Kartel's "coloring book" both to raise the critical issue of colorism and to highlight the ways in which the media and the music industry inform how Blackness is made visible and on what terms. This deployment of color has its parallel in the way in which Black women are allowed to occupy space in the dancehall industry, a fact that Spice has also put "outta door" in her music.

With Spice's entrance into the reality television scene in the United States, a new dancehall star has picked up the baton, along with a healthy dose of controversy among the socially conscious "respectability" hawks and the dancehall faithful alike. Ishawna (Ishawna Natalia Smith) has taken her place among the top female dancehall deejays, and like Lady Saw, Spice, and many others before her, she launched her career by answering the bell with a song that met and exceeded the degree of sexually explicit lyrics typically associated with male performers in the dancehall. She has several songs to her credit, but "Equal Rights" put her squarely in the center of a dancehall firestorm because of its personal and sexual politics. Her "vershan" of Peter Tosh's 1977 well-known call to arms and solidarity raised many eyebrows, while undoubtedly also producing a number of knowing grins among women. "Equal Rights" became a de facto anthem for many rude gyals during the watershed moment of the Tambourine Army, the anti-domestic violence women's rights organization, and the Jamaica's Survivor Empowerment March. All these utterances of women's political, social, and sexual freedom found their amplification by reverberating against heterosexist, patriarchal institutions that systematically threatened and even shamed women into silence not only in Jamaica but also globally. The sexually explicit lyrics in "Equal Rights" called, without apology, for women's sexual and political needs to be addressed head-on (all puns intended).

But as with Terry McMillan's fictional romance, Ishawna's relationship with her then fiancé, the well-known producer Foota Hype, took on larger-than-life proportions when he publicly asserted that their separation was due to what he perceived as her "sexual deviance," and not his womanizing and abuse as she claimed. Very quickly, the discourses of shaming and personal threats that frame a number of women's movements globally came to life and migrated seamlessly, and painfully, from her hit singles to the airwaves of Jamaica—amplifying a sonic shift that was taking place between the public politics of gender oppression in professional and political institutions and the private "bedroom politics" of intimate relationships, physical abuse, and the policing of Black women's sexuality. Ishawna's song, with its unabashed call for equity in the arena of sexual satisfaction—"Me say equal rights and justice / nuff ignorant people ah goh cuss this / Mi p***y tight, cut up yuh cocky like cutlass / But if you want head my youth, you haffi suck this"—was released in 2017, exactly forty years after Peter Tosh's album by the same name. Yet what became abundantly clear was that the sociopolitical environment of oppression and exploitation, from which Tosh's album emerged, has not changed significantly for Caribbean women so many years later.

Gardening in the Garrisons, (Un)Visibility in Contemporary Caribbean Art

Chapter 6 examines the work of two Caribbean visual artists who are actively creating their own modalities of insurgency that draw on an array of traditional and emergent media of expression. Their work, I argue, is aimed at creating a new Caribbean aesthetics of taste. The mythology of the Caribbean as paradise was first produced visually, followed by the marketing of the region as a "tropical paradise," and the primary vehicle for this promotion was (and still is) Black bodies, usually juxtaposed alongside an array of "goods" from the region—fruits, rum, coffee, and, more recently, exclusive resort experiences. These representations typically fluctuate between sexually suggestive, compliant, and gleeful servants or totally laid-back unconcerned locals. Artists Chris Cozier and Ebony G. Patterson are decisively recrafting this aesthetic in unique ways, always with an eye toward reenvisioning the visual and political landscapes of their generation.

For Cozier, born in 1959 on the cusp of Trinidad and Tobago's independence, was disillusioned by the 1980s when the sweetness of the promise of sovereignty proved to be a sour reality. Borrowing from the iconography of the post–oil boom landscape in Trinidad and Tobago, Cozier's work remixes these images so that the painful ironies infusing the day-to-day lives of Trinidadians are painfully evident. In his series of drawings *Tropical Night,* Cozier provides an unforgiving perspective on the unfulfilled promises of post-independence rhetoric while also chronicling the cultural landscape that has emerged in its wake. The muted colors of the 7 × 9 inch drawings push back against the visual renderings of the Caribbean that we have come to expect and even demand, all the while, liberally borrowing from the region's iconography: we see representations of the hummingbird, a Carnival costume-clad woman, handmade posters announcing a Sound Clash, and the ubiquitous breeze blocks that frame the yards and homes, adding an aesthetic and pragmatic flair to the architectural landscape. But there are also images in the *Tropical Night* series that seem to come out of a dream or, worse, a nightmare. They remind us that underneath the bright sunshine and blue waters of Trinidad and Tobago lies a darker reality: the recurring semiautomatic weapons wielded by an army in military fatigues, the silhouette of the Midnight Robber, the traditional Carnival masquerader, or the Red House with smoke bellowing just above, clearly an evocation of the attempted coup by the Jamaat al Muslimeen on July 27, 1990.

Ebony G. Patterson was born in 1981, nearly a generation after independence in Jamaica and only a year after one of the bloodiest elections in the country's history; she came of age in one of Jamaica's most turbulent political and economic periods. At first glance, Patterson's pieces appear to be the antithesis of Cozier's work, if only because of the explosiveness of color and glitter/shine that dominates the surfaces of most of her works. And yet, as we know from the Caribbean literary canon, the Edenic landscapes that enthralled colonial explorers and postcolonial tourists alike are also the sites of many notorious acts in the history of the Caribbean. The "picturesque New Jamaica" that emerged through purposefully manipulated renderings of its landscapes developed the "aesthetics of concealment, long a part of picturesque aesthetics, [which] provided a ready-made mask through which planters and the artists they commissioned could disguise the conditions, violence, and brutality of the plantation" (Thompson 2006, 39). Olive Senior's *Gardening in the Tropics* (2005) is a collection that imagines the garden as the bedrock for the region's brutal history, from the conquistadors right up to the dons who control the garrisons in Jamaica. This vision of the garden as the archaeological site of Caribbean history (past and present) is one that Patterson and Senior, both Jamaican artists living and creating abroad, in the United States and Canada respectively, share despite the forty-year generational span between them. In the section from which the book takes its title, each poem begins "Gardening in the Tropics" and then proceeds to unearth a broad archaeology of Caribbean history that lies buried in the most unlikely places, all mixed up and hidden at times by the "amazing fecundity" of herbs, flowers, weeds, and woods and the occasional don or politician (2005, 86).

On first encountering Patterson's work, I thought to myself that viewing it is like walking into one of Senior's poems, so layered and entangled were the vines, flowers, roots, beads, and baubles. One gets lost trying to follow the surreptitious patterns in each tapestry, but then suddenly, the outline of a hand emerges, then a torso, and soon an entire body is buried beneath this maze of color, finery, and beauty. The deceptive beauty that shrouds these burial sites has become a trademark of Patterson's work, which, as she says, is founded on the premise that beauty is what draws her audience in and brings them near, and then the horror of what her work represents reveals itself: young children from the urban areas of Jamaica who were murdered and their bodies discarded among the garbage, shrubs, gullies, and sundries of the urban centers and rural cane piece. Her landscapes are untamed, disorderly, and explosive, designed to have the opposite effect of what Thompson identified as the "aesthetics of concealment." And yet her works have the same effect of concealment, if only momentarily, which is largely responsible for the disconnect between tourists who frequent Jamaica with no awareness of the sharp contrasts between the picturesque surroundings of the resort and the concrete hardness that frames the lives of Jamaicans living (and dying) in Tivoli Gardens, Trenchtown, and Augustown. Her evocative visual reimagining of the Jamaican landscape is paralleled by a discursive urbanization rendered through her remixing of names and discourses of gardening into bladez, treez, and shrubz in tapestry installations with titles such as "in di grass—beyond the bladez." The invisibility of these lives lost, often through direct and indirect state-sponsored violence, is the subject of two interactive installation pieces, "Invisible Presence: Bling Memories" (2014) and the "Of 72 Project"

(2012), which were shown in public spaces in Jamaica and Trinidad and Tobago before they were ever shown in a gallery or museum. Both pieces elicited the participation of members of the communities from which these lives were taken.

Buyers Beware introduces readers to a wide range of avenues for exploring and reinterpreting the power of consumption to frame what citizenship and belonging mean for Black Caribbean subjects both in the region and in the diaspora. All the while, this book assumes there is an unyielding mutability about Blackness, particularly as it is represented and performed in popular culture. Blackness, like Caribbeanness, is as much about the performance of cultural scripts influenced and shaped by confluent histories, discourses, and traditions. These confluences are manifest through embodied expressions and experiences or what Michelle Stephens (2014, 30) refers to as "the circularity of the act of objectifying and subjectifying one's skin, [which] is a process of simultaneously witnessing and performing, seeing and being seen." The cultural texts analyzed in this book are invested in these acts of "witnessing and performing," each in their own unique manner. What brings them together is that they all represent insurgent modes of embodied resistance that rise to the occasion to disrupt the reification of Blackness in contemporary Caribbean popular culture. In and of themselves, these representations, however, are not sufficient to disrupt the desire and even demand for the performances of Blackness that are visible primarily through established orders of signification. Blackness that signifies "Other/wise" is wayward, perverse, "outta order," and, most importantly, difficult to digest socially, culturally, and politically.

1

Is Not Everything Good to Eat, Good to Talk

Sexual Economy and Dancehall Music in the Global Marketplace

What is to stop the youths and them out
of control?
Full up with education, yet no earn a
payroll.
The clothes pon their back have countless
eye-hole.
Could go on and on, the full has never
been told.
It's a competitive world for low budget
people,
Spending a dime, while earning a
nickel,
With no regard for who it may tickle,
My cup is full to the brim.
I could go on and on the full has never
been told.

Buju Banton's (born Mark Myrie) artistic and spiritual journey from slackness to roots-and-culture deejay chronicles several of the complex negotiations taking place between musical artists and the global record industry. Known as a conscious vibes artist, Buju's ascendance to the top of Jamaican popular music is one of the island's untold stories, one that chronicles the struggle to survive in the marketplace. His is not simply a tale of individual sacrifice but an instance of how artists use cultural value to mediate the hegemonic force of market values in the age of global capitalism. Buju is one of the most successful dancehall-deejays-turned-conscious vibes-artists, and his song "Boom Bye-Bye" (1992) provides an opportunity to explore how market values influence the cultural values expressed in Jamaican cultural commodities produced for "glocal" consumption.[1] The increasing desire for cultural commodities, particularly diverse or exotic music, clothes, and foods, is part of the market appeal of Jamaican dancehall music for Americans. The song initially received substantial airplay on the radio and in dance clubs, but when news of its (translated) content hit the airwaves, it was immediately taken out of rotation by most major radio stations and banned in the United States for its homophobic lyrics. However, it remained a staple in dancehall sessions at clubs where Jamaicans and other West Indians were the primary patrons. The furor launched an international debate among cultural critics and ordinary citizens about the competing value systems of Jamaican culture and those of the global marketplace, most specifically the record industry. When called on to apologize for the lyrics in his song, Buju refused, pointing out that they were an artistic expression of his beliefs.

Some believed Buju's refusal to apologize for the song would spell the decline of his appeal to Americans and the demise of dancehall music in the U.S. record industry. However, Buju's refusal to bow down sent a loud signal to Jamaicans at home and in the United States that, despite the power of American markets to make or break imported products and even entire markets, dancehall music would reflect Jamaican sentiments and culture, no matter where it traveled. Here, the reference to *bowing* needs to be read in all its complexities. The obvious meaning for the term *bow* is the physical act of bending the head in greeting, respect, agreement, or submission and acquiescence. In dancehall parlance, bowing also represents cunnilingus or fellatio. The song's international appeal, so encouraged in the music industry, ran head-on into its ideological antithesis: cultural value or, some would say, artistic freedom. Shortly after the controversy, Banton made an important career and spiritual shift, deciding to turn his creative energies away from slackness (glorifying hetero sex, cars, money, and fashion while also being adamantly opposed to homosexuality and lesbianism) and toward the conscious vibes roots-and- culture model of Jamaican popular music, which takes social, cultural, and spiritual uplift as its emphasis. It professes an anti-institutional sentiment in relation to the Roman Catholic Church, militarization of the nation, and government policies, and it is also unapologetically anti-gay. Conscious vibes artists like Capleton, Sizzla, and Tony

Rebel are closely associated with or are believers in Rastafarianism. Note, however, that the line separating these two forms of Jamaican music (conscious vibes and dancehall music) is not at all solid. Although Buju's music has taken a notably different turn, much of the anti-Western, anticolonial, and antigay sentiment remains but is veiled in ethical, moral, and religious discourses that are also part of the conscious vibes brand of reggae music.

Banton's career and his song "Untold Stories" on the *Til Shiloh* album, to be explored later in the chapter, chronicle the discourses being negotiated in Jamaica. An increasing number of dancehall songs attempt to negotiate the same cultural-value and market-value terrain identified in the controversy over "Boom Bye-Bye" and in the responses to it. Parsing some of the competing and, at times, contradictory discourses of value that are part of this critical approach, albeit in the context of the larger cultural landscape of Jamaican dancehall music, is critical to understanding the stakes and stakeholders in this analysis. A good place to begin this analysis is with an examination of the closely knit yet seemingly opposed discourses of economics and sexuality in Jamaica popular and national culture.

The outcry evoked by Buju's "Boom Bye-Bye" raised a series of questions about market value and cultural value in the new global village. The lyrics that drew the attention of cultural critics and gay rights activists are in its chorus: they express an antigay sentiment, which is not uncommon in dancehall culture:

> Boom bye-bye inna batty bwoy[2] head
> Rude bwoy no promote no nasty man dem haffi dead
> Boom bye-bye inna batty bwoy head
> Rude bwoy no promote no nasty man dem haffi dead

When the song lyrics were translated into English, an array of cultural critics in Jamaica, the United States, and England published commentaries, and three significant points of view emerged from this cross-cultural exchange. First, the dominant concern expressed by critics in Jamaica and by Jamaican critics in outposts in the United States was what appeared to be American and British cultural hegemony, which arose after the lyrical content of Buju's song was labeled homophobic and a form of hate speech. Second, from this argument emerged a public discussion about cultural authenticity and the mistranslation of Buju's song by American and British academics. Finally, enmeshed in this discussion but buried under the surface was a simmering debate, already underway in the thriving dancehall culture of Jamaica, about the collision of market and cultural values in Jamaican national and popular culture.

The cultural critiques launched at "outsiders" for imposing their interpretations and values on Jamaican culture, while knowing very little about the contexts and traditions out of which its music emerged, highlight the extent to which market categories such as *world music* and *world literature* circulate in many institutions without much attention to the processes that manufacture these commodities. In his book *Encountering Development: The Making and Unmaking of the Third World*, Arturo Escobar (1995, 59) reminds us that globalization is an institution "composed of systems of production, power, and signification that should be seen as cultural forms through which human beings are made into producing subjects." This is not only true for common laborers but also for intellectual workers, as the proliferation of academic books and journals attests, and it is certainly the case for musicians in the record industry.

The phrase *cultural value* demarcates a range of socially accepted practices, ideologies, constructions, and beliefs that appear with a degree of regularity in the cultural landscape such that their point of origin and purpose are ingrained as part of the "internal politics" of a country such as Jamaica. *Market value* is based on a similar set of accepted practices, ideologies, and constructions whose frequency in economic systems institutionalizes them in the landscape of the global marketplace. The controversy over "Boom Bye-Bye" was an instance in which several of these ideologies and constructions collided in the most unlikely places: radio stations, dance clubs, popular culture magazines, and academic journals.[3] This chapter examines the manifestations of these two systems of value in Jamaican national and popular culture.

Despite the seemingly antagonistic relationships between the communities represented in these two modes of expression and value systems, the processes of globalization have blurred the lines separating them. Buju's song "Untold Stories," quoted in the epigraph, signifies the economic distress experienced by Jamaicans, naming their experiences among the untold stories about the underbelly of global capitalism, many of which are experienced in Jamaica and its outposts on a daily basis.[4] Waves of Caribbean migration to the United States have continued in response to the increased difficulty of existence for "low-budget people" in the competitive global economy. Moreover, the phenomenon of "spending a dime while earning a nickel" highlights the devaluation of the Jamaican currency on the world market and the subsequent flight of workers to the North for relief. Yet, economic migration within the Caribbean region and to the North is not a new phenomenon. From the building of the Panama Canal to migration to Cuba, the Dominican Republic, small islands like St. Lucia and St. Kitts, Western Europe (especially Britain), the United States, and Canada, the Caribbean region has been integrated into global capitalist economies for centuries.

One product of this long history of migration is the vast and lucrative exchange of culture and cultural commodities. Annual celebrations of Carnival in New York, Miami, Washington DC, Toronto, and London are the most famous examples of this cross-cultural trade. Caribbean-style Carnival (ole mas, steelpan, calypso) exists as a subculture within the multicultural melting pot of the United States. However, as the scope and financial viability of Carnival have grown, gaining the attention of corporate sponsors and political recognition within "local" communities, it has quickly been glocalized to maximize the flow of capital across cultural, geographic, and national boundaries. The music industry is probably one of the best examples of culture being understood primarily in terms of market demand. Moreover, the advent of music videos, which ushered in an era of flashy cars, expensive clothes, exotic places, and exotic people, provided the opportunity for global citizens to consume Black popular culture. Most importantly, music videos provide audiences a window through which to view and witness reproductions of countercultures at a safe yet lucrative distance from the conditions represented in the lyrics of rap artists and dancehall deejays.

In the fast-paced world of global markets, music produced in "local" communities is simultaneously reproduced and registered (or interpreted) via the internet, television, and the mobility of human beings in a variety of frequencies (cultural contexts) in *outernational* or glocal communities. The constant making and remaking of identity between and across citizens, cultures, communities, and markets have created a situation in which national (official, institutionally supported) and popular (unofficial, community-based, and community-supported) cultures are increasingly indistinguishable. Yet these cultural interactions are the markers of increasingly unequal economic relationships between countries in the North and those in the South. One is left to wonder how the large proportion of people who are not "plugged in" keep abreast of these changes.

Dancehall music has emerged as a vehicle for filling the information gap among poor Jamaicans. In his essay "Mr. Reggae DJ, Meet the International Monetary Fund," Andrew Ross argues that one of the social functions of dancehall deejays in Jamaican popular culture is to keep poor people abreast of the developments in local politics. He makes a very important point about the influence of deejays, one that takes the debate beyond the tendency to point an accusing finger at them for the state of immorality in the country. Ross (1998, 208) asserts that their influence

> goes to the heart of concerns about how culture is produced and disseminated, by which I mean culture in the broadest sense of prevailing values, civic loyalties, and modes of behavior, expression, and respect for authority. Who governs the reproduction of culture among educable youth is a concern for any state, but above all for an effectively recolonized state. . . . Unable to rely upon the diminished moral authority of the state, elites are more willing to demonize the "straight talk" of the dancehall MC than to blame the economic violence of structural adjustment programs for the fraternal distrust and incivility that emerge from the sustained hardship and impoverishment of Jamaica's poor.

As Ross notes, deejays give voice to the experience of Jamaica's sufferers, though not necessarily in socially sanctioned discourses of economic readjustment and moral uprightness. More than simply providing Jamaica's poor with updates on the "runnins" in the country, deejays critique everything from politricks,[5] fashion, and religious institutions to the legal and health systems while also providing religious education, sex education, and lessons in survival for Jamaica's poorer citizens.

The state has long seen dancehall culture as part of the problem, not the solution to Jamaica's moral decay. While government agencies struggle to find solutions to Jamaica's economic crises, many of the country's youth have begun to participate in the new forms of "social welfare" programs emerging throughout the country: the drug trade, weapons smuggling, and other criminalized activities. The drug trade provides sufferers and low-level criminals in Jamaica the opportunity for "upward mobility" and independence from Jamaica's politicians. Elements of the underworld, once controlled by politicians, have developed their own forms of social relief programs by supporting those who are loyal to their dons. In response to the government's narrative of senseless killings, moral decay, and glorified violence among the lower classes, deejays like Bounty Killer, appropriately dubbed "the poor people's governor," aim their lyrics of condemnation and fury at government corruption, economic policies, and U.S. government interference. The starting point on this social trajectory that has transformed Jamaican society and dancehall's place within it was when Buju Banton ascended to the top of the music industry chart at precisely the moment he was convicted for conspiracy to possess cocaine with the intent to distribute.

Austerity measures implemented in the 1980s contributed to a social and economic national crisis as anxieties about productivity and consumption in the national economy began to overwhelm the government's ability to ensure the most basic rights of its citizens. This period reflects a critical moment in Jamaica's development, when the country moved from a socialist nationalist agenda toward a more explicitly free market, global economy. This shift had a tremendous effect on popular cultural modes of expressing national identity. Although Buju's 2010 album *Before the Dawn* was in circulation long before his legal troubles began, the sentiment expressed in this chapter's epigraph encapsulates an ongoing struggle against several significant cultural forces: state repression (Jamaican and American), an ongoing war against drugs (spearheaded by the United States), and according to many of Buju's supporters, continued "persecution" for his views on homosexuality. Although none of the songs on his Grammy award winning album, *Before the Dawn,* explicitly refers to homosexuality, Buju and his music became a flashpoint in representations of power negotiations between states, citizens, markets, and industries in Caribbean popular culture. His utterances—dancehall discourses on sexuality, Rastafarian religious rhetoric, and Black transnationalism—represent a confluence of responses to the austerity measures and political changes of the late twentieth century, projected onto the stage of the popular in Jamaican culture through efforts to police the sexuality of Jamaican citizens, especially women. Buju's statements thus reflect a range of anxieties that converge in social constructions of sexuality and masculinity in the years following the implementation of social and economic policies that many felt compromised Jamaica's sovereignty and the moral center of its citizens.

Anxieties about "being consumed" (in all senses of the term—culturally, sexually, dietarily, politically, metaphorically, and literally) begin to take precedence in the primary discourse on sexuality and citizenship in the late 1990s. Ironically, increases in the prices of popular food items among the working classes such as coconut water, oxtail, saltfish, and ackee—paired with the large-scale importation of foreign agricultural produce—made inevitable the yoking together of economic uncertainty within Jamaica and the unbridled power of structural adjustment policies around the globe. Mimi Sheller's (2003) *Consuming the Caribbean* provides a productive analysis of the close connections between consuming goods produced by bodies that labor in remote locations and the policies and conditions that consume (destroy) laboring bodies to meet the demands of global consumers. Mobilities of consumption shifted drastically, and as a result, commodities, desires, and experiences no longer flowed in one direction from South to North. There are now numerous economic, technological, and cultural tributaries along which goods, services, and experiences travel and are exchanged. Moreover, these new pathways expanded the possibilities for many whose power to consume was, for hundreds of years, severely limited. With these changes, there is an increased need for critics to understand how (and where) discourses and practices of consumption inform alliances among industries, nations, individuals, and communities. Therefore, knowing which cultural commodities (and representations) are highly valued and why is crucial to any critical engagement with popular cultural studies.

Just one day before Buju Banton appeared in a Tampa, Florida, courthouse to face drug trafficking charges for the second time, he was awarded a Grammy Award for *Before the Dawn*.[6] Under house arrest and permitted to leave his home only to see his lawyer and for medical reasons, Buju could not attend the ceremony to accept his award. Despite his absence from the ceremony, there were still venues for fans and detractors alike to voice their (dis)approval. The World Wide Web was buzzing with jubilation from those who supported Buju's music and his battle against real and perceived injustice and condemnation from GLAAD and other gay rights groups. Well before awards night, a popular blog (my.firedoglake.com) had announced Banton's nomination for the Grammy:

> The Recording Academy, which awards the Grammy awards has, once again, discredited and dishonored itself by rewarding "kill LGBT" performer Mark Myrie, aka "Buju Banton," with a Grammy nomination for 2011. The nomination this year is for "best reggae album" for "Before the Dawn." Buju was nominated for "best reggae album" in 2009 for "Rasta Got Soul." So far, Buju Banton has not won a Grammy.

> The "Before the Dawn" album was released while Buju Banton was in U.S. federal custody on charges of conspiracy to distribute 5 kilos or more of cocaine and aiding and abetting each other and knowingly and intentionally possessing a firearm in furtherance of, and carrying a firearm during the course of a drug trafficking crime.
>
> Buju's first trial ended in a mistrial. He is scheduled to be retried for the same charges and additional charges starting February 14, 2011. The Grammy Awards Show is on February 13, 2011. ("Grammys Reward 'Kill LGBT' Performer" 2011)

His physical absence from the ceremony further increased the number of responses to the award win on Twitter, Facebook, and a host of other blogs. The sentiments expressed at my.firedoglake.com, like thousands of responses posted online, reflect some of the deeply contradictory, competing interests involved in "valuing" the freedoms of citizens from sovereign territories while also remaining competitive in the global music industry.

When competing notions of freedom (artistic, national, sexual, religious) are pitted against one another, lines of allegiance blur, and in the interest of keeping all eyes on capital gains, partnerships between unlikely constituencies are forged. In response to calls to denounce homophobia in music from gay rights organizations, the Recording Academy stated that it honors artists "regardless of politics" and that "artists of a variety of political or cultural perspectives ha[d] been nominated or featured on the telecast" (Brown 2010). The focus on "political or cultural perspectives" is a multicultural approach that fails to address the deeper, more complex, problems of negotiating the troubling relationship among censorship, hate speech, freedom of expression, and the rights of sovereign states and their citizens.

To be sure, the lyrical sentiments about sexuality expressed in Buju's music are not uniquely his; similar lyrics appear with regularity in Jamaican reggae and dancehall music and in the work of U.S. hip-hop and rock artists. However, contrary to popular belief, Jamaica has not always been the bastion of homophobia that many activists allege. Natasha Barnes (2009, 121) poses two useful questions useful in analyzing when and why homophobic lyrics began to emerge in dancehall music. First, why is ideology at stake in a cultural phenomenon that seems the least "political" of any modern Jamaican musical expression? Second, why and how does homophobia make such a public emergence in dancehall themes and languages, given its virtual absence in the history of musical and oral traditions on the island? Barnes describes the political and social climate that existed before the 1990s in Jamaica, when "gay-hatred is absent because gay, lesbian and transgendered islanders knew well the virtues of keeping their sexuality a secret" (122). She also notes the social panic generated by HIV/AIDS as a "homosexual" disease" (122), a monumental shift in global consciousness about gay sexuality that affected large and small nation-states alike and coincided with the rise in popularity of dancehall music. However, Barnes argues that neither of these socially rooted/routed explanations accounts adequately for the homophobia of the late twentieth century. Instead, she situates her critique in the lyrical tradition closely linked to "toasting," where the deejay voices over recorded music, and rhyme and rhetoric are essential tools of the trade.

I argue, however, that this tradition is not sufficient by itself to account for the virulence of heteronormative discourses that begin to overpopulate the cultural landscape of Jamaica in the 1990s (Barnes (2009, 123–132). Songs like "Wicked in Bed" and "Boom Bye Bye," which are central to Barnes's analysis, are symptomatic of a dramatic shift not only in the way dancehall lyrics represented sexual identity but also in the changing market value of sexual desire, consumption, and expression. They are the precursors to another generation of music that would prove itself to be even more lyrically dangerous. When Barnes asks, "How is Buju Banton's 'Boom Bye Bye' 'responsible' for the indifference of the many middle-class Jamaicans who hate dancehall as passionately as they hate homosexuals?" (123), she presumes that we ought to be more concerned with middle-class indifference than working-class Jamaicans who love dancehall as passionately as they love to reject the pretensions of respectability politics espoused by Blacks in Jamaica. This perplexing question highlights the unlikely alliances that emerge in consumer and popular cultural representations. Buju Banton's "Boom Bye-Bye" is a watershed song that signals a shift from the previous decade, when many dancehall songs expressed masculine braggadocio and tales of sexual conquest, to the songs produced between 2000 and 2010 that articulated not only antigay sentiments but also emphasized policing *all* forms of sexuality, even heterosexual sex. Responding to Barnes's questions about this particular song requires a consideration of the popular culture that emerged out of the social moment in which Jamaica's infrastructure was being disassembled. Furthermore, we need to carry out this critical analysis through a constitutive lens, rather than a cause-and-effect paradigm. Deborah Thomas (2011, 171) describes this relationship most fittingly in her analysis of violence in Jamaica:

> The Jamaican state's decreased ability to meet the social, educational and occupational needs of its citizens has articulated with the reassertion of racial hierarchies internally and national hierarchies globally . . . (Sassen 2000; Trouillot 2001). Because racial hierarchies have not disappeared, and because racial discrimination is still acutely felt not only at individual but also structural levels, racial vindication is still a critical project. That this is a project that is often expressed through the elaboration of notions of appropriate masculinity and femininity, and that it is implemented in complex and diverse ways—ways that often confound analysts and activists—reflects not only the persistence of racial distrust but also a changed generational vision in which "uplift" is often felt to be as constraining as "downpression" (Ulysse 1999). This

> is not a zero-sum game, as should be clear by my attempts to show that one of the axes around which both respectability and "racial respect" seem to cohere is that of sexuality.

I quote Thomas at length here because her analysis of the structural nature of violence in Jamaica is absolutely central to the earlier questions raised by Barnes and other critics about why discourses of homophobia appear in dancehall music in the specific historical context that they do. State power is exhibited primarily through its capacity to protect and provide rights and representation. When that power is compromised, other parallel hierarchies become even more entrenched through culture and, I argue, modes of consumption. Buju's song is not "responsible" for the indifference of the middle classes, but it is certainly symptomatic of a realization among Jamaican citizens that the rights and provisions ensured to them as citizens are under threat.

For middle-class Jamaicans, maintaining their own status in Jamaican society as "respectable" citizens is often articulated through discourses about poor Jamaicans as "unproductive," "undisciplined" citizens. For poor and working-class Jamaicans, who desire "respect," the dominant modes of expression emphasize the scourge of "nonproductive" sexuality (lesbian sex, homosexual sex, abortions, and other transgressive modes of sexual gratification) while also proposing possible remedies, some of which are violent in nature. The discursive disparities between "unproductive/nonproductive" and "respectability/respect," as Thomas warns us, are not merely semantic. By policing women's sexuality, reproduction, and labor while also promoting aggressively heteronormative conceptions of the body politic, Black women's bodies emerge as the stage on which these desires are enacted (Thomas 2011, 170).

The 1990s found Jamaica still reeling from two decades of austerity measures on which unprecedented levels of support from the World Bank and the International Monetary Fund were conditioned. Fallout from these policies was easily visible in the popular cultural expressions that swept across the country, and the acronym "IMF" took on a number of new meanings.[7] It is not a coincidence that dancehall music increased in visibility and popularity at precisely the time when the country's poorest citizens had fewer and fewer avenues to express the impact of these policies on their families and communities. The discourses that emerged in popular representations of this period reflected several economic, religious, and social anxieties about national identity, respectability, and, most certainly notions, of masculinity.

Dancehall culture influences (and is influenced by) overarching discursive traditions that have shaped the racial, gendered, and (trans)national terrains of Jamaica since before independence. The distinction between respectability and respect, which Thomas makes throughout her analysis of violence in Jamaica, is of utmost importance. Both discourses are drawn out of constructions of race and class that have a long-embedded history in the Caribbean, and Thomas (2011, 170) provides a critical lens through which we can better understand the subtle, yet significant, differences between respectability and respect:

> *real* respect would entail a validation of racial subjects who are still confronted with the legacies of slavery and colonialism and the recognition of the integrity and legitimacy of a class-coded set of cultural practices and values that diverge from those "respectable" practices that have been (and, in many cases, still are) promulgated by political and cultural elites, middle-class professionals, and most religious communities as the proper foundation for citizenship.

Telling those Untold Stories: Truths, Metaphors, and Consuming Rhetoric

For the purposes of this critique, I consider the "class-coded cultural practices" that appear in dancehall music as nationally approved modalities of citizenship for Jamaicans at home and abroad. There is no greater avenue for expressing class, race, ethnic, and national stratification than through the palate, and it is the palate that brings me back to the rhetorical questions with which this chapter opens. If discourse (or what comes out of the mouth) is one mode of expressing shared but contradictory political agendas, then it stands to reason that an analysis of consumption (what goes into the mouth, the home, the closet) can also teach us a few important lessons about how national, sexual, and class identity are performed. A cursory survey of the catalog of dancehall or hip-hop music since the 1990s would reveal the overwhelming preoccupation with practices of consumption in Jamaica. Buju's question, "what is to stop the youth and dem outta control," has the discursive effect of weakening some of the distinctions often made between reggae and dancehall music by linking both to a continuous political history of racial and class struggle, albeit one articulated in very different discourses and cultural practices. By blurring the once firmly installed lines of demarcation and yoking together a rather (un)holy trinity—dancehall music, Rastafarian culture, and Black transnationalism—Banton opens a space to read these cultural moments as equally invested in palatable expressions of Jamaican citizenship and identity.

Where the public image of poverty has historically been that of the malnourished Black or brown faces of the "Third World," Bounty Killer's album *The Fifth Element*, released in 1999, featured "Anytime," a song that showed up on the state's radar because it featured this malnourished body as an armed subject with the means to change his or her current circumstances. It was immediately interpreted as a threat to its authority and certainly for its ability to foment civil disorder. When "Anytime" was released, poor Jamaicans heralded the song's brash honesty and its "plain talk, bad manners" approach to Jamaican politics.[8] The lyrics leave very little room for cultural or market mistranslation:

Jack Ass unno nuh tired fi pressure poor people
Well Babatunde have a message fi yuh see
Never let your problems get you down
Gotta stay focused and hold your ground
Though it seems hopeless, there is no progress
We still a hustle round town
We do what we do so we stay alive
We sell what we sell so we haffi survive
We tired a the f**kery[9] and we fed up from 'bout 95
So, tell them seh anytime,
Mi hungry again them ah goh see meh nine
Police outta road sey dem a fight crime
And holiday a come and mi nuh see the first dime
Tell them seh anytime the government policies ah undermine
Poor people plight that a sure sign
Corruption and war a goh reach its prime
Imagine, after mi try my best to survive the street
Sometimes mi wonder how some people dweet
Nuff time it burn mi, mamma clean dirty floor so the kids can eat
Five Christmas now mi don't drink nuh sorrel
Landlord and mamma deh ah courthouse a quarrel
Chin ah send a kriss[10] chrome nine inna barrel
What you expect me to do?

Bounty's lyrics are indeed chilling because they not only describe the level of poverty and distress of Jamaica's poor but also signify sufferers' preparedness to change their conditions by violent means if necessary. Moreover, the narrative provides an alternative historical background to the nature of the violence in Jamaica suggesting that it is in direct response to governmental corruption and one that is commensurate with the kind of treatment they are receiving from those in power. Bounty's references to the "hard labor" women face to make ends meet—labor that, despite their best efforts, fails to achieve their most basic needs—point to the futility of hard work in a system where human (particularly women's) labor is so devalued. The passing yet powerful reference to weapons imports, "Chin ah send a kriss chrome nine in ah barrel" puts the cause and effect in more direct proximity to each other. That is, in the absence of food and work, weapons are the next best means for survival.

The explicit threat in the chorus that "anytime the government policies undermine, dem ah goh see meh nine" challenges the state's authority at several levels: it blatantly charges the state with neglect; it throws the illegal arms trade in the state's face by asserting that the trade is both a viable and necessary mode for survival; and, most important, it threatens the state with retaliation. We know, however, that this retaliation is actually felt by and aimed directly at other sufferers and working-class Jamaicans. Where the state feels the impact of this retaliation, it is through its reduced capacity to uphold civil order, which in turn has long-lasting implications for business investments in a country that depends on external investors and tourism dollars. Last, and probably most important, the song directs our attention to the burden of government policies and corruption on the day-to-day existence of poor people in Jamaica. The fusion of corruption and war, when juxtaposed against the state's power ("police outta road say dem ah fight crime"), is meant to direct the listener's attention to the irony of fighting crime on the streets when, in fact, crimes are being committed against poor people by the government and its policies. The internal contradictions between state power and the people the state is supposed to serve, therefore, are rendered all the more starkly.

Given these contradictions, Bounty's rhetorical question at the end of the song works effectively to institute another order of power, one that is (ironically) exercised through the same modality as that of the state's "protective services": violence. Globalization, which has enabled the free movement of goods, weapons, services, and people across geographic boundaries, cannot guarantee the legality and equity of these movements. The opportunities provided by free-trade agreements are supposed to provide relief for poor people. However, as many have noted, the relaxing of trade restrictions between the United States and Caribbean countries has also resulted in an increase in the exploitation of workers and easier access to high-powered weapons. Despite the emergence of Economic Protection Zones (EPZs), which were supposed to create jobs for Jamaicans, low wages paired with the continued escalation of the cost of living meant that even those who were working full-time needed to supplement their salaries. In her 1995 book *Born fi' Dead*, Laurie Gunst points out that shortages in employment and escalating housing and food costs meant that women (in particular) were forced to find ways to subsidize their incomes. The references in Bounty's song are not simply meant to evoke a sympathetic response to hard labor. What the song makes clear is the extent to which women's labor, while fueling the global economy, does not provide them with the basic means to support themselves and their children. Many women have chosen to go abroad in search of better opportunities, leaving their children to become "barrel children," so named after the shipping barrels containing foreign goods.

The market demand for products from abroad—Nike apparel, Tommy Hilfiger jeans, Nintendo PlayStations, and other such commodities that arrive in barrels every few months—is one manifestation of the enormous impact that commodity culture has had in Jamaica. Yet, many women have been able to turn the imbalance between consumption and production in Jamaica into profitable businesses by becoming informal commercial importers (ICIs). Dancehall culture ensures the ICIs a steady demand for name-brand clothing and, as Bounty's song notes, name-brand weapons imported from the United States. The irony, of course, is that many of the goods sold as name-brand clothing and accessories in the Caribbean are, in fact, black-market reproductions.

With the advent of increased economic avenues for women to secure some measure of economic stability for themselves, they have become more independent and, according to many songs, more sexually demanding. The need for money also opened a new market for women who saw finding a "sugar daddy" as a short-term economic solution for their problems. As Laurie Gunst (1996, 38) notes, "Jamaican women, like their sisters everywhere, were the miners' canaries for their country's poisoned air. Super Cat, the undisputed don of dance hall, came out with a hit song called "Boops" about the way ghetto girls had to find a sugar daddy if they wanted to eat. "Boopsism" became the talk of the town, a code for female despair." The growing rate of unemployment among men in Jamaica and the increasing feminization of the labor force by female-intensive industries such as garment and textile manufacturing, tourism, and data processing meant that Jamaican men also had to resort to creative and desperate ways of surviving the lean times. If finding a sugar daddy was the solution for women, political gangsterism and the drug trade provided a similar form of unemployment relief for many young men in Kingston. This new trend provided the inspiration for many dancehall songs that emerged from this period.

If we take all these factors into consideration, we can begin to see how the affairs of the state affect the national "body politic" in Jamaica. Under these conditions, the realities of social (dis)ease become more and more evident. In the Caribbean region, popular culture has long been a barometer for the political and social climate; in Jamaica, dancehall music became a purgative for the poor to release the toxins that were invading their social, cultural, and economic systems on a daily basis. The lyrical bravado that circulated in the political garrisons was the elixir used by dancehall artists to express the trends and concerns of those without a political voice. With a dire shortage of socially acceptable yardsticks of manhood—namely the ability to work and provide for one's family and self—many young men resorted to metaphorical gunplay.

Fusion and Con/Fusion: Gender, Sexuality, and Consumerism

From no gyal cyar call yuh furniture face,
Not dis mouth, not dis face
Want hear de shottah[11] whey ah keep tings straight
Not dis mouth, not dis face
From yuh know yuh conscience nah carry no weight
Not dis mouth, not dis face

From no gyal have no secret fi yuh mouth,
Want fi see di rudebwoy hands ah push out
For no gyal cyar see and point yuh out,
Want fi di lighter dem flash all about
From yuh nah keep sissy man as yuh frein'
Mek me see de hand dem cause ah pure gyal we bend.

—Cobra, "Not Dis Face"

My aim here is to consider the relationships among ideologies about sexuality in the Caribbean, popular cultural representations of sexuality, and consumer culture in Jamaica. The discursive intersections in these debates participate in a set of complex negotiations as they present themselves not just in Banton's music but also in other Jamaican dancehall songs composed between 1990 and 2010. Another significant turn (whether upward or downward is open for debate) in dancehall lyrics is the positioning of women's sexual desires in relation to the "value" of "work/wuk."[12] Recognizing the centrality of women in dancehall lyrics as objects of desire and for the performance of masculinity is crucial for understanding both the literal and lyrical contexts of songs, particularly those that take sexuality as their subject matter. Although most dancehall songs have a seemingly mandatory salute to the "stallions" and to women who can "handle de wuk," a growing number are dedicated entirely to sexual conduct and, more specifically, to the prohibition of oral sex as a cultural norm. This prohibition emerges as a direct response to the perceived threat to masculinity represented by women's sexual and emerging economic power. First and foremost, women's bodies are the site for articulating wealth, national prosperity, and lyrical and sexual prowess. Second, women are the bearers of the nation, both figuratively and literally, in that they give birth to the nation's future. Women also make up a large portion of dancehall audiences, and their presence makes both the state and the church uncomfortable.

The obsession with women's sexual practices in Jamaican dancehall music is no less fanatical than the moral policing by religious organizations that, like the government, stand in firm opposition to abortion, homosexuality, and sex work. However, there is another interesting twist in this saga of cultural values and moral policing. As Cobra's song "Not Dis Face" suggests, the discourse of shame and emasculation associated with sexually satisfying women through oral sex has spread to include the public shame, nay threat, of politicians being "fingered"[13] as committing any or all these forms of perceived social and cultural transgression. Cobra's song articulates the significant intersections between masculinity, sexual prowess, and violence in Caribbean cultural discourses. Moreover, the public discourse of shame, which has its roots in Catholicism, plays an interesting part in negotiations of power and authority. The possibility of being pointed out "outta door" seems to be the motivating factor in the song. The call-and-response pattern in Cobra's song opens a space for the men in the audience to perform their identities and, in doing so, creates a shared discourse of sexual conduct, particularly among "shottahs" and "rude boys."

To explain the preoccupation with sexual conduct in Jamaican popular music, Peter Noel (1993, 30) argues that in "West Indian culture many people still cling to Old World ethics. Their beliefs, morals and suspicions are rooted in the canons of the Roman Catholic and Anglican churches, whose teachings on homosexuality are more virulent in the former colonies than in Europe or America." The forbidden nature of homosexual conduct creates curiosity and temptation and, therefore, the need for the protection and salvation provided by God, the state, and citizen. Popular culture, as Noel notes, is one of the tools for administering both guidance and protection: "In the West Indies there are many ways to broach the forbidden. Dancehall—the new 'hard-kicking, raw and wild' style of reggae—contains references to all manner of sexual prohibitions, including fellatio: 'No ice-cream sound.' As for cunnilingus: 'How a man fi live inna oman hole like ah crab?' On the other hand, it's perfectly acceptable to 'hear di y'ung gyal ah bawl when she get up to nine inch tall'" (30). The double standards expressed in these perspectives on sexuality are founded on an ideology of the "natural" order of things or nostalgia for the "way things used to be." This failed romantic period, although never identifiable in concrete terms, still circulates within institutions to construct boundaries and codes for moral, sexual, and cultural behavior.

Given the human propensity toward temptation, institutions such as the state and the church are charged with the responsibility for implementing these behavioral codes. But what happens when both the state and the church can no longer provide this protection? The erosion and delegitimization of the state's social welfare programs and the conservatism of the churches in dealing with economic and political crises in Jamaica have left many wondering about where poor people can turn for guidance, direction, and support. In this vacuum, how then are cultural values maintained, policed, and administered? To whom does the responsibility fall for ensuring the "order of things?" I argue that popular culture has stepped in to fill this gap, but not necessarily in the ways we might imagine.

As Noel points out, dancehall music represents "unofficial" cultural codes of conduct, both lyrically and literally. For example, Spragga Benz's hit song "Cyan Get No Gyal" is one of the few songs dedicated solely to sexual codes of conduct. It fuses several institutional discourses to install what seems to be a new social order. However, on close examination, the song nonetheless reinscribes the same conservative ideologies espoused by both the church and the state:

> What ah nastiness, like we bettah change de national dish
> To Jackie and saltfish
> Chorus: Some boy cyan get no gyal if him no eat

Nuff man nah say dem look and ah do it
Mariana tell me she gi him de treat
True yuh see dem in a Lexus outta street
Meh cyar believe di ting dem weh Jamaica embrace
Man doh know demself dey need to pull em dem lace
We catch a boy already he say prayahs and grace
Now true dem have de money, dem a bow and dem ah taste
Dem ah waste!

The lyrics stress cultural values as the fabric of Jamaican society. However, the discursive fusion of sexual labor and economic labor, as represented in the material symbol of the Lexus, elides a direct engagement with the issue of power in both economic and cultural systems of operation. The question of productivity in the context of dancehall music is largely described in terms of a man's ability to "gi di gyal wuk" and women's ability (and flexibility) in "tekin di wuk." In this context, "wuk" has little to do with sexual pleasure for women unless we count the constant references to the sexual gratification of women who "bawl fi mercy" as they are ground, slammed, and "spread out inna bed."[14] Spragga's charge that the national dish be changed from "ackee and saltfish" to "Jackie and saltfish" suggests that women are now a culinary "treat" for some men in Jamaica.

The obvious comparison between the cost of the literal saltfish and its slang equivalent, punanny, is significant because the two common denominators here—availability and accessibility to local Jamaicans (and dancehall don-gaddas who depend on foreign markets for their income)—are under threat because of poverty and the constant devaluation of the Jamaican dollar. Although a successful dancehall artist who has managed some crossover appeal benefits from the continued devaluation, "home-grown" artists, who produce primarily for Jamaican audiences (at home and abroad), do not manage as well. Moreover, a deejay's ability to put in "overtime" makes him a "stallion," "thoroughbred," or a "productive," ambitious citizen. Oral sex, however, is not part of the discourse of "wuk" and is, as this song suggests, a sure sign of man's lack of ambition as a social and sexual worker. In other words, men who have oral sex with women do so because they are not up to the "wuk" or are incapable of handling the amount of "wuk" before them; that is, they suffer premature ejaculation or sexual dysfunction. The absence of employment is indeed a threat to the national economic agenda and to popular sentiments about sexuality because without work/wuk the state cannot maintain itself, its citizens, and its identity.

There is, however, an inherent con/fusion in state-administered codes of sexual, cultural, and market conduct, particularly as they pertain to homosexuality. These codes of conduct join (or create a fusion) social and cultural values with legal prohibitions in such a way that these prohibitions appear as the natural order of things constitutionally (hence, the con). In her discussion of sexual-offense legislation in Trinidad and the Bahamas, M. Jacqui Alexander (1994, 22) touches on a delicate yet explosive connection between governmental legislation and women's bodies, which suggests that women's national identity is linked to their willingness to be "productive" citizens. The form of this productivity is of singular importance:

> We can read state practices as attempts to propagate fictions of feminine identity, to reconfigure women's desire and subjectivity and to link the terms of the nation's survival to women's sexual organs. This is what Geraldine Heng calls, in the specific case of Singapore, "the development of a sexualised, separate species of nationalism, a nationalism generated from the productive source of the womb." To understand it in Heng's terms, the indictment of prostitutes and lesbians inscribes "a tacit recognition that feminine reproductive sexuality refuses, and in refusing registers a suspicion that sexuality is non-economic, in pursuit of its own pleasure, sexuality for its own sake, unproductive of babies, is unproductive of social and economic efficiency" (Heng and Devan 1992, 363–364). It registers a suspicion of an unruly sexuality, omnipotent and omniscient enough to subvert the economic imperatives of the nation's interest. From the point of view of the state, it is a sexuality that has to be disciplined and regulated in order that it might become economically productive.

I quote Alexander at length here for several reasons. First, this passage offers us a register for exploring the varied yet close relationship between the gender politics of the state and popular articulations of a collective national gender ideology. Second, the recent proliferation of songs that pay attention to appropriate guidelines for sexual intercourse—specifically, those that discourage oral sex—and link fellatio and cunnilingus with non-Jamaican culture and "foreign" influences con/fuses the discursive location of these sentiments about gender, economics, and sexuality.[15] The intersections between unofficial gender ideologies and those that are institutionally sanctioned complicate Alexander's assertions because they show the fissures and contradictions in the locations and the narratives produced therein.

The "foreign" influence and in/fusion of American culture in Jamaican society are under attack in Spragga's description of the voracious appetite for foreign imports; namely, "peaches," "plums," and "punanny":

> Mr. Man meh cyar believe is so low yuh reach
> Ah tell yuh is Sodom and Gomorrah dem ah teach
> Nuff ah dem *bite and suck on like it ah leech*
> Me hear when dem ah nyam it dem ah *nyam it like peach*
> Hear me tink dem likkle gyal dem by houses
> Man ah come inna di dance in di *batty-man trousers*
> Nuff ah dem a freak and ah *suck off gyal toeses*

Even though Kim have de gum
Still nah goh chew it an' me *nah bite de plum*
Get fi understand dem broddah *love stretch de tongue*
Dem de nastiness dat Capleton ah fyah pon. (Emphasis added)

The reference here to the conscious vibes Rastafarian artist Capleton (aka The Fireman), who regularly advocates purification by fire to rid Jamaica of foreign influences like the Roman Catholic Church, the IMF, and corrupt politicians, is intended to highlight the beliefs shared by two cultural establishments: dancehall music and Rastafarian conscious vibes music. Although not as biblically empowered as most references to Sodom and Gomorrah are in other songs, Capleton's prescription for Babylonian principles and practices and homosexuality is meant to evoke a similar wrath and scorn.[16] Furthermore, the evocation of "batty-man trousers" here suggests that oral sex, even between a man and a woman, is seen in the same light: it is an unproductive and, most important, (un)Jamaican activity, because it does not serve God, or people, or country. Men who "suck off gyal toeses" or "stretch di tongue" are also cast into the realm of sexual uncertainty. The terms of sexual conduct, according to this song, suggest that men who perform oral sex have no potential to be sexually "productive." Moreover, their sexual appetites call their status as Jamaican citizens into question.

The lyrics of Baby Cham's and Bounty Killer's "Another Level" articulate some of the tensions between workers, capital, and culture or, as Escobar (1995) characterizes it, production, power, and signification. "Another Level," released in 2000, opens by admonishing listeners to remember that

Hard work, the key to success
Yuh have some boy no put in nuttin' at all an expec fi be di best
We gonna show dem why we rated among de greatest
Mi go ah foreign and big up mi nationality
Mi luv di money but mi nah bow fi vanity
Mi see di posse dem come wid animosity
Pressha mi, pressha mi, but meh nah leggo mi sanity.

Oral sex, according to many dancehall songs, is one manifestation of foreign influences that impinge on the moral well-being of "sufferers." The imagined distance between the sexual practices and preferences of Jamaicans at home (inna yard) and those of Jamaicans living or visiting from foreign (or "farin" in Jamaican parlance) is rendered as a discursive and cultural difference between those who will bow to get ahead and those who will not.[17] In this instance, to "go foreign" is to travel someplace that requires a visa; that is, to go abroad to the United States, England, or Canada. But it is also to travel a metaphorical distance away from what is sexually accepted at home in Jamaica, the implication being that "sexual deviance" is the result of foreign influence. Sexual deviance is thus another force against which poor people must constantly struggle, much in the same manner as they struggle against government corruption. "Another Level," stresses the relationship between "sexual perversions" and "economic distress" by juxtaposing "biggin up yuh nationality" against "bowing fi vanity," which implies inequities between market values and cultural values. When artists, common laborers, and others "go ah foreign" in search of better wages and opportunities, the unequal power relationships between migrant workers and big industry nation-states are accentuated through below-minimum-wage compensation and the deunionization of workforces. In short, these cultural and industry workers face a market in which their production, while having a high market value for industry, has little value in relation to the cost of living in Jamaica. As the song expresses, in this situation the only "sanity" is to be found in the "nationality" or cultural value of being Jamaican, which is evoked as the great equalizer, capable of balancing the weight of hegemonic forces.

The inequity between Caribbean artists and markets and North American record producers and labels, which assume that the audience for all music is first and foremost American, demands a certain uniformity in the production of goods, in this case music and lyrics. Listeners expect each song on an album to be a unique addition to the overall theme and tempo of the compilation. Hence, the release of singles prior to the entire album release gives listeners a sense of the range of the entire product, while each song is different in sound and content. Current trends in dancehall music, however, seem averse to many of these demands. From the use of single deejay "riddims," which are reproduced and "ridden" by various artists, to the common practice of "dropping" new styles for specific shows depending on the audience (whether the performance is in the United States, Jamaica, or Trinidad), dancehall artists produce lyrics as much for their local constituencies as for a larger market.[18] In many dancehall compilations, the music itself is identical—but it can be slowed down, sped up, rhymed over on different beats, thereby making the same rhythm sound different. It is not at all uncommon, therefore, to have an entire CD recorded to a single rhythm. This practice is consistent with earlier genres of Jamaican music like dub where artists repurposed older songs to give them new life and social relevance. As in other forms of Caribbean music, such as calypso, the techniques imply an ongoing conversation between artists and their community of listeners.[19] In fact, although record labels seldom record the songs performed during concerts in Jamaica and for Jamaican audiences in the United States and Britain for commercial release, they are frequently bootlegged onto CDs and sold on the black market. Whether we choose to recognize it or not, these practices are part of a large and prosperous informal commercial industry that exists not only within the U.S. economy but also globally. Therefore, what were once understood to be "local" productions have now changed *locale* and are now not part of the fluidity of economic systems seeking to maintain their cultural and political values within Jamaican communities in the metropoles.

Another interesting juxtaposition of political and economic policy with sexuality and moral uprightness in "Another Level" highlights the "slippery" nature of literal and lyrical language in dancehall music. Baby Cham's lyrics summon the biblical wrath of the Almighty against "sexual misconduct" and government corruption:

Tell di broddah weh f**k up di economy
Fe go read Chapter 3 Deuteronomy
Tell em sey we have to secure we family
Government corruption ah goh down like sodomy

Here, the fusion of political corruption and sodomy, as well as the juxtapositions of economic success and forbidden sexual practices with religious prohibitions, is a powerful discursive tool for policing and distributing both punishment and salvation. Moreover, the implicit insistence on the "family" as the nucleus of this perspective reasserts the "unproductive" aspects of homosexuality and, by extension, governmental bowing to foreign demands, both of which are cast as antithetical to the biblical, moral well-being of the nation. The religious righteousness expressed in this verse of the song closely parallels the sentiments of churches toward "perverse" sexual activity; however, the comparison ends there when we consider the possible economic alternatives often suggested in other dancehall lyrics (robbery, becoming a shottah, and the drug trade). What, then, is the relationship between these two constituencies—dancehall artists and religious leaders—and those they are said to represent, particularly women? What are the shared values and agendas between these constituencies? And finally, are these values and agendas necessarily "nationalist"?

Oral sex between two men, and between a man and a woman, is represented as a consequence of the systemic absence of productive work for men. In a heterosexual framework, the shortage of work is characterized as compromising the role of men as providers who, because their economic power is not well defined, cannot hold up their heads in the home and, by extension, in their bedrooms. As a result of the lack of good jobs, men in Jamaican culture "succumb" to gay culture, which is always understood to be a foreign import into Jamaica, in the name of economic gain. "Ghetto Pledge" by Bounty Killer and Baby Cham, commonly referred to as the "poor people's national anthem," expresses a similar sentiment:

Mi haffi rate every youth wey hold di faith

Cause we haffi mek Jamaica feel proud
Whe Cham say?? Bun a fyah pon ah fool and on ah fake
Wey a walk in a batty man crowd

Cause di people dem piss and when dem ah get pissah
De police ah go get diss, di shotta dem no missa
De youth dem fi kriss and tings could ah krissah
Dats why ah whole heap ah dem gwine turn boogah fellah.[20]

Both Spragga's and Baby Cham's songs seem to con/fuse discourses of hard labor and proper compensation, which brings me to my second point of engagement with Alexander's assertions. Where Alexander stresses the state's efforts to control sexuality so as to meet the aims of the nation, Spragga's treatise against oral sex is also a directive against politicians and legislative acts influenced by foreign interests and industries. Thus, although buggery is a felony in Jamaica, "since tourism is the island's main industry, gay visitors frolic without fear of the police" (Noel 1993, 30); hence, the disbelief and confusion expressed in Spragga's assertion that "mi cyar believe de ting whey Jamaica embrace, man doh know demself, dey need to pull up dem lace." "Pulling up laces" is a reference to the "cultural slackness" of the state, which, in its efforts to maintain a positive market value, does not uphold the laws it is responsible for administering. The indifference expressed through the tradition of political violence in the name of the state and the state's legislative adherence to colonial sexual codes of conduct both work effectively to discipline economically distressed bodies and constituencies into prescribed performances of respectability while simultaneously denying them respect in the form of living wages, safe living and learning environments, and equitable safety and protection under the law.

Despite the discursive and ideological similarities between Jamaican popular and national culture, stark differences and disagreements emerge at the level of praxis, particularly regarding how workers (politician, ganja farmer, tourism worker, or gun man) and lovers (stallion, whore, batty man, "p***y watchman"[21]) are defined. In the end, men who cannot uphold their political and economic roles as (and with their) member(s) of society are relegated to the den of sexual and political iniquity. However, when these seemingly separate categories are fused (gunman/battyman, matey/wife, don/politician), the line that separates these constructions seems less and less sturdy. This is the problematic that many of these songs attempt to negotiate through explicit assertions that "gunman and batty man" have no business with one another (figuratively and literally).

On another level, the figure of the batty man demarcates social, political, and cultural violation because homosexuality violates the patriarchal state and its ability to "re/produce" itself and its discourses of Jamaican identity. If, as these songs suggest, the wealth of the nation depends on the productivity of its citizens, we must ask ourselves how socially and state-sanctioned methods, such as the "seeding"[22] of women, help achieve this task. Responses to the recent appearance of saltfish (punanny in popular cultural terms) as a preferred delicacy within the political economy of Jamaica are virtually absent from the majority of dancehall songs, save for a few written by female deejays such as Lady Saw,

Ishawna, and Spice that emphasize the prowess of women who "tek wuk" or maintain full-time "wuk" from men while other, less talented women are constantly "unemployed" (see chapter 5). The discourse of employment effectively consolidates a certain measure of empowerment and affirmation of women's bodies, by which "pum-pum power" has the capacity to expand and even reframe language inherited from the traditionally patriarchal space of the dancehall. A fundamentally different aspect of this reframing, however, includes a revaluation of pum-pum.

We need to consider the ways in which discourses of resistance also work to reinscribe hegemonic practices, particularly where women are concerned. If we do not examine the cultural, economic, and discursive linking of gender and sexual politics in relation to nationalist politics and nationalist constructions of sexuality, we can easily assert dangerous romanticisms about Black women's lived realities. For example, in his essay "Rasta, Ragga and Reinventing Africa," Louis Chude-Sokei (1994, 82) argues,

> From a Western liberal-feminist perspective these lyrics, because they are boldly heterosexual and disdainful of bourgeois sentimentality, seem very sexist and objectifying of women. However, down there in the mire of postcolonial reality, where power is a rare but prized commodity, these women find both affirmation and power in the fear that their sexuality creates in men. It allows them the freedom to navigate around a world of brutality, violence, and economic privation.

If we agree with Chude-Sokei's claim that dancehall lyrics can indeed be read as an affirmation of Black female sexuality in Jamaica, then we cannot deny the very limited freedom women have in constructing their own sexuality, controlling their resources (their bodies and their labor), and certainly in protecting themselves from economic, political, and physical violence. To return to my earlier claims about market value and cultural value, the limited opportunities for women to participate on their own terms and in their own body language are connected to the hegemonic practices of market value.

There is also a false dichotomy between Western feminist ideology and popular cultural expressions that are "boldly heterosexual and disdainful of bourgeois sentimentality" (Chude-Sokei 1994, 84). Arguably, there are several popular cultural statements that fuse these two political positions, reaffirming the anxieties expressed in many of the songs discussed here. What does such a pop culture landscape look like? Where and in what modes of popular cultural expression might we best examine the realizations of these anxiety-producing representations? The immediate response might be to turn to dancehall lyrics by female deejays. However, this is not the most productive place to begin, particularly because of their limited market circulation—their music does not yet have the same opportunities for global distribution and airtime as enjoyed by male artists—and the small number of female dancehall deejays on the market at any given moment. To capture a similar market share of consumers, we would need to consider another equally popular cultural commodity. In the interest of engaging a popular form not often critiqued with the same "high" regard as popular music, I consider the often easily dismissed genre of "chick lit" romances. In this genre of popular fiction, women are represented as purveyors of market values, and because of their increased financial power, they are the desiring subjects in search of men, power, and all the other accoutrements of success that usually dot the pop culture representations of the world. More importantly, the world of chick lit and its offshoots (sistah lit, dick lit, and nanny lit), for ill or good, represents a new cultural frontier where women *determine the meaning of equality and freedom*, though not necessarily in ways we might imagine or deem acceptable.

2

Buyers Beware, Hoodwinking on the Rise

Epistemologies of Consumption in "Sistah Lit"

They had a Chinaman called Dick
Hung Lo
He got married in Mexico
His wife divorce him pretty quick
She like bamboo but not chopstick
She like the big bamboo
I give me woman some sugar cane
Fruit of the trees I did explain
The only thing to my surprise
She like the flavor but not the size
She like the big bamboo
—The Mighty Skipper, circa 1950

The significance of disseminated images for patterns and modalities of consumption is central to my analysis in this chapter. Consumer patterns in the global marketplace depend increasingly on images that influence desires for services and commodities and even the expectations of pleasure. Music, films, literature, commercials, photography, fashion, and other cultural artifacts shape expectations of places, people, and experiences. My analysis of "market goods"—sex, food, medicine, fashion, and music—centers on two popular fiction novels: Terry McMillan's *How Stella Got Her Groove Back* (1996) and *Balancing Act*, a novel coauthored by Jonathan Plummer (McMillan's ex-husband) and Karen Hunter. My critique considers how visual economies of desire inform the cultural and political palates of consumers, particularly in the United States. Popular fiction also shapes consumers' palates and their visual expectations, particularly with regard to the Caribbean region. New genres unapologetically seek to develop markets and canons of consumer goods and practices that women the world over use to measure their successes in the pursuit of "womanhood." The political economy of "chick lit," "sistah lit," and "dick lit" cannot be underestimated, given that popular literature controls the lion's share of the publishing market. Arguably, popular fiction is the literary equivalent of "tourism" for readers, allowing them to edify themselves in an entertaining context.

Suzanna Ferriss and Mallory Young (2006, 9) define these genres as follows. In *chick lit*, narratives are framed by consumer culture media, especially self-help, advice, and lifestyle books and magazines. It targets twenty- and thirty-something professional, heterosexual, single (usually white) women and is focused on how these women struggle to achieve what their mothers could not; professional success and a fulfilling personal life (symbolized by marriage, a boyfriend, or significant other). *Sistah lit* shares some of the features of chick lit but reflects the lives and realities of African American women whose experiences with the world of relationships, fashion, and self-help advice differ significantly from those represented in *Vogue*, *Cosmopolitan*, *Vanity Fair*, and *Elle*. Yet the fashion and self-help magazines—*Essence*, *Ebony*, *Jet*, and, more recently, *Heart and Soul*—featured in sistah lit novels still often include insights from *Vogue* and similar publications, in large part because white women continue to be the standard by which *all* women are judged. This fact is a central focus of many sistah lit narratives in which Black women are struggling to raise their children, support their extended families, and succeed in a society that consistently devalues them.[1] In these novels, the romantic relationship is constructed as the most likely place for these women to find serenity and reaffirmation in a world that rarely, if ever, sees Black and white women through the same lens. Most often, however, there is little solace to be had in these relationships. In fact, after following social formulas for finding the "perfect man," protagonists are never able to find "Mr. Right" precisely because their expectations are not only unreasonable but also are nearly impossible to meet.

Dick lit is often described as contemporary fiction written by men about emotions and relationships for female audiences. Steve Almond, author of popular books such as *The Evil B. B. Chow and Other Stories*, *My Life in Heavy Metal*, and *God Bless America: Stories*, provides one of the more astute critiques of dick lit in a guest column written in 2003 for the publisher Melville House Books:

> However you view the genre, we can all agree that men simply don't talk about their feelings in the same way that women do. . . . They are allowed—even, to

> some extent, pressured—to live further from the chaos of their feelings. Accordingly, they don't read much. And when they do read, it's more likely to be non-fiction, Tom Clancy, historical novels, or the *Sports Illustrated* Swimsuit Issue. . . . This gender bias is also in place on the supply side. By which I mean, when men write literary fiction, they tend not to place the primary focus on romantic entanglements. They write, instead, about war, or professional ambitions. These areas, after all, are officially sanctioned male domains.

If we extend these insights to consider how and where Black male authors are encouraged to cast their lot, the conversation becomes even more complicated. There is certainly a large market of readers for popular fiction by African American men that focuses on African American women's professional lives, relationships (heterosexual, homosexual, and lesbian), family dynamics, and communities. Whether they are characterized as part of the dick lit category depends largely on understanding how white and Black masculinity have been defined historically, particularly in relation to expressing pain, hurt, and vulnerability. Acknowledging emotional vulnerability may make white male authors suspect, but Black authors (both male and female) have to navigate a long, complex tradition of stereotypes in American popular culture that represent Black men as emotionally dysfunctional and serially unfaithful and Black women as fierce and strong—the "mules of the world" according to Zora Neale Hurston ([1937] 2006).

Given these stereotypes, meeting the primary conventions of sistah/chick/dick lit—creating Black male protagonists who are worthy of the attention and desire of Black female protagonists—is a particularly difficult task. How do these authors create protagonists who are masculine, "Black" enough, exceptional sexual partners, sensitive (without being "soft"), good financial providers, faithful, and handsome while also being "believable"? Black female protagonists seem to have limited options: they can lower their expectations and aim for regular everyday men with their flaws, continue to search for a Mr. Right who does not exist, be continually disillusioned with the whole process, or decide to escape the scene altogether by dating or marrying outside their ethnic or racial communities. Terry McMillan and Stella follow the last option, turning to the Caribbean as a likely location to find their slice of paradise.

McMillan is considered the progenitor of the sistah lit genre. Her most notable contributions to the genre are *Disappearing Acts* (1989) and *Waiting to Exhale* (1992). Critical examinations of this genre mark the overdue arrival of Black women's experiences and concerns in the popular fiction landscape, even though *How Stella Got Her Groove Back* is not usually included in the canon of sistah lit discussed in these critiques. However, Lisa Guerrero does cite it as a gold standard of the genre in her essay, "'Sistahs Are Doin' It for Themselves': Chick Lit in Black and White." Her provocative opening assertion that "most fans of contemporary women's fiction can immediately answer the following question: how *did* Stella get her groove back?" serves as a reminder that readers of chick lit know what is most important (2006, 87). Guerrero does not return to a discussion of McMillan's novel, so her essay never specifies how Stella got her groove back; however, are we to assume that the answer—she leaves the United States—is obvious? I would argue that this elision occurs because Stella has transcended the concerns that plague Black women in most sistah lit narratives. Arguably, not only has she solved her relationship issues but also her response to being single makes her a female prototype of the kinds of men that many of the women in *Waiting to Exhale* are trying to escape or avoid: she is a highly successful business professional who, rather than feeling her life is incomplete because she is not partnered, decides that playing the field is to her benefit because she has the power and the resources to determine the rules of the game and what "winning" means. The world is her oyster, and true to the Edenic trope, she turns to the Caribbean to find her "pearl"—whether it takes the form of a sexual partner, escape from stress, or her piece of heaven on earth is totally up to her as the mistress of her domain.

As Faith Smith notes in her discussion of the 1998 film adaptation of McMillan's novel, Stella (and Terry McMillan) can travel to the Caribbean to indulge her desire for pleasure in any way that she chooses:

> Imperialist fantasies of the Caribbean reveal themselves in the sustained focus on the body of the upper-middle-class-elite-turned-beach-bum who catches Stella's fancy. Ironically, this focus rereads the classed and gendered Jamaican in ways that are potentially liberating, but the film is less interested in local subtexts than in facilitating the America tourist's three-day, two-night groove. *Black professional women now replace the succession of European and American male adventurers who traditionally consume the bodies of exotic and available Caribbean females.* (Smith 2001, 47; emphasis added)

The Caribbean region has been produced—some would argue overproduced—as a paradise. In McMillan's novel, it is a place of luxury, excess, mystery, and sensuousness. At the other end of the spectrum of visual images are films like Wes Craven's *The Serpent and the Rainbow* (1998), which depicts Haiti as a place of poverty, disease, underdevelopment, violence, and corruption. Despite the differences in these representations of the Caribbean, they have thoroughly penetrated consumers' desire for the region as a vacation destination and, at the same time, fed their fears of it as an unsafe place for visitors. Somewhere in the midst of these representations lies a far more complex space.

Jamaica has become a trope representing the entire Caribbean, a signifier that is both loaded and empty. Jamaica's reggae and dancehall cultures have been heralded as the voice of the region, leaving behind (at least in terms of market sales, "branding," and "visibility") equally relevant cultural traditions such as calypso, zouk, and soca, to name a few. When most Americans make the effort to "place" or locate people within their imaginations in the Caribbean, Jamaica is the starting point and measuring stick for the region. Some would argue that this is because of the country's geographical proximity to the United Sates, but this is only true if you ignore Cuba, as Americans have been encouraged to do by the U.S. government. Others might point to Bob Marley and argue that the success of reggae music has emblazoned Jamaica's iconography onto the minds of people the world over. My concern here is not so much accuracy as the ironies of consumerism and capitalism, particularly as they relate to cultural commodities. In the end, regardless of the motivation, what is heralded as Jamaican or, more broadly, Caribbean is a fabricated ideal designed to reflect the cultural, social, and political values and institutions that Americans can digest within their low-calorie (read: low tolerance), high-fashion (read: high cultural capital) consumer diets.

The connection between how the Caribbean is viewed and how it is consumed is not merely discursive. Building on Mimi Sheller's critique of consumption, Krista Thompson's *An Eye for the Tropics* (2007, 48–49) traces a complex cartography of shifts in the visual economy of the region. The Caribbean became a location of desire for tourism at the same moment that demand for consumer goods from the region began to rise. Thompson charts the processes involved in turning what had been viewed/seen as zone of tropical death into a location where the mercantile elite could both increase their wealth and flaunt it, while at the same time acquiring a tremendous amount of cultural capital. Food—more specifically, fruits—that were intended for export and consumption, much like the slave labor that fueled the plantation economy, became an essential element in this shift in the region's visual economy.

In 1871, Captain Lorenzo Dow Baker introduced bananas, a previously unknown fruit, to consumers in the United States. By 1899, Baker's Boston Fruit Company, which at its peak shipped more than sixteen million stems of the fruit to the United States, had become the United Fruit Company, a major player not only in the fruit export business but also in the tourism industry (Thompson 2007, 48–49). The company had two sales aims: to sell (1) exotic fruits (bananas pineapples, oranges, cocoa, etc.) to U.S. consumers and (2) the visual image of the Caribbean as a safe, clean, exclusive, comfortable place filled with natural beauty. It achieved both aims: "Crucially, the United Fruit Company's reach also extended to the tourist trade, as their steamships doubled as passenger ships for tourists. The company also acquired two hotels on the island [Jamaica]. It built the Titchfield Hotel in Port Antonio in 1897 and assumed ownership of the Myrtle Bank Hotel in Kingston in 1918. Subsequently, the American company controlled a significant percentage of both the fruit and tourism trades" (49). This initially small development beachhead influenced not only how the Caribbean would be seen but also how it would be consumed. As Thompson notes, no expense was spared by the mercantile elites in their remapping of the visual terrain of the Caribbean. The space had to be made more readily consumable for investors and tourists alike. Fast-forward to the twentieth century, the argument could well be made that the efforts of the United Fruit Company and its British counterpart, Elder Dempster and Company, represent one of the most extensive and successful marketing campaigns of the late nineteenth and twentieth centuries. Today, few vacation destinations are as popular as the countries of the Caribbean.

You Are What You Eat: The "All Inclusive," "Authentic" Vacation Experience

As globalization has transformed the appetites and patterns of consumption, the "dietary" preferences for cultural goods and sexual services have become more complex. The desire for new "dietary supplements" to feed the ever-growing appetites of global markets can be mapped through shifts in the palates of consumers. All-inclusive vacations provide visitors with "all you can eat," but menus rarely feature local Caribbean cuisine. American tourists prefer foods they identify with, tastes they are familiar with. Their appetite for "spicy," "exotic" experience is satisfied by extracurricular activities in the resorts, journeys into less familiar places, and even experiences that might include hair braiding, sex with strangers, illicit drug use, or attending religious ceremonies.

In "Globalization, Tourism and the International Sex Trade," Beverly Mullings asserts that the desire for truly "authentic" vacation experiences has led to the production and consumption of "far-off" places: "Particularly since the 1980s an increasing number of travelers have begun to demand travel experiences that are closely tailored to individual tastes. The 'new middle classes,' as these travelers are often described, emerged in the 1980s as new cultural intermediaries initiating and transmitting new consumption patterns, including the search for 'authentic' holidays in developing countries" (Mullings 1999, 59). The idea of vacationing as a mode of relaxation, as a space to recuperate one's energies, has since the 1980s mutated into seeing travel as an opportunity to achieve and attain cultural capital through consumption. As many vacationers have learned, however, complex and at times dangerous social, political, and cultural milieus do not cease to be dangerous simply because visitors plan a vacation in these areas. The most egregious examples of this danger include the deaths of adventure seekers who travel to regions of the world that are in the midst of civil wars and other military disputes.

But there are also less tragic—but more ironic—examples of the new phenomenon of adventure-seeking travelers. Take, for example, the scandal of Terry McMillan's divorce from her Jamaican-born husband, who announced in 2005 after seven years of marriage that he was gay. McMillan's well-publicized marriage to Jonathan Plummer, a young Jamaican twenty-three years her junior, provided the subject for her best-selling novel *Waiting to Exhale*, in which she showed readers, and eventually movie-goers, the world over how they could "get their grooves back" in exotic places like Jamaica where beautiful, available Black men were waiting to meet Black and white American women. She received more than a million dollars for the film rights. The movie version stars Angela Basset as Stella and Taye Diggs as Winston Shakespeare, her young Jamaican love interest. One has to wonder about McMillan's sense of humor (or maybe irony?) in naming her male protagonist. Does she see him as a poet or a gifted dramatist of his time?

The story has a boy-meets-girl narrative structure but with an interesting twist: the "boy" in the novel is not a stereotypical beach dread (a fit, dreadlocked beach bum) who sells sex and sometimes marijuana (ganja) to tourists looking for "something new."[2] Winston is from a middle-class Jamaican family and seems to be living a rather comfortable life in Jamaica before he meets Stella, who is trying to escape burnout produced by her corporate job; for example, when he gets a job at the Windswept resort, his parents (who, we are told, once owned ten horses) send a car to pick him up so that he can come home and collect his things (McMillan 1987, 150, 163). Nor are the experiences of the Black woman in this novel typical of those provided by the stereotypical beach dread who is concerned only with sexual gratification; rather they are closer to those provided by the infamous character Dexter St. Jacques in the movie *Raw*, made famous by Eddie Murphy: he plays a lover who is well endowed and meets Stella's sexual and emotional desires as well.[3] Like many other tourists, Stella travels to Jamaica to get away from her mundane existence and find fun in the sun, a young lover, and her "groove"—but she ends up finding much more.[4]

McMillan devotes a great deal of her book to guiding her audience through the terrain of conspicuous consumption—music, books, clothes, mobility, food, and language—that is essential to American popular cultural identity.[5] In particular, Stella's "diverse" range of music preferences provides an interesting portrait of what cultural consumption means to African Americans in this novel. As she packs for her trip to Jamaica, we are introduced, through an extensive catalog, to the breadth of her music appreciation. She despises most hip-hop because of its misogynist lyrics and use of the word *niggah*, which, she is keen to point out, "we have never used and I don't allow to be used in our house" (50). Stella's taste in music, like her son Quincy's, suggests a "seasoned palate":

> I do appreciate some hip-hop, a little SWV TLC Xscape R. Kelly Mary J. Blige Brownstone Boy II Men Jodeci etc. etc. etc. I also like a lot of music by white people, which a lot of my friends don't understand. Quincy loves that rock group Green Day and Aerosmith and Hootie and the Blowfish and I kind of like them too and I love Seal *even though he is African but British* and mostly white people buy his music and I love Annie Lennox Diva over and over and Julia Fordham and Sting and hell good music is good music. (50; emphasis added)

There is a peculiar confusion in the statement that she loves Seal "even though he's African but British." There is little basis for this conditionality, so it is difficult to discern whether the contradiction in loving his music lies in Seal's

Africanness, his Britishness, the fact that mostly white people buy his music, or her awareness that she likes his music for the same reasons she likes that of white European artists. It is quite possible that the contradiction lies in the suggestion that she, an African American, likes his music for the same reasons that white people do: even though he is African, "good music is good music." The idea that race can transcend cultural boundaries appears to need qualification when racial difference emerges from a "third space" ("Third World") that is neither the United States nor England ("First World"). The subtexts that inform this effort to differentiate among social class and cultural identities are not the focus of McMillan's novel. In fact, we are constantly distracted from asking what, in Pierre Bourdieu's (1984) terms, is the "habitus" that links Stella not only to other white people in America but also to Seal, who is "African but British." I suggest that we can find the answer to this question by looking closely at the culinary formation of desire that informs consumption patterns in McMillan's novel. The consumption of music and food is as intricately and intimately connected to the body politic as it is to the consumption of Black inter/national culture.

After Stella returns from her groove-getting excursion to Jamaica, she begins to come to terms with the idea that maybe, just maybe, she is emotionally attached to her young lover. Her second trip involves a different kind of "retail therapy" as she seeks to separate herself from other travel companions. She upgrades the three plane tickets (for herself, her best friend, and her son) to first class, "for a mere three thousand dollars," to ensure her enjoyment on the flight in case she dies in a crash before realizing her dream of making love to Winston once more (285). With the tickets upgraded, she loads up on snack food. Her snack selection, coupled with her philosophical musings, provides another occasion for critical reflection on the relationship between the patterns and ethics of consumption, the expectations of consumers, and the real situations in which exist the goods, services, and bodies being consumed:

> If I could have another chance to press and seal my lips against Winston's just one more time which if God really is fair He or She would grant me a final pleasure before I go and if there's time an hour or two of some nuggies would be like frosting on the cake if it's not asking too much. . . . So while I buy two packages of Oreo cookies a super-saver size Kit Kat one Three Musketeer a Butterfinger a Pay Day three bags of Lay's potato chips—plain, barbeque and sour cream and onion—I add all this stuff up and I come to the conclusion that I have earned the right to some happiness and by golly I'm going to get me some. (284–285)

As in the laundry list of music, the absence of punctuation and the inventory of junk food (and other commodities) highlight the fact that consumption is the yardstick by which "happiness" is measured. Given the many flavors of potato chips and kinds of candy bars, along with the uniquely American concept of the super-saver, the inclusion of sex ("nuggies") should not be surprising. Discursively, it is merely one of the many "sweet treats" on the list. Sex functions much like the "frosting on the cake": it is high-calorie intake with no nutritional value whatsoever.

McMillan's novel shares several stylistic conventions with the diaries kept by domestic servants during the Victorian era. According to Anne McClintock in *Imperial Leather*, these diaries provide remarkable insight into the extent to which progress was measured by a growing preoccupation with commodities, the things that effectively kept the boundaries between classes stable. Writing about Hannah Cullwick's diary, for example, McClintock (1995, 169) asserts, "If the diary as a genre is dedicated to the idea of the individual, the syntax of Cullwick's early diaries bears witness to an erasure: the sovereign 'I' of individual subjectivity is missing. A typical day's entry from her early diary for Saturday July, 1860, reads as follows":

> Opened the shutters & lighted the kitchen fire. Shook my sooty things in the dusthole & emptied the soot here. Swept & dusted the rooms & the hall. Laid the hearth & got breakfast up. Clean'd 2 pair of boots. Made the beds and emptied the slops. Clean'd & washed the breakfast things up. Clean'd the plate; cleaned the knives & got dinner up.
>
> Clean'd away. Cleaned the kitchen up; unpack'd a hamper. Took two chickens to Mrs Brewer's & brought the message back. (McClintock 1995, 170).

The preeminence of objects that needed to be cleaned and ordered, as McClintock notes, takes precedence over the life of the domestic servant, making the system of value abundantly clear to the reader. The inventory of commodity items, knives, plates, beds, and boots, implies that Cullwick's entire being is measured in relation to things, rather than people, or what Karl Marx called commodity fetishism.

Although McMillan's novel differs significantly from Cullwick's work in historical context and content (in terms of the commodities listed), the overwhelming emphasis on and accounting for objects in the two works draw our attention to the power of commodity fetishism during the colonial era and during the new era of globalization. There is a fundamental difference, however, between the Victorian emphasis on labor and the contemporary capitalist emphasis on consumption. The "I" of individual subjectivity, far from being erased, is now so large that it overwhelms all other subjects in its presence. The relentless list of objects and goods gives way to the "I" that determines the meaning and value of all goods being exchanged and consumed.

This pattern is repeated time and time again as Stella enters malls, department stores, grocery stores, music shops, and specialty stores. Ironically, it also occurs when she gets excited about seeing Winston: she recounts the cologne he was wearing, his clothes, and the music that was playing. This emphasis on material objects, according to McClintock (1995, 170), is "what Marx called commodity fetishism: the central social form of the industrial economy whereby the social relation between people metamorphoses into a relation between things." Although the junk food listed and itemized is for Winston, neither Stella nor the readers are encouraged to consider why these items are either unavailable or too expensive for Winston and other Jamaicans. Junk foods are not quite the trinkets traded with "natives" in the New World, but they function in the same way: they are small objects of trade and affection meant to indicate the goodwill of the visitors. To be clear, I am not casting Winston (or other Caribbean people who participate in these kinds of relationships) as unconscious, easily duped, naive victims of tourists. By outlining the social and political subtexts that inform the popularity of these kinds of narratives about the Caribbean, I am suggesting instead that these subtexts should raise questions and eyebrows among readers of chick/sistah/dick lit, but they rarely do.

Despite losing her job after her return home from her first trip to Jamaica, Stella sends Winston gifts of jewelry, clothes, and sneakers, all of which he wears when he visits her at the hotel during her second trip. Although there are no explicitly stated exchanges of goods for sex, the narrator draws our attention to what Winston is wearing, which certainly encourages such an interpretation. The food chain is such that Winston consumes what Stella provides, and Stella in turn consumes him, a pattern that is strikingly similar to those we see in films like Laurent Cantet's *Heading South* (2005). The exchange of commodities for the happiness Stella so desperately feels she deserves (and is intent on getting) seems to be one of "fair trade," in the global market sense of the phrase. In accordance with the spirit of fair trade, Stella is improving the quality of Winston's life by contributing to his capacity to maintain his lifestyle while unwittingly providing him the support—a free ticket to the United States, a visa, and possibly later a green card—that will allow him to compete on the global market. However, McMillan, like Stella, does not seem to anticipate that the desires and palates (even of Caribbean consumers) can and often do change, based on market conditions and the availability of other options.

Anancy and the Tale of Dietary Caution: How Terry McMillan Lost Her Groove

Reading McMillan's novel through the lenses of colonial commodity fetishism, socioeconomic discourses of development, and global exchange highlights the complex nexus of negotiations taking place between vacationers and the workers they encounter during their stay. McMillan's novel does not operate simply as a text about sex tourism. On the contrary, *How Stella Got Her Groove Back* carefully maps out emergent modes of social and economic exchange, sexual desire, market demands, and the contact zones in which all these registers are fused and at times confused, particularly when life begins to imitate art, with equally unexpected and undesirable endings.

Sociologists have sought to differentiate the categories of relationships between tourists and those with whom they develop sexual partnerships. The advent of romance tourism, as distinct from sex tourism, has encouraged a further delineation between male and female sex workers, who are paid largely for their willingness to have sex with tourists, and those who act as romantic partners: "Male sex workers are involved in romance rather than sex tourism, because there is often a level of emotional involvement that is not often present in sex tourism. This division of sexual labor is tied to an aim driven industry where companionship, for women, is of equal importance as sex for tourists who are men. These holiday relationships tend to be longer term, involving a much higher level of social and economic commitment on the part of both parties in the exchange. . . . Some relationships may last for many years and result in marriage or migration" (Mullings 1999, 66).[6] As Mullings suggests, these sexual liaisons are complicated by the power inequities resulting from differences in class and culture between visitors to and residents of the Caribbean and other developing countries. Exchanges and negotiations are enmeshed in these power structures and necessarily determine the tenor of relationships, regardless of romantic desire, genuine affection, and sexual desire. It is virtually impossible to demarcate where desire for a better life (through migration, marriage, or both) ends and where romantic desire begins, as evidenced by the very public relationship, marriage, and divorce of Terry McMillan and her young lover, who is indeed Winston Shakespeare's real-life counterpart.

The absence of a local subtext in McMillan's novel contributes to her inability to see Plummer as anything more than a loaded/empty signifier similar to Jamaica itself in this economy of desire. In her novel there is very little mention of what Jamaica is like beyond the resort environment. It is as if Jamaica does not exist beyond the people who work in the hotels, restaurants, and on the beaches. Stella, who is allegedly falling in love with Winston, never makes an effort to learn anything about Jamaican culture or his status within that space. Instead, she fashions him in her own (or maybe her son's?) image, going to the mall and buying him music, a CD player, and brand-name clothes, only briefly stopping to ask herself, "What if he thinks I'm doing this to impress him or to buy his affection?" (255). Alas, this moment of reflection is quickly dismissed as she responds to herself, "Why would he think that, Stella? And besides, this stuff doesn't even add up to my car payment" (255). We might wonder what it might mean for Stella (and other readers/viewers) to think, *I wonder what kind of music he likes? What if his taste in music is different from my own?* All of this assumes that the setting of the novel (more than two-thirds of the novel is set in Jamaica) and the film actually matter to Stella and other vacationers like her.

Throughout the novel there is an already-known quality about Jamaica, one that pervades most popular texts about the region. This knowledge is based on access to capital and the notion of "earning the right" to happiness. Why think about Jamaica beyond the resort if you can afford not to?

After publication of her book and the news of her whirlwind relationship with Plummer, McMillan became a poster child for Jamaican all-inclusive vacations that were guaranteed to rest, relax, and restore all grooves. As part of the promotion for her book and the film, McMillan traveled around the United States, singing the praises of her relationship with her newfound love, with the object/subject of her affection standing by her side. Similar to colonial travelers who brought back specimens—birds, fruit, fabrics, even human beings—from the New World, McMillan reveled in the spectacle of the public's response to Plummer's presence. He was the "gold" that so many Black women traveled to El Dorado (the Caribbean) in hopes of claiming. McMillan wanted her readers and viewers to see him shine, and at the time Plummer seemed more than willing to play his part.

McMillan's real-life romance followed a similar trajectory to that presented in the novel, but in 2005 the real-life marriage ended, and a new part of the drama that seemed ripped from the pages of a best-selling novel began. The end of McMillan and Plummer's marriage marked the beginning of a torrent of complex negotiations for authority, ownership, rights, and citizenship, all of which her novel seems gleefully ignorant of when the two lovers meet. This is not to suggest that they are not of importance, rather the romance narrative of the "sistah lit" genre seems committed to leaving these political details behind in favor of sexual frolicking and the idealism of age being "just a number." McMillan filed for divorce in Northern California's Contra County Superior Court, citing her husband's "fraud" as the grounds for the separation. According to McMillan, Plummer, now thirty years old, lied about his sexual orientation when they married. Plummer had recently revealed to McMillan that he was gay, a fact he claimed to have realized only after several years of marriage to her.

Two moments in this drama about the relationship between sexuality, globalization, and consumerism are instructive. McMillan's court declaration reads like a bill of sale for a product that was damaged or, at least, not as advertised. After all, if consumers cannot depend on truth in advertising, what is left? McMillan declared, "It was devastating, to discover that a relationship I had publicized to the world as life-affirming and built on mutual love was actually based on deceit, lies, and obtained by fraud. I was humiliated to realize that Jonathan was not attracted to me and possibly had never been. . . . I reacted angrily and sometimes impulsively, as many would."[7]

In turn, Plummer sought a restraining order based on the allegations of harassment listed in his declaration, some of which he admitted are "not fit for public consumption":

A. She came to my place of business and left:
   a. A jar of hot pepper sauce she labeled "penis juice";
   b. a bottle of Island Spices Seasoning where she circled the word jerk and wrote "appropriate";
   c. a bottle of Jamaican pepper sauce on which she wrote "Fag Juice Burn Baby burn" ("'Stella' Exhales in Nasty Divorce" 2005)

It is too easy to highlight the emphasis on these consumable Jamaican goods, all of which are inseparable from Plummer's sexuality, doing so distracts attention from more critical issues at play in this legal matter. And yet, my earlier comments about reserving the "spicy" adventures for the resort have great relevance here. Like her protagonist, McMillan engaged in this relationship precisely because she saw the Caribbean as a place where she could free herself of any inhibitions about choosing a sexual partner. In this "extralegal" Edenic space, the rules that would normally govern her interactions with potential partners are no longer valid. McMillan claims that she was hoodwinked and that Plummer fraudulently claimed to be something other than he was. I use the term "hoodwinked" to critique McMillan's sexual expectations because it is a double entendre: it both refers to being duped and draws attention to the popular terminology in Jamaica for the penis, *hood*. This signification highlights how the phallus in this instance becomes a tool in the repertoire of the trickster (Anancy spider) to wield to outwit predators or competitors. But the pun can be extended to draw our attention to the practice of "looking under [or in this case beyond] the hood" (or sex) before buying a bill of "goods." I do not mean to suggest that on closer "inspection" McMillan would have been able to "discover" Plummer's sexual identity. This cautionary tale invites us to consider the production of hypersexualized Black bodies in the Caribbean, specifically, and of poor bodies in other parts of the world. I emphasize the physical body here because, from all accounts, the physical and sexual "encounter" between Stella and Winston, and McMillan and Plummer, was easily scripted into well-documented fantasies of travel, leisure, adventure, and consumption.

He Said, She Said: Balancing Cultural Currency and the Sexual Diet

With the divorce behind him, Jonathan Plummer took to the airwaves to tell his version of the story, even appearing alongside his ex-wife on the *Oprah Winfrey Show*. Most of their interview focused on why it took Plummer more than twenty years to "discover" he was gay, something that Winfrey simply could not believe. For his part, Plummer attributed his late sexual epiphany to his Jamaican upbringing and the regulations governing private and public life in Jamaica: he explained that he was "from a culture where it is very conservative, and we never thought about being gay. It's not a good thing in my culture just because of our way of life. People look down on it" (Plummer and McMillan 2005). He went on to make several other primetime guest appearances on other shows, including the *Wendy Williams Show*; in each appearance the conversation shifted to Jamaica's intolerance of gay people and the growing phenomenon of Black men "on the down low." At around the same time, during the heated divorce proceedings, the public was given access to dozens of pages of court documents that Plummer filed in an effort to get a restraining order against McMillan; these filings indicate McMillan was doing her part to highlight the extent to which Americans could also be intolerant of homosexuals.

Shortly after the divorce and McMillan's lawsuit against him were settled, Jonathan Plummer coauthored *Balancing Act* (2007) with Karen Hunter, coauthor of the best-selling nonfiction book, *On the Down Low: A Journey into the Lives of 'Straight' Black Men Who Sleep with Men* (2005). Rather than following the prototypical boy-meets-girl paradigm, *Balancing Act* revolves around a community of men and women in the fashion industry whose sexual relationships have as much to do with power and social and professional status as with pleasure and desire. The novel borrows the romantic notion of finding the perfect Black man from the sistah lit genre, only to put an unexpected twist on it. In this case, the "perfect Black man" is a Jamaican man who is "discovered" by a young African American woman who owns a modeling agency. The protagonist, Tasha Reynolds, has made a successful career out of being a purveyor of masculine fetishism. Although *Balancing Act* does not approach McMillan's craft and her masterful manipulation of the conventions of contemporary popular fiction, it provides similarly productive moments for considering how popular culture shapes what we consume and desire and how we know ourselves as consumers.

Most texts about the experience of tourists in the Caribbean emphasize the experiences of the tourist. Jamaica Kincaid's *A Small Place* (1988) is the best-known exception: it is a Caribbean literary text that offers the reflections of Jamaicans on tourists who visit the region. There are few contemporary popular fiction texts that provide a similar critique, most likely because consumers find everything they disdain in this perspective, one they would prefer to have relegated to the fine print in the background. This is not to suggest that popular fiction is not a useful genre for critiquing American culture for its consumption. Quite the contrary: the beauty of popular fiction is the frequency with which these texts provide opportunities for cultural analysis based on popularly known (and accepted) stereotypes, not simply as stereotypes but as counternarratives that have the capacity to expose the complex assumptions that underlie popular representations of race, class, and sexuality.

If Winston Shakespeare was Stella's "boy toy" in *How Stella Got Her Groove Back*, then *Balancing Act*'s Justin Blakeman has improved his literary lot tremendously through his strong, albeit deeply problematic, narrative voice. When Tasha Reynolds "discovers" Justin on a roadside in Jamaica selling sugarcane, she promises to make him famous if he follows her to New York and works for her as a model. For all her expertise and talent, however, Tasha's opening salvo lacks the lyrical skill (or "game") typically associated with pimps—even though the promise of fame in the big city that she extends is eerily similar to the stereotypical line that pimps use to lure young, unsuspecting women (and sometimes men) away from home. Another tactic Tasha deploys that borrows from popular representations of pimps in film and television is the devaluation of Justin's current social condition to encourage him to believe that her offer is infinitely better than anything available to him in the near or distant future. Tasha makes it clear to Justin that work is not the same thing as *labor* and that *she* is the one who decides which qualifies and is to be rewarded. In her eyes, agricultural labor does not qualify as meaningful or productive work because it lays waste to Justin's otherwise appealing body, which could generate income for her rather than for himself or his family . Although employment, rather than romance, provides the pretext for their encounter, their exchange highlights the thin line between sexual work and other forms of labor, especially for Black "Third World" subjects:

> Tasha wanted to spend a little more time with Mr. Perfect Jamaican; she needed to study him to see if he had any weird disgusting ticks [sic], any hygiene issues, any missing teeth. . . .
>
> "Okay, I got a better offer for you," she said.
>
> "Now lady, I don't even know you. What kind of man do I look like?"
>
> "Oh please don't flatter yourself!" said Tasha. She didn't crack a smile. She wanted him to know that sex was the furthest thing from her mind. "Young man, I *am* interested in your body. But it's strictly business!" (Plummer and Hunter 2007, 11)

Without ever inquiring about Justin's current employment or social and familial obligations, Tasha determines that what she is offering him exceeds any available possibilities in Jamaica. Like Stella's Winston, Justin never mentions his family's business or the land they own. But why not? One would assume that in the conventions of the genre, having such a background would make them even more "ideal men." I argue, however, that their strategic withholding is a means of obscuring their power, thereby better positioning themselves to maximize the generosity of their "patrons" without jeopardizing the class security and respectability they enjoy in Jamaica. For both protagonists, their wealth is a nest egg in case things do not work out in the end.

Although the pimp/prostitute paradigm is readily apparent in the exchange between Justin and Tasha, his interpretation of their encounter is strikingly different from that of Winston in McMillan's earlier novel: Justin is unwilling to acknowledge the uneven power balance in this relationship. In an ironic twist of cultural transliteration similar to what occurs with Stella's ambivalence about liking Seal's music (*even though* he is African but British), Justin subverts the viewing lens to focus on the relative similarities between the Caribbean and the United States ("Second World" and "First World") by introducing Africa as a truly "Third World" locale. This construction relies heavily both on the audience's familiarity with tropes of the Caribbean (as a paradise) and Africa as its antithesis (impoverished, underdeveloped, malnourished) and also its assumed ignorance of the kind of power imbalances that make "worlding" possible. Stunned at Tasha's audacious invitation to take advantage of this "once in a lifetime opportunity" to become a star, Justin thinks to himself,

> *Who does she think she is? That superior attitude, as if she is coming here to rescue someone? Like she's in Africa, saving a starving child. Who does she think she is? Angelina Jolie? Madonna? F**k that.*
>
> *Do I look like I have flies on my eyeballs and a protruding stomach? Those damned Americans. Every year they come to this island with their shit.*
>
> *"Yah, mon, where can I get some weed?"*
>
> *I get stopped at least a dozen times with that one. And if it's not thinking that every f**king body in Jamaica smokes weed, then it's thinking every man will f**k your brains out. That damned woman with her book ruined it for us—now all we get are these women thinking they can get their groove back.* (Plummer and Hunter 2007, 13; emphasis in original)

The image of the black child with "flies on [their] eyeballs and a protruding stomach" belongs to a globalized visual culture that has the power to bring disparate audiences together through a shared (mis)recognition of race and poverty.[8] In these commercials, the face of poverty is almost always Black, and the message, "save these children," is conveyed through a narrative of patronage. The visually impoverished body is an essential part of what is "said" to the viewer because the image directs the gaze onto the Black child and speaks that which the child cannot utter on his or her behalf: the children in these images are too weak to speak for, much less help, themselves. Gayatri Spivak's brilliant critique embedded in the sentence, "White men are saving brown women from brown men" (1994, 93), cautions us about how language codifies and silences Black and brown bodies by turning them into metaphors for a number of imperialist practices. As in the Hindu practice of sati, or widow sacrifice, the true history of Black diasporic subjects cannot compare to the invented colonial narratives represented in paintings and photographs, on television screens, and romance narratives.

The fact that Justin evokes this imperialist stereotype as a response to his own interpolation into a similar discourse speaks volumes about the effectiveness of these visual regimes. Despite his upper-middle-class status, he is infantilized and emasculated by a system of signs that silence and erase his reality. And yet the starved, weakened body of a malnourished African child is the visual (and physical) *antithesis* of what Tasha actually sees in Justin's body. Tasha sees a body she thinks she knows and interpolates Justin into a system of signs that overdetermine his status as an immobile, disempowered, underdeveloped subject/object starving for the right nutritional diet; naturally, she is the only one who can "rescue" him. In an attempt to restore his respect and respectability, Justin reduces the economic and social distance between the Caribbean and the United States by evoking the stereotype of African poverty. In the meantime, he attributes Tasha's (mis)recognition of him to a lack of sophistication (i.e., class consciousness). He expects that *even though* Tasha is American (but Black) she should know better than to participate in this kind of misguided behavior. After all, as he sees it, she is neither Angelina Jolie nor Madonna (read: white, wealthy, with a desire to save Black children).

Both Winston and Justin belong to landholding families, and therefore, we can surmise that they are upper-middle-class Jamaicans. However, as mentioned, McMillan's novel provides very little insight into how Winston's family acquired their land and even less about his social formation. He is a blank slate on which she projects her fantasy. This knowledge gap is integral to how the Caribbean is consumed in popular fiction, but I suggest that, in these romances, it can also be used as a weapon for Caribbean consumers to take advantage of opportunities in the marketplace. *Balancing Act* attempts to fill in some of these narrative gaps, but in a curiously provisional manner. The narrator informs readers that "Justin's family claimed to be descendants of Queen Nanny of the Maroons" (Plummer and Hunter 2007, 8). This historical reference is intended to consolidate the Blakeman family genealogy as part of a rebellious tradition and yet locate them solidly in the Jamaican upper middle class. According to their family narrative, they own land that was once Maroon land and subsequently used it to build their wealth, stature, and respectability.

The rest of Justin's social background is set against the backdrop of two sex scenes, each of which speaks volumes about gender and class privilege in Jamaica. In the first instance, thirteen-year-old Justin is caught in the laundry room of his parents' home with their Dominican maid Maritza, on her knees giving him fellatio. She is promptly fired, while Justin receives quiet affirmation from his father who "grinned as [his] mother was ranting about appropriate behavior and class and discretion" (Plummer and Hunter 2007, 36), chastising him for his lack of discretion. The lesson he takes from this experience is that this kind of behavior is inappropriate *only* if he is caught. The second instance is almost identical to the first, but when the shoe is on the other foot, Justin is not nearly as cavalier as his parents. He walks into the assistant headmaster's office and finds his girlfriend Nannette, a "girl with proper breeding on her knees after school in the dean's office, giving the headmaster head." She tries to win him back by "giving him some lame excuse about being coerced by Fellows, who threatened to give her detention if she didn't comply. But Justin wasn't buying it. It didn't make sense" (26). He never recovers from witnessing his first love *in flagrante delicto* with another man with more authority but is of a lower class. In fact, after ending this relationship, Justin stops dating for years and, for the time period covered in the book, does not has another steady girlfriend.

Although *Balancing Act* provides significantly more insight into the social environments of all its protagonists than McMillan's *How Stella Got Her Groove Back*, there is what Thompson refers to as an "aesthetics of concealment" at work in how these sexual encounters are presented throughout Plummer's novel. According to Thompson (2006, 39), in producing "picturesque" images of the Caribbean, "planters and the artists they commissioned would disguise the conditions, violence, and brutality of the plantation." Although the setting for exploitation has shifted from a plantation economy to other forms of globalization for profit (i.e., tourism, domestic work, garment and information industries, etc.), the discursive strategies of concealment function in a similar way In *Balancing Act*, it occurs through an aesthetic of overexposure whereby the exploitive conditions of consumer culture are disguised through explicit sex scenes. There are few scenes of sexual intercourse in *How Stella Got Her Groove Back*, because McMillan uses consumer goods to distract our attention; in contrast, *Balancing Act* uses sex in the same manner that McMillan uses food, clothing, music, and other commodities. This narrative strategy effectively allows conditions of exploitation to be "hidden in plain sight" because sex functions as a signifier through which power is negotiated.

Oral sex and sexual positions are modes of concealment deployed throughout the novel. Justin's sexual encounters are represented through a series of sexual transgressions initiated by various women in his life: rarely is he an agent in the development of his sexual consciousness. Although Maritza is introduced to the reader as "a closet freak" who lures him into the laundry room, the narrator tells us ironically that they "met in that laundry room every afternoon until his grandmother caught them" (Plummer and Hunter 2007, 36). This suggests that their sexual encounters had become part of the daily chores Maritza was performing for the Blakeman family. Despite the fact that Justin is thirteen, he seems conveniently oblivious about his power and position as a Blakeman and, by extension, her employer. However, he certainly recognizes that his class status makes him a desirable catch for the girls in his class. When he sees Nannette on her knees "giving the headmaster head," the value of her proper breeding suddenly diminishes in his eyes, so much so that he refuses to even entertain the possibility that she may have been coerced into the act.

When Justin and Tasha first have sex, she fully expects to exercise her power as she usually does: with her on top of her sexual partner. However, for the first time in the novel, Justin becomes an agent and takes a more active role in a sexual act: "Tasha had Justin just where she wanted him, on his back as she went to work on his member, which seemed to swell another inch if that was possible. . . . She wanted to mount him badly but before she could, he flipped her over. It was a smooth, martial-arts-like move. Tasha had no idea how she'd ended up on her stomach. She *never* ended up on her stomach" (Plummer and Hunter 2007, 59).

Here, sexual positions are not simply about pleasure or desire; they are also about exhibiting one's power. Even the act of penetration is cast as another kind of negotiation of identity. All the sex scenes with Tasha involve her being penetrated, but the narrator repeatedly describes Justin as "servicing her," which suggests that regardless of their sexual positioning Tasha is always already "on top."

The practice of concealing "in plain sight" is not confined to the Caribbean, domestic spaces, or heterosexual sex. When Justin has a homosexual affair with Dorian (which, of course, Dorian initiates), every scene of their sexual relationship is rendered through explicit accounts of fellatio. Although Justin is a very eager participant, he has one inhibition: "The one thing Justin knew for sure was that he *never* wanted a man to penetrate him. That was just *too* gay. And Justin, even in the arms of this man, kissing and licking and stroking this man, didn't consider himself gay" (Plummer and Hunter 2007, 118). Dorian ends their relationship for fear that he will lose his modeling contract if Tasha finds out he is "responsible" for Justin's homosexual explorations. Once Justin can no longer rely on the security and protection that Dorian provides for him as a lover (specifically, a safe, comfortable space to explore his sexuality), he begins to frequent the back room of an arcade, while Dorian has sex in parks and bathrooms with strangers, because he enjoys being a "faceless, nameless, sexy body who [can] do whatever he want[s]" (122).

The obverse, however, is not true for the women in the novel. While Tasha's sexual desires seem focused wholly on Justin, she has another romantic interest, a woman named Anne a creative consultant in the industry who occasionally works with the Reynolds Agency. While Justin is in London, modeling at a fashion show, Tasha calls Anne to get help on an impending cover shoot. When Anne arrives, ready to work, Tasha seems distracted, and she is totally taken aback by Anne's beauty: "Tashsa continued to stare, amazed by what a black woman and a German man had produced" (Plummer and Hunter 2007, 93). The two have sex shortly thereafter, but Anne seems fully aware that this encounter may well be a one night stand and is "content to hold on to the memory of that night and content to never bring it up again, even if it was just that once" (Plummer and Hunter 2007, 96). As it turns out, it was just that once because Tasha, ever concerned with her public appearance and persona, could not let anyone find out that she had slept with Anne. They carry on their business relationship with no mention of what had transpired between them until Tasha decides to tell Anne on an out of state date that she has found the perfect mate in Justin. Anne immediately responds by asking her how Justin, someone she controlled totally, could ever be an equitable partner to her. By the end of the date, Tasha has chosen Justin over Anne and, though drunk, is ready to move on with her seemingly perfect life. Despite the sting of the rejections, Anne decides to drive Tasha, who is totally drunk, back home, and she calls Justin to help Tasha up to their apartment. Anne hands Justin the keys and leaves, knowing that it is over between her and Tasha.

Ann decides to walk home in order to clear her head after the events of the night, cutting through Central Park as she had done hundreds of times during the day. She is so deep in her own thoughts that she does not realize a man approaching her with a gun in his hand. By the time she recognizes him, he has already grabbed her, put the gun to her head, and has begun dragging her into deeply wooded area. What ensues is a brutal beating and rape, and Anne is left for dead in the park. Fortunately, from her hospital bed, Anne decides to seek revenge on Tasha, who she feels is partly to blame for her rape because, yet again, she put Tasha's well-being before her own. The rape scene is a pivotal moment for all the main characters in the novel. Plummer and Hunter take the unusual step of giving a detailed account of the trauma that rape victims often endure from the police, nurses, and the legal system. The narrative is thus keen to highlight the extent to which women are vulnerable to sexual violence, committed not only by individuals but also by institutional power structures. This description of the rape and its aftermath is particularly striking because it is the only explicit critique of gender and sexual privilege and power in the entire novel. The brutality of the scene would imply that this kind of critique would not be necessary because it is so obvious, yet great care is taken to detail every part of the legal and medical processes that Anne undergoes, after which she comments that the experience "made her feel like she was being raped all over again" (Plummer and Hunter 2007, 155).

While at the hospital, Justin encounters Anne's closest friend, Darryl, who tells him everything that happened the night before, including the date and the affair between Anne and Tasha, and the fact that Tasha had just broken off the physical relationship with Anne shortly before the rape occurred. Justin is floored when he hears the details from Darryl, and he hardens his resolve to break it off with Tasha, not simply because she has cheated on him, but also because he has been sleeping with Dorian, another male model in Tasha's modeling agency. When he returns home, with the shock of Anne's assault fresh in his mind, Justin tells Tasha he is leaving her, declaring, "I think I'm gay! And from what I hear, so are you!" (Plummer and Hunter 2007, 186). Tasha's response to Justin is captured in a litany of derogatory terms, punctuated by a recounting of all she has done for him, the claim that she *made* him, and the accusation that he was nothing before he met her. In this regard, Tasha's vitriol is strikingly similar to Plummer's account of McMillan's "faggot"-laced tirade in his deposition requesting a restraining order against her.[9] To Tasha's verbal assault, Justin finally replies, "You act like you plucked some porch monkey out of the jungle and civilized him. I wasn't Tarzan when you met me. And I'm going to let you in on something else: *I was far from poor*" (185).

Thus, Justin finally acknowledges his class status in Jamaica and, in so doing, suggests that withholding this information was his means of maintaining some (minimal) control of his narrative. The conclusion of the novel can hardly be described as a happy ending, but it is certainly a profitable one for several of the other characters, who begin to realize the amount of power they have always had but were unable or unwilling to acknowledge. Once again, this critical insight is rendered through an ironic yet effective sexual analogy. Anne's new assistant, Darryl, becomes a mentor of sorts to Justin, providing him with an important lesson about sex, exploitation, and power: "'Without her bottom bitch, Miss Tasha will fall,' Darryl said. 'No disrespect to you. But you were her bottom bitch—you were her top money earner, the one she depended on. She may have made you feel like you needed her, but she needed you'" (Plummer and Hunter 2007, 210). Again, the pimp/prostitute analogy is an obvious point of reference, but the lesson Darryl is trying to impart to Justin is simple: even though Tasha is "on top," her power extends only as far as Justin allows it to, because it is his labor that determines her success.

However, it soon becomes clear that Justin is not only a bad student but is also easily duped. I return to the pivotal point of Spivak's question: "Can the subaltern speak?" For all intents and purposes, the answer in Justin Blakeman's case is unequivocally no. Justin accepts an invitation to Tasha's house, where she offers him a chance to reform his ways and continue their relationship. When he refuses, she assaults him, and when he fights her off, she has him arrested for allegedly attacking her. Not long afterward, the narrator tells us, "Darryl and Anne saved Justin. He was on the brink of losing not just his possessions, but also his mind. And they came along and gave him something he sorely needed—friendship and a purpose" (Plummer and Hunter 2007, 210). Even when Justin is given a chance to claim his own self-determination by joining the Becker Agency, Tasha soon dangles in front of him another "offer" that he may not be able to refuse: Dorian. After inviting Justin to her apartment to bury the hatchet, she invites him to come back to work for him, but he refuses saying, "I know you've noticed that I'm doing pretty okay without you" (222). Tasha, not one to be outdone, retorts "You could do *so* much better" and walks away from Justin into her bedroom, only to summon him a few minutes later:

> He walked into the huge bedroom and didn't see her, but the door to her master bathroom was open. He slowly walked to the threshold of the bathroom.
>
> There, in the huge marble tub, was Tasha.
>
> On the other end was Dorian.
>
> "Come on in," Tasha said beaming. "There's definitely room for one more" (222).

We never find out if he accepts her offer and his role as a Black man in constant need of being saved. That is left up to our imaginations. Ironically, what emerges by the end of *Balancing Act* is a realization of the anxieties expressed in dancehall songs: women are now the predatory force in the global marketplace, and they have voracious appetites. This is not to suggest, however, that they are now protected from being exploited, violated, or adversely affected by the unrelenting weight of institutional inequities that still position them on their backs, so to speak.

Critically examining popular fiction allows us to interpret the extent to which sex and sexuality are a trope for negotiating the terms of exchange and engagement. Sheller reminds us of the ways in which sexuality can be deployed as a tool or weapon to balance unequal power dynamics in the global marketplace:

> Against the forces of a world economy that commodified Black bodies, sucked the marrow from their bones, and tried to turn them into will-less workers, *resistance took the form of taking a claim in one's own body. Using one's own sexuality for personal gain and profiting from the sexual display of oneself are ways of "turning a trick."* In contrast, to work for another, to become an object controlled by forces outside oneself suggests a disciplined body, a body without agency, a zombie. (Sheller 2003, 155; emphasis added)

This interpretation of the political economy of sexuality is played out in a very significant cultural context that must be considered as part of this cautionary tale. What Sheller describes as "turning a trick" has long been part of the discourse of the street, of the pimps, prostitutes, and patrons who buy, sell, and barter sex in the global marketplace. There is also another subtext, one that draws on the Caribbean tradition of "anancyism." In Caribbean oral traditions, Anancy spider uses wit and cunning to succeed against other, larger predators. In a global economy in which smaller, developing countries become the playgrounds for vacationers and travelers in search of "authentic" experiences, there will always be room for a hustle. Indeed, many would argue that in developing countries there is no chance for survival without some kind of hustle. Whether the hustle is being a police officer by day and a bouncer by night, selling baked goods without a license, marrying for money or a green card, selling drugs, or selling pirated music and counterfeit designer goods, it is part of a thriving global informal economy.

The moral of the story here is an old one, a cliché even: buyers beware—not all that glitters is gold. This is a lesson that McMillan learned from Plummer's demand for a share of the income earned from the sales of *How Stella Got Her Groove Back*. In Jeannette and Richard Allsopp's *Dictionary of Caribbean Usage* (2003, 30) a definition of *Anancyism* includes a brief quotation from the Jamaican newspaper, *The Daily Gleaner*, which reads, "Nowhere in the vast literature of anancyism is there an instance of Anancy paying for anything. Ananciologists have justified this attitude to life by arguing that Anancy is a small creature who . . . has to employ his wits to protect himself against much larger predators and competitors." The legal documentation presented by McMillan during her divorce proceedings includes a detailed listing of all the monetary support McMillan provided to Plummer. The unspoken assumption was that

McMillan, not Plummer, set out terms of this arrangement, including the prenuptial agreement and his "allowances." Based on these "agreements," McMillan understood herself to be in possession of a loyal (hetero)sexual subject. Her reaction, therefore, was as much about how people would perceive her as it was Plummer's coming out. To be sure, many have questioned and will continue to question how she could not have known that he was gay, implying that her "gaydar" somehow malfunctioned. It may simply have been the case that she, like Stella and Tasha, saw the commercials advertising what Jamaica had to offer and was not interested in anything beyond the fact that she had "earned the right to some happiness." (Plummer and Hunter 2007, 285). Others might justifiably argue that even if Plummer had married McMillan to obtain citizenship, had he not also worked hard (as her husband, lover, partner) and "earned" his own right to happiness? The phenomenon of the Black male as an "embodied commodity" was certainly realized as a lived fantasy through McMillan's novel, so much so that it sparked a new trend: "the whole tableau was so inspirational that thousands of itchy women started flocking to the Caribbean, scouring the beaches for their own special bronzed groovemakers" (Gerhart 2005).

What lessons, if any, are learned when vacationers gorge themselves and then complain to the management that the food is no good, the sun not bright enough, the groove no longer there? As Sheller (2003, 181) asks, "Does metropolitan culture in fact again reproduce its domination, reconstitute its centres of knowledge and power, and erase the (neo)colonial relations of violence that enable this proximity in the first place?" These are among the questions that are not asked of popular texts that invent and reproduce the Caribbean as a place of exotic others whose reason for being is to "service" and make real the fantasies of visitors. Whether we read McMillan's narrative and real-life drama as a case of hoodwinking or "playing dead to catch corbeau alive," the moral of the story may well be that the shifting tides of globalization obscure the intricate international flows (and definitions) of labor, sexual identity, and capital. Practices of consumption can be and often are interpolated into cultural and discursive registers that are beyond the reach and tastes of many consumers. For some, however, the instability of signs, economies, and identities provides an interstitial space from which they can weave creative, intricate webs of identity that serve as bridges for them to cross over obstacles and (national, sexual, and economic) boundaries.

3

"Who's On Top?"

Power, Pleasure, and the Politics of Taste

> Appetite comes with eating, my Friend, and Toussaint, who before did not desire more than The Ysland of Santo Domingo[1] for his rule, is now planning to successively incorporate the neighboring Ysland of Jamaica . . . then Cuba, then Puerto Rico, and finally the whole Globe.

White women's desire, once only suggested in nineteenth-century narratives, serves as the basis for an industry of popular representations that feature Black and white women as consumers seeking to have their desires fulfilled through travel to exotic places and participation in erotic (forbidden) experiences. However, these erotic desires are by no means limited to tourists from abroad, regardless of class. Dany Laferrière's fiction engages the paradigm of desire as a driving motivation for travel; whether one has the desire to escape the monotony of life in the North, to feel powerful because of one's value as a tourist or as a wealthy Haitian, or to be considered "desirable," no one is free from the effects of what he refers to as "the dictatorships of desire." *Heading South* and *Le gout des jeunes filles* provide complex frameworks for considering agency through sexualized bodies that signify or perform what Giatry Spivak describes as strategic "withholding" during intimate sexual exchanges.[2] These acts of withholding guard these otherwise overexposed Black bodies from representation, and thus interpretation, as victims in these postcolonial narratives. In many of the sexual encounters, the primary consumers know little, if anything, about the lives of their sexual partners. As such, this seemingly intimate exchange is shown to be more superficial than the foreigners participating in the exchanges are even aware of. In this regard, there is a space for these Haitian boys and girls to exercise a degree of agency in their lives beyond these sexual escapades. Laferrière's young protagonists are keenly aware of their tenuous positions in the consumption pyramid of Haitian society and in their relationships with other global consumers, especially Americans. What is so striking about his narratives is his singular attention to how the experiences of consuming and being consumed shape the consciousness and subjectivities of young people. Strategic withholding functions like a value-added tax (VAT) applied to consumers by those with limited access to the traditional means of power and agency. I suggest that Laferrière's overriding concerns about sexuality reveal much deeper questions about the circuits of consumption among the middle classes in the Caribbean region. There is an implicit social system of value circulating in these texts that overrides the dollar value of commodities, particularly security and sex, and in so doing redistributes the implicit power of these commodities among those who are more likely to be consumed than consumers.

In the French, *Le gout des jeunes filles* literally translates to "The Taste of Young Girls"; however, the book's English title is *Dining with the Dictator*. The novel's title change, from the French to the English, signals a change in the relationship between readers and the versions of the Caribbean they can comfortably consume. Given the ambiguity of the term *le gout* ("the taste"), the title change shifts the agency ascribed to the young girls in the novel and places it squarely into the hands of the dictator. The emphasis on sex and sexuality is seen in other provocative titles by Laferrière, most notably *Why Must a Black Writer always Write about Sex* and *How to Make Love to a Negro without Getting Tired*. Many of his titles highlight the political assumptions underlying various modes of cultural representation that espouse a practice of fair trade among producers, consumers, and markets, particularly within the literary world and, by extension, the publishing industry. In this chapter, I also examine the trend of recasting popular fiction in cinematic forms that exchange (or trade) the discursive underpinnings of representations of racial, sexual, and national identity for more aesthetically disruptive representations, such as older white women who unabashedly express their sexual desires. Older bodies that would be considered undesirable and asexual in the United States, and certainly in Hollywood, replace the perfect physical cinematic (Black and white) bodies that traditionally populate these narratives, as in *How Stella Got Her Groove Back*.

In contrast to Jamaica, which is often described as a desirable vacation destination, contemporary imaginings of the Caribbean rarely represent Haiti as a place of relaxation, fun, and sexual adventure. More often, when Haiti appears in the popular imagination it is constructed as a proverbial "underworld" in which political corruption, violence, poverty, and vodoun have a stranglehold on the country. Anxieties about Haiti's "darkness" belong to a long tradition that dates to well before the November 1803 founding of the first Black and the second oldest republic in the Western Hemisphere. The realization of Haiti's dream of independence was received as a nightmare, particularly by slaveholding countries. The events that culminated in the 1803 Haitian Revolution were preceded by a series of rebellions that began in 1791 with a mulatto revolt against the French. To be clear, theirs was not simply a struggle to end slavery: they wanted full civil rights that would give them equality with the whites. This request fell on deaf ears, and in March 1791 a few hundred mulattoes (led by Ogé) revolted to bring about this change. However, they were brutally executed by the colonial militia (Williams 2020, 247).

The next rebellion, and the most critical one in terms of Haiti's current place in the American imagination, occurred a few months later in August 1791. According to numerous accounts, this rebellion was preceded by a voudoun ceremony led by the Jamaican-born slave, Dutty Boukman, in Bois Caiman; that was the beginning of the twelve-year battle that eventually defeated Captain-General Charles Leclerc's army. Writing to Napoleon in distress, just a few weeks before his death in 1802, Leclerc had this to say about the events transpiring in Saint-Domingue: "Here is my opinion of this country. We must destroy all the negroes in the hills, men and women, sparing only children under twelve, destroy half of those living in the plains and leave behind not a single man of color who has worn a uniform—without this the colony will never have peace."[3] By the time this letter reached Napoleon, however, the last of his forces had been defeated, and after three hundred years of enslavement, in November 1803, Jean-Jacques Dessalines declared Saint Domingue[4] free and reclaimed its indigenous name, Haiti.

The phantasmagoria captured in the epigraph speaks to the extent to which the fear that their wives, daughters, property, and power would be consumed took hold of planters and politicians in Haiti, as well as those in power in countries around the globe. To most Europeans, the Haitian Revolution seemed unimaginable: it overturned the epistemic and ontological foundations of the world as they had known it for hundreds of years. The sentiment expressed in the epigraph also captures the sense of dread about the potential of an indiscriminately "devouring" Black nation-state. Whites were not terrified that simply by eating/tasting freedom, Toussaint and the Blacks of Saint-Domingue would desire more. Instead, as the epigraph asserts, they understood that "appetite comes with eating," and they envisioned that an "undisciplined" economic, political, and cultural palate could only lead to excessive indulgences. However, according to Sybille Fischer (2004, 4), this fear was not rooted in the political implications of the Haitian Revolution but in rumored sacrifices, rumored rituals, and the brutality of the uprising: "In the letters and reports of white settlers, the revolution is not a political and diplomatic issue; it is a matter of body counts, rape, material destruction, and infinite bloodshed. It is barbarism and unspeakable violence, outside the realm of civilization and beyond human language. It is an excessive event, and as such, it remained for the most part, confined to the margins of history."

What is important here, particularly for thinking about how Haiti is represented (and consumed) in a contemporary context, is the response to the revolution that focused on its terror/horror. No space or effort was given to considering the possibility that the so-called excesses of the revolution were commensurate with the level of terror and suffering exacted on the enslaved populations of Haiti. In fact, Dessaline suggested precisely this when, in his January 1, 1804, proclamation of Haiti's freedom, he asserted, "I have given the French blood for blood."[5] I return to the question of "excess" later in this discussion because it is an essential part of the existential debate about freedom and subject formation.

Necro-Politics and Necro-Romance in Popular Representations of Haiti

The immediate response to the terror evoked by the Haitian Revolution was to take action to control the spread of news about the rebellion. The fear was that knowledge of the event in Haiti would promote similar attempts at rebellion and the destruction of plantations by slaves in neighboring countries. According to Fischer (2004, 4), "In response to the revolution, a cordon sanitaire was drawn around the island to disrupt the flow of information and people." But this effort was only partially successful, as whites who managed to escape the rebellion fled, some with their slaves, to neighboring countries. In 1825, twenty years after the Haitian Revolution, France recognized Haiti's independence. The United States did not recognize Haiti as a sovereign, independent nation until 1862. However, during the period of the blockade, both France and the United States were involved in bustling economic partnerships with Haiti, although they were permitted only marginal access to the country. The history of relations between the United States and Haiti is a long and remarkably complicated one, marked by occupation by U.S. military forces; American intervention in Haitian governmental structures and elections, coup d'états, and dictatorships; and waves of immigration to and droves of deportees from the United States. The large-scale political power struggles, when coupled with well-earned blame and mistrust, make for a complex relationship of interdependence. How are we to understand the trajectory of events, from the Haitian Revolution to the recent earthquake in 2010, and how Haiti is imagined and represented in popular culture? With more than three hundred years of history, scholarship, and documentation from the Haitian perspective of the revolution to draw on, there is one moment that has had an unusually powerful influence on the way Haiti is imagined: the voudoun ceremony in Bois Caiman that precipitated the first stage of the Haitian

Revolution. Well over three hundred years later, it continues to shape popular imaginings of Haiti and the numerous (national and natural) catastrophes that seem to have a stranglehold on the country.

Despite the wealth of historical accounts that detail the organization of the rebellions and Haiti's diplomatic, economic, and political institutions—which were similar to those associated with the formation of the United States, the only republic that is older than Haiti—the belief persists that Haiti achieved its freedom through "otherworldly" transactions. There are numerous ways to interpret the term "otherworldly," and fiction writers have expounded in richly imaginative ways to suggest that the ceremony at Bois Caiman was a call to African ancestors to aid the Haitians in their struggle. This perspective of the ceremony was memorialized in Alejo Carpentier's 1949 novel, *El reino de este mundo*.

In their essay "Necropolitics," Achille Mbembe and Libby Meintjes (2003, 12) outline, in careful detail, the rise of modern terror and its relationship to the state's willingness and ability to exercise what Foucault refers to as *biopower*, or that domain over which power (namely the state) has taken control:

> Any historical account of the rise of modern terror needs to address slavery, which could be considered one of the first instances of biopolitical experimentation. In many respects, the very structure of the plantation system and its aftermath manifests the emblematic and paradoxical figure of the state of exception. This figure is paradoxical for two reasons. First, in the context of the plantation, the humanity of the slave appears as the perfect figure of a shadow. Indeed, the slave condition results from a triple loss: loss of a "home," loss of rights over his or her body, and loss of political status. This triple loss is identical with absolute domination, natal alienation, and social death (expulsion from humanity altogether).

Among the numerous examples of modern terror that they include in this analysis are Nazi concentration camps and South African apartheid; however, they pay particular attention to the critical aims of the plantation system as they pertain to two critical aspects of exercising sovereignty over colonized bodies: "Sovereignty meant occupation, and occupation meant relegating the colonized into a third zone between subjecthood and objecthood" (Mbembe and Meintjes 2003, 26). However, this third space was drastically reconfigured by Haitian slaves on the eve of the final battle for independence. Mbembe and Meintfes, like George Bataille, believe that the subject only realizes his or her full potential in freedom through the realization that "sovereignty is the refusal to accept the limits that the fear of death would have the subject respect" (Bataille and Hurley 1988, 16). By winning their independence through war and rebellion, Haitians had conquered not only the French but also death and, in so doing, entered the realm of what Hegel terms the "becoming subject."

The events that transpired in Haiti obliterated the foundational structures on which Enlightenment reason was founded. The rebellion against their enslavement called into question the assumed "animal" nature of Blacks because they fought with full knowledge that if they failed, they would be killed. Their willingness to go forward despite this knowledge, according to Mbembe and Meintjes (2003, 14), is the critical point of departure between human beings, and nonhuman beings:

> Within the Hegelian paradigm, human death is essentially voluntary. It is the result of risks consciously assumed by the subject. According to Hegel, in these risks the "animal" that constitutes the human subject's natural being is defeated.
>
> In other words, the human being truly *becomes a subject*—that is separated from the animal—in the struggle and the work through which he or she confronts death (understood as the violence of negativity). To uphold the work of death is precisely how Hegel defines the life of the Spirit. The life of the Spirit, he says, is not that life which is frightened of death, and spares itself destruction, but that life which assumes death, and lives with it.

I quote Mbembe and Meintjes's article at length here for two reasons. First, their deployment of Hegel is particularly useful for my discussion of the contemporary fixation on the voudoun ceremony at Bois Caiman and why it has become, for many, an emblem of "Haiti's troubles." Like Mbembe and Meintjes, I am interested in Hegel's thinking about death and subject formation insofar as it allows a better understanding of the concept of sovereignty. However, the second reason I quote at length is that I am also interested in how Hegel's theories about subject formation and sovereignty offer a framework for interpreting the various ways that Haiti continues to function as an outlier in the exceptional and improbable struggle to maintain one's humanity in the face of social death.

The evocation of ancestors on the eve of the revolution was both a religious and political act. However, accounts of the rebellion, as Fischer points out, sought to diminish the deeply political and religious nature of this struggle by focusing primarily on its excesses—the brutality, body counts, and destruction of property. The open embrace of the world of dead is a means of ending the state of "non-life" or the "living dead" that slavery posits. This might be considered a perverse interpretation of Hegel's notion concerning the life of the Spirit as a "life which assumes death, and lives with it "(Fischer 2004, 12). Rather than rejecting the overemphasis on voudoun as a central element of the Haitian Revolution, I want to consider the possibility of reading voudoun as a symbolic cultural practice that provides an important institutional structure for fragmented, subjugated communities, then and now, to occupy and experience—in short, to live—their humanity. In this framework, the embrace of death is more of a transitory space, rather than an end of life. In the Haitian voudoun pantheon, there are lwas (like Papa Legba) who occupy both spaces, keeping one foot in each world, while others act as intermediaries between the living and the dead. Moreover, the evocation of voudoun is an enactment of the enslaved's "capacity for self-creation through recourse to institutions inspired by specific social and imaginary significations" (13).

Social significations are often misread or reinterpreted in cultural systems that run contrary to the political and cultural contexts out of which they have emerged. Nowhere is this more evident that in the contemporary appropriation of voudoun in the popular imagination as the reason for every natural/political disaster that has ever occurred in Haiti. The televangelist Pat Robertson's infamous statement on *The 700 Show* of the Christian Broadcasting Network, made just days after the 2010 earthquake in Haiti, reflects this sentiment:

> Something happened a long time ago in Haiti, and people may not want to talk about it. They were under the heel of the French, Napoleon the Third, and whatever. They got together and swore a pact with the devil. They said we will serve you if you will get us free from the French. True story. And so the devil said, "Okay it's a deal." And the Haitians revolted and got themselves free. But ever since, they have been cursed by one thing after the other and desperately poor. The island of Hispaniola is one island, cut down the middle. On the one side is Haiti, and the other side is the Dominican Republic. The Dominican Republic is prosperous, healthy, and full of resorts, et cetera; Haiti is in desperate poverty—same island. They need to have, and we need to pray for them, a great turning to God, and out of this tragedy, I am optimistic that something good will come.

In an effort to mollify the public outcry that ensued after news of these comments made its way across the media airwaves, Chris Roslan, spokesman for the Christian Broadcast Network, issued a press release later that day that read in part,

> On today's *The 700 Club*, during a segment about the devastation, suffering and humanitarian effort that is needed in Haiti, Dr. Robertson also spoke about Haiti's history. His comments were based on the widely discussed 1791 slave rebellion led by Boukman Dutty at Bois Caiman, where the slaves allegedly made a famous pact with the devil in exchange for victory over the French. This history, combined with the horrible state of the country, has led countless scholars and religious figures over the centuries to believe the country is cursed.

Note that this press release Roslan never actually states that what Robertson said was erroneous, improbable, or even offensive (even when taken "out of context"). Instead, it provides a genealogy of how this "belief" developed, locating it in a tradition of scholarly thought, religious authority, and "hard evidence" presented through "history." Curiously, the release does not cite the names of any historians or religious scholars, other than Pat Robertson and the Christian Broadcast network. There is also a discursive shift from a voudoun ceremony to a pact with the devil (because this seems to be the only way one can evoke spirits for strength and support—a practice that we are encouraged to assume is far outside the Judeo-Christian belief system).

As if the religious mythology were not damning enough, Robertson's comments hint at other popular and negative representations of Haiti. His reference to the Dominican Republic as a "healthy, prosperous, and full of resorts" is no doubt informed by the myth that voudoun practices were the likely source of the spread of AIDS in Haiti. A cursory glance at media representations in the United States during the 1980s speaks volumes about how Haiti was imagined in the earliest days of the HIV/AIDS epidemic. The intertextual relationships between popular narratives and scientific research are now often discredited because of the current stringent standards set for medical researchers. However, as Paul Farmer highlights in his 2006 book, *AIDS and Accusation: Haiti and the Geography of Blame*, quasi-scientific links made between "popular" imaginings of Haiti and the spread of HIV/AIDS had a tremendous impact on policy makers, medical professionals, and ultimately patient care. Farmer recounts the emergence of this kind of culturally influenced medical research: "In North America and Europe, other commentators linked AIDS in Haiti to 'voodoo practices.' In the October 1983 edition of *Annals of Internal Medicine*, for example, physicians affiliated with the Massachusetts Institute of Technology related the details of a brief visit to Haiti and wrote, 'It seems reasonable to consider voodoo practices a cause of the syndrome.'"[6]

A close discursive analysis of this claim certainly raises questions as to why it would be "reasonable" to consider voudoun as the cause of AIDS. Farmer (2006, 2) himself asks, "Did existing knowledge of AIDS in Haiti make such a hypothesis reasonable? Had voodoo been previously associated with the transmission of other illnesses?" Undoubtedly, popular representations of Haiti and Haitians have influenced the way communities of scientists, religious leaders, and politicians configure Haiti in their policies and research.[7]

Haiti's representation as a vector of disease, on the one hand, and as an ideal location for the extraction of natural and human resources, on the other, speaks to the contradictory nature of representation and the uses to which the "large reservoir of cultural imaginaries" (Mbembe and Meintjes 2003, 26) have been put. One of the best-known cinematic representations to combine these three agendas and discursive communities—scientific, religious, and political—is Wes Craven's 1998 cult classic *The Serpent and the Rainbow*. Although this chapter does not provide an in-depth analysis of Craven's film, I evoke it here because it is a critical text for understanding how the same market-driven "aesthetics of taste" described in the epigraph have come to represent the relationship between Haiti and the rest of the world. In other words, insatiable appetites are not found in Haitians, but rather in governments around the globe—not unlike those that barricaded Haiti after its revolution—which are terrified by the prospect of a Black nation seeking self-determination and freedom. The embargo was intended to deprive Haiti of its right (and ability) to control its natural and human resources. A similar appetite is at the center of *The Serpent and the Rainbow*, a biopic about a Harvard-trained anthropologist who travels to Haiti to fulfill his insatiable desire to corner the ethno-pharmacology market. The film situates Haiti as a country of "darkness," overrun with corruption, drugs, violence, mysticism, sex, and (of course) sun—a well-crafted combination of several of Haiti's historical representations.

Papa Doc Duvalier's regime provides the backdrop for the central narrative about Wade Davis, a white American anthropologist seeking to discover the secret potion used in the process of zombification, with the intention of reproducing it as a wonder drug that would transform the pharmaceutical industry and the health care profession. Based on Davis's book of the same name, *The Serpent and the Rainbow* is heralded as one of Wes Craven's cult classics, both because of its dark, gruesome (political) nightmares and how it situates Haitian society and culture as a newly emerging market that could be of use to global pharmaceutical industries in the Western Hemisphere. In the film, Haiti figures as pathway, vector, and test group for scientific inquiry into a range of religious and cultural practices and beliefs.[8] Although it is implied that Duvalier employs zombification to oppress Haitians, the primary concern for the scientist is not ameliorating the oppressive conditions in the country; instead his focus is on the value and marketability of the potion for the U.S. pharmaceutical industry.

Haiti is presented as the proverbial "boogey man," governed by "black magic," vodoun, and other worldly forces, the least of which is exploitation by U.S. institutions and industries. However, even in the context of the "dark science" of the film, sexual encounters figure prominently as part of this enticing landscape: even the "rational" scientist cannot escape the allure of his "guide" through the treacherous "underworld" of Haiti under Duvalier. After all, scientists need sex too, and what better source than the native informant whose job it is to provide Davis with inside information about Haiti and voudoun. By the end of the film, sexuality has to be viewed as another site of critical engagement with the different ways in which Caribbean commodities are consumed. As Craven's film suggests, sexual intercourse, like food consumption, involves the intimate entrance into "native" (physical, spiritual) bodies. But these questions remain: What "inside information" does sexual intimacy provide, and how is it decoded, disseminated, and valued on global markets?

Hens, Cocks, and Yard Fowls: Dining and Consumption in *Heading South*

The aesthetics of taste are closely connected to the politics of pleasure, power, and sexuality, but several complex negotiations inform the dynamics of these exchanges. For example, how are cultural palates shaped and through what processes? What role, if any, do gender and age play in shaping tastes, desires, and expectations of travel and entertainment? If what we ingest—food, spirits, pharmaceuticals, and so on—is one point of entry for ethical debates about power, mobility, and consumption, then can sex be examined as another point of ethical critique for visitors and "natives" alike? If consuming "authentic" food items from the Caribbean is one method of experiencing local culture, then how are we to interpret the consumption of bodies, cultural artifacts, and practices? Dany Laferriere's vast body of writing takes up these questions in several provocative, and some would argue perverse, contexts. The strategies deployed by the "underprivileged" to negotiate systems of power among upper-middle-class Haitians, tourists, foreign nationals, politicians, and hustlers are often manifested through sexual relationships.

Laferrière's young protagonists are keenly aware of their tenuous positions in the consumption pyramid of Haitian society and in their relationships with other global consumers, especially Americans. His singular attention to how experiences of consuming and being consumed shape the consciousness and subjectivities of young people is a crucial part of his aesthetic as a novelist. In the short story collection, *Heading South,* and *Dining with the Dictator,* the young protagonists engage in what I define as a "strategic withholding" that functions similarly to a value-added tax (VAT) traditionally applied to consumers by the state at every step of the production process. Among those with limited access to traditional means of power and agency, the practice of strategic withholding provides protection from overuse and depletion, particularly in jobs that are physically demanding. Where systems of taxation have historically been the domain of economic agencies within government structures, individual citizens—often women, children, and others who are economically vulnerable—have developed systems of informal taxation that create opportunities for them to be compensated more equitably for their labor. In other words, citizens have begun to usurp the government's power of taxation literally and figuratively in an attempt to slightly tilt the playing field away from primarily benefiting the state.

Laferrière's overriding concerns about sexuality reveal much deeper questions about the circuits of consumption among the middle class in the Caribbean region. In both *Heading South* and *Dining with the Dictator,* there is a circulating but implicit social system of value that overrides the dollar value of intangible commodities (particularly pleasure, security, and sex) and attempts to redistribute the "use value" of these commodities among those who are less likely to be consumers than they are to be consumed. In lieu of equitable opportunities and access, Laferrière's protagonists adopt a perverse brand of "fair trade" that is remarkably similar to the model used to demarcate goods and labor grown, marketed, and imagined globally under more "equitable" conditions for laborers.

The short story from which the collection takes its title, *Heading South,* is later reimagined as a thoughtful film adaptation of Laferrière's representations of consumption, sexuality, and power. Its genealogy has been a source of confusion for viewers, but it is based on three short stories that first appeared in a 1997 collection titled *La Chair du maître* (The Flesh of the Master). In 2005 these three stories were republished, along with several new stories, as *Vers le sud* (Heading South) to coincide with the release of Cantet's film. Despite their shared genealogy, the two texts are distinctly different, and Canet borrows liberally from several stories in the collection to build composite characters for his film. As Elizabeth Walcott-Hackshaw notes in her discussion of Laferrière's collection,

> Apart from the middle-aged women, there is also Sam the businessman, ready to exploit the dire economic conditions of a family-owned hotel about to go bankrupt. Sam is described as "a vulture only seen when something has already died." The American consul Harry gives visas in exchange for sexual favours from young Haitian girls. In Haiti, Americans have the power to buy literally anything they like, both property and people. The history of this American exploitation of Haiti is recalled by Albert, the Haitian maitre d'hôtel at the beach resort where the women stay. Albert's father fought against the Americans during the first American Occupation from 1915 to 1934.

The complex systems of exploitation represented in this passage highlight the interconnectedness between the personal, the political, and the commercial in countries that are forced to rely on foreign tastes and investments for their stability. The array of commerce systems that stretch across the stories show the extent to which commodity fetishism shapes the day-to-day lives of citizens who are economically vulnerable: the currency of choice ranges from visas, influence, education, and employment to food, sex, clothing, property, and even art. Through this broad range of capital, Laferrière reminds us in subtle and not so subtle ways that, even in a political economy where hard currency is scarce, other vital commodities are used to conduct the daily business that makes life livable or, in the case of Haiti, treacherous.

As Walcott-Hackshaw's critique suggests, Laferrière's social mapping moves between historical flashpoints that include the Haitian Revolution, the U.S. occupation, and the Duvalier dictatorship to highlight how circuits and technologies of consumption are explicitly linked to larger projects of colonialism, destabilization, and globalization.[9] This last point takes us back to Cantet's film *Heading South*, which re-creates Haiti as a proverbial sexual playground for three middle-aged white women on holiday.

The three women in the film—Ellen, Brenda, and Sue, played by Charlotte Rampling, Karen Young, and Louise Portal, respectively—seem to have found their heaven on earth among the "gods": Legba, played by Ménothy César, and Neptune (played by Wilfried Paul), a local fisherman who frequents a beach resort Haiti during the 1970s Baby Doc era. This film has not received the critical attention it deserves, particularly considering the wide acclaim given some of its cinematic predecessors, particularly *How Stella Got Her Groove Back*. This has everything to do with the ethical dilemmas at the root of *Heading South*, which decidedly disrupt what Krista Thompson (2015) calls the "visual economies" so often associated with all-inclusive vacation locations in contemporary films about the Caribbean. Part of the visual disruption emerges from the uncomfortably youthful appearance of the young Haitian boys who are Ellen and Brenda's objects of affection. The young men in the film appear to be *barely* of age to consent to sexual activity, which is a clear effort to maintain some degree of faithfulness to the novel, which identifies the boys as being underage. In Laferrière's stories, the young are represented as young stallions whose primary job is to service older women, who are often described as "choice birds." It is important to note, however, that this description applies not only to white female tourists but also to female members of the Haitian ruling elite. In fact, one of the main protagonists, Fanfan, who is seventeen years old, tells us in *Heading South* (Laferrière 2009, 4):

> I like my women more mature. I like watching them lose their cool. Especially those who take themselves seriously. For some time now, I've had my eye on a really choice bird: the principal of the school my sister goes to. . . . I know she is a respectable person, but I want to see her private side, what's hidden behind her mask, the dark side of her moon. So, I sit very still in the room. I know she's spotted me. I've often caught her looking at me out of the corner of her eye. I play the innocent.

The introduction to Fanfan is intended to put readers on alert about the stories they will read about Haiti, the disempowered, underprivileged working classes in the country, and the relationships they have with the ruling elites who, as the narrator tells us, "barricade themselves in their fancy houses up on the mountainside" (Laferrière 2009, 3). Fanfan, the son of a seamstress, is brutally conscious of the limited options the social structure of Haiti provides for him and others like him, who are moderately well educated but are not part of "the golden circle" whose wealth, power, and influence entitle them to rule the entire country. For the youth who populate these narratives, innocence has little use for those who wish to succeed in life, a lesson that Fanfan learns from as young as age twelve. The "choice bird" he has set his eyes on is Madame Saint-Pierre, who is French but who came to Port-au-Prince so long ago that she "seems to have taken on all the cruel customs of Haitian high society" (9–10). But Fanfan is in no hurry to consume his prey once he realizes she has fallen victim to his innocent charm. Instead, he plays with Madame Pierre until she can no longer bear his torture and maneuvers her into succumbing to her desire. Although she realizes that he is young enough to be her son, carnal desire far exceeds any maternal instincts she may harbor. In the end, it is Madame Pierre who initiates the sexual relationship between herself and Fanfan, but Fanfan is the one in complete control. The mother hen becomes a "yard fowl" who throws her middle-class airs of decency to the wind, virtually stalking Fanfan for a chance to get him into her car where she can taste him with "her huge carnivorous mouth" (4). There is no pretense of romance in Laferrière's stories. Nor is sex confined to the bedroom, or hotels, or homes: it is often part of a public performance no different from those of the musicians and artists whose appearances dot the landscape of his stories.

Laferriere's novels and short story collection map the interior structures of power, desire, and commerce that make it possible for countries like Haiti to advance, though not necessarily in the ways readers might define as progress. Moreover, his writing manages to keep visual literacy at the center of the narratives he constructs. The cinematic referents in Laferrière's work make us very conscious of the extent to which the visual informs not only the form but also the content of his writing. In fact, several of his stories are titled as "screenplays"; others assume the format of the "mockumentary" deployed in Cantet's film. The intertexuality of Cantet's film and Laferrière's stories produces several disruptions in the "visual regimes" often associated with representations of the Caribbean. These disruptions are achieved through the stark contrast between the visually underdeveloped, vaguely underfed bodies of the young boys who populate the beaches and the hotel rooms of the women, who themselves represent the antithesis of most Caribbean romances. They do not conform to the perfect "beach body" aesthetic that attracts (male and female) movie viewers to the theaters. They are middle-aged, battle weight problems and sexual dissatisfaction, and feel unwanted by their husbands or men in general. In short, they face many of the same struggles—unhappiness in their relationships, dissatisfaction with their work lives, or simply needing some excitement and satisfaction in their lives—that moviegoers are trying to escape by entertaining themselves with romances.

If viewers feel uncomfortable watching children having sex in Cantet's film, in Laferrière's short stories the question of sexual agency is far more complicated. The children in the collection of short stories are noticeably younger than they are in the cast of the film. In one narration, Brenda discloses that Legba "didn't look like he was more than 15 years old" when she met him (Laferrière 2009, 129). Cantet manages to keep his viewing audience uncomfortable by highlighting middle-aged women's sexual desires and sexuality: older white women are the new consumers of exotic, youthful Black bodies in the Caribbean. Yet he tries to minimize the age difference between them by casting older actors, who look like teenagers, to play the prey. Viewers are easily distracted by the changing patterns of consumption, from white men who flirt with exotic women in resorts to white women who sleep with young boys on secluded resorts in Haiti. In the mockumentary segment of the film, the three women speak directly to the camera, describing their participation in sex tourism in Haiti in candid monologues. In one of the most revealing accounts, Brenda, a divorcée from Savannah,

Georgia, describes meeting Legba, who is a composite of Fanfan and other young boys in the collection of short stories[10]:

> The first time I came here was with Mark, my husband. It all started when Mark took pity on this young boy who hadn't eaten in two days. He invited him to eat at our table. Albert [the restaurant manager] wasn't too happy about it. The boy didn't look a day over fifteen. Mark told him he could order anything he wanted. You should have seen him, I've never seen anyone eat so much in my life.

Brenda notes that Legba seems to take their (she and her husband's) "adoption" for granted and then immediately recalls inviting him to go swimming with her:

> He took me to a secluded beach. We were lying in our bathing suits on a big rock basking in the sun. His body fascinated me: long, lithe, muscular; his skin glistened. I couldn't take my eyes off him. The later it got the more I was losing my mind. I remember every move I made as if it were yesterday. I edged my hand over and placed it on his chest. Legba opened his eyes and immediately closed them again. That encouraged me and I moved my hand down his body. Such soft young skin, he was motionless. Then I slid my two fingers into his bathing suit and touched his cock. Almost immediately it started getting hard, growing in the palm of my hand until it just popped out. He breathed faintly, but very regularly. I looked around to see that no one was coming, and I threw myself on him. I literally threw myself on him. It was so violent I couldn't help but scream—I think I never stopped screaming. It was my first orgasm. I was forty-five.

That Brenda's description of the magnanimous act of feeding this young boy, who "hadn't eaten in two days," is almost immediately followed by her recounting how she sexually assaulted him on the beach is significant.[11] The "we" of the opening statement, disappears, and an all-consuming "I" that devours the previously malnourished young Black male, assumes control of both the sex act and the narrative.

The food chain is clearly outlined in this exchange: initially the act of fattening Legba is presented apparently as an act of care and concern, but by the end of this scene we are left to wonder whether Brenda's magnanimous act of feeding this young man is in fact merely a means to her ends of sexual gratification. The violence of this exchange lies not only in the sexual act but also in the way Brenda narrates the incident. Brenda's recollection that "Legba opened his eyes and immediately closed them again. That encouraged me and I moved my hand down his body" leads viewers to wonder how, through the gesture of opening and closing his eyes, does Legba give Brenda consent to his body. What is lost in translation from story to film is the intertextuality between Laferrière's appropriation of discourses of conquest, a common part of "first encounter" narratives in the New World, to describe contemporary "innocent encounters" between tourists and locals. Brenda's narration of the scene in the story is more akin to the genre of travel writing seen in Christopher Columbus's diaries.

Brenda's use of a passive voice just as she begins to consume Legba sexually is an effort to veil her position of power and her "right of access" to his body as a paying customer. She recounts the experience as though Legba is indeed participating, only to assure us later that he did not move or say a word: "Encouraged, I moved my hand down to his stomach. I felt an incredible thrill of pleasure traveling up from the young man's soft skin through my fingertips. I tried to stay calm but couldn't. Legba didn't move a muscle. It was as though he was making me a gift of his body" (Laferrière 2009, 131). The last sentence harkens back to Columbus's interpretations of indigenous Indians who, by showing him where to find food and small amounts of gold, allegedly indicated that he should take all that was theirs for the king and queen of Spain.

However, one could just as easily interpret Legba's unwillingness to participate actively in the sex act as an acknowledgment that his sexual violation is the "debt" he must repay for having been fed. Indeed, Brenda extracts her pound of flesh, "throwing herself on him" in such a violent way that she screams throughout the process. Though she is the hunter, who exacts gratification by consuming her prey, the narrative voice situates Brenda as the victim who suffers death, or *la petite mort*. We have no clue as to whether Legba climaxes during the assault; after all, this is not the concern of the "I" narrating the incident. In the story, Brenda is recounting this incident to the police officers who are questioning the three women after Legba's dead body washes up on the beach. His near-total erasure from his first sexual encounter with Brenda is recounted only after his total erasure in death, and even then, the story is still about Brenda's loss.

By shifting from a reader's perspective to that of the viewing audience, the film situates the viewers as the audience to which the mockumentary is addressed, not the police officers. We, then, are asked to occupy the gaze of "authority" and "witness" simultaneously. This cinematic move is of critical importance for two reasons. First, it effectively makes the viewing audience a third-party witness to sexual assault and thus implicates the viewer as a participant, if only at the level of being a voyeur. Second, it aligns the viewing audience with a missing protagonist in the cinematic adaptation of this story, Brenda's husband. Whereas the film suggests that Brenda, Sue, and Ellen are driven and controlled by their desire, Laferrière tells a very different story, particularly in the exchange between Legba and Brenda. In the short story, "Heading South," from which the collection takes its title, Brenda's husband Bill takes Legba and Brenda to the secluded beach after lunch. Furthermore, it is Bill who gives Brenda a "wink that [she] took as a kind of permission" and encourages her to "give in to [her] obvious inclinations" (Laferrière 2009, 130). We never hear Bill's account of this experience; indeed, we hear very little from him throughout the film. That Cantet chooses to exclude this important power play between the husband and wife makes for a very different reception of the sexual interactions in the film because they all seem to be initiated largely by the three women. However, for all three, even if it is only implied in their monologues, the lack of attention and satisfaction from white men in the United States (or Canada) is the underlying motivation for their frequent visits to Haiti.

Neptune, Sue's romantic interest during her vacation, is one of the few characters in the film whose physical appearance resembles that of the traditionally buffed, well-proportioned beach boy, but he is by far one of the oldest men on the resort, second only to Albert, the hotel manager. However, Neptune's physique, like that of the main protagonist Justin Blakeman in *Balancing Act*, is not the result of hours in the gym but of a tremendous amount of rigorous manual labor—not in the cane fields like Justin, but out at sea, as a fisherman who works to feed himself and other Haitians. The soft lighting and camera angles focused on the Black male body that are a critical part of romance narratives about the Caribbean are replaced by the dimly lit bedroom that Neptune returns to after an early morning of fishing. When he undresses and climbs into bed with Sue, his physique is barely visible because the room is so dark, despite the fact that the sun is shining brightly outdoors. Much of the obfuscation used in the film is Cantet's attempt to represent Laferrière's revisions of conscripted narratives about race that inform many of the fictions about Black people in the Caribbean and the United States. These fictions include romantic ideas about Caribbean Blacks being more "docile" than Black Americans.

Consuming Blackness as a cultural aesthetic while simultaneously evoking stereotypes about Black Americans allows these three white women to position their "liberal" perspectives as anything but racist, at least while in Haiti. An excellent example of this range of romance appears in Sue's "confession" in the mockumentary portion of the film:

> I've tried every diet known to science and I still look like a blues singer from Harlem. And I've never set foot in Harlem. I'm really crazy about Neptune, and Neptune is as black as the ace of spades. To me when I say black men, I mean American black. All American blacks think about is cutting white throats, and we do everything we can to help them do it. Neptune is the first man who ever paid me a compliment about my weight. To him, being big isn't a fault. It's a quality. He's a fisherman. He has a little sailboat. He fishes not far from here, near the Île de la Gonâve. His philosophy is very simple: fish, eat, drink, sleep like a baby, and f**k like a lion. Not a bad life, eh?

This "confession" engages in several romantic fictions, which function as what I term "comfort narratives," or palatable modes of consuming Blackness, that allow the three women to inhabit their power in Haiti while minimizing their powerlessness in their respective home countries. The assertion that "all American blacks think about is cutting white throats" suggests that the Black Haitians do not harbor similar thoughts or, better yet, that the historical founding of Haiti as an independent nation-state did not involve a brutally violent resistance that reflected the terror that framed slave life in Haiti. In Sue's island romance, Neptune's tattered fishing boat is transformed into a romantic-sounding "sailboat" and he into a child. That is, of course, until he is f**king, at which point the romance of Black subjects being closer to "nature" is evoked, and he is transformed into a beast of the jungle and "lionized." The "natural order of things" remains conveniently undisrupted; most importantly, Black male sexuality is contained by this order, as we are told that Neptune, like other Haitians, eats only enough to supply the needs of larger economies whose appetites are super-sized.

We are left to wonder how these women can go on vacation with such a sense of security in a country where the slitting of white throats was not only actualized but also a critical part of achieving independence. And Haiti under Baby Doc Duvalier could hardly be described as an idyllic Caribbean island. In fact, even when the political and social turmoil gripping the country threatens to disrupt their paradise, they conveniently brush it aside, choosing to ignore the interventions as a brand of naïveté exhibited by local Haitians. Thus, much of the "romance" in the film relies on the stories the three women tell themselves and the reader/viewer so that they can imagine themselves as desirable, powerful, in love, safe, and exceptional as compared to other Americans or Canadians (Sue is cast as a Canadian in the film, presumably to account for her being able to speak French).

Charlotte Rampling's character, Ellen, is the only one of the three women to willingly embrace the politics of being a sex tourist. She is the most forthright about her desire and presents an insightfully brutal critique about the power dynamics at play between white North American women who come to Haiti as tourists and the men they encounter in Haiti:

> If I had my way I'd rid the earth of everything that's dirty, and there is more of what's dirty here in this town than anywhere I've ever been. So why, dear God, did you plant, in this dungheap, a flower as radiant as Legba. I turned fifty-five last month. I can tell you there are worse things in life. And this young man is as beautiful as a god. Do you think I could find anyone like him in Boston? Don't tell me I could because I've been in every bar in that snobbish whore of a town a hundred times, and believe me there is nothing in the North for women over forty. Nothing, nothing, nothing, you bunch of bastards!

Ellen's overwhelming sense of dissatisfaction with her life in North America does not make her unique among the three women. Rather, it is her privilege as a highly educated woman who teaches contemporary literature at Vassar that marks her as a woman who would seem to be less likely to participate in the kind of exploitation they are all engaged in while on vacation. Surprisingly, after berating women who are obsessed with getting married, having children and acquiring all of the material symbols of wealth, who eventually "wash[ed] up on a beach somewhere in the Caribbean like so many overstuffed sperm whales." Rather than imagining herself as above these kinds of women, she acknowledges that, although she does not share in their obsessions, she does share their desire for sexual gratification and companionship.

Ellen is very open about her complicity in exploiting Haitian boys but rationalizes by casting herself as a victim of her own desires:

> I love love so much—love or sex, I don't know which anymore—that I've always told myself that when I'm old I'll pay to get it. I just didn't think it would happen so soon. That boy was Satan personified. The Prince of Light. But the kind of light that can kill You. He showed me what hell was like. I'd never been afraid of suffering, but this was too much. I'd given him everything. In return he humiliated me in ways I'd never imagined possible. He dragged me through the mud. I took it all.

The complexities of Laferrière's commentary on Haitian society consistently register throughout the entire collection of short stories. The network of negotiations taking place among the Haitian women and men in *Heading South* is absolutely crucial to appreciating the inner workings of social hierarchies in Haiti. However, within the inner world of the resort, we only catch a very brief glimpse of the workings of the country because the resort functions as a sovereign state within Haiti. In the few instances in which the worlds collide, there are dire consequences for Legba. In fact, prior to Brenda's journey into the town, Legba skillfully maneuvers between the world of the resort and Port-au-Prince. He goes into town regularly to play football and visit with his friends, who are all aware of how he earns money at the resort. In fact, during a chance encounter with his ex-girlfriend, we learn that she too is caught in a web of transactional sex, but one that is controlled not by American tourists but rather by Duvalier's henchmen. She is summoned by Colonel to be his mistress and makes a conscious decision, knowing that as she says, "They give you gifts, smiles, roses," but all the while she knows these gifts are like "a machine gun against your neck."

In Haitian voudoun culture, Legba is the master of the crossroads, controlling the gates between the mortals and the lwas. But he is also known as a trickster figure who walks with a limp, some say caused by the difficult work of navigating these pathways. In the film, Legba skillfully maneuvers between the streets of Haiti, where corrupt police take advantage of the poor, and the world of the resort, where tourists attempt to do the same. However, when the balance between these worlds is compromised, both he and his young girlfriend are violently reminded by the "gods" (the henchmen of the Colonel, presumably Baby Doc Duvalier) that the pathways of power are governed by powers far greater than them and far, far greater than American or Canadian tourists.

In one of the few scenes in the film in which we see Legba outside the resort, he runs into his ex-girlfriend who is being driven in a luxury car by one of the Colonel's henchmen. When she summons Legba into the car, he enters apprehensively and attempts to reprimand her for accepting the advances of the Colonel. She promptly reminds him of his own complicity in the systems of exploitive exchange, telling him that what he does for money, she does to stay alive—literally. Her reprimand proves to be dangerously accurate as we find out a few scenes later in the film. During one of their romantic flourishes, Legba takes Brenda into town where they shop and hold hands while walking through the marketplace. As they are walking, Frank (the driver of the car he was previously summoned to enter) sees Legba and gives chase, forcing him to leave Brenda behind. Brenda returns to the resort, alive but shaken, and recounts her harrowing experience, telling of the gunshots she heard while Legba was being chased.

The next day when the sea spits up both Legba's and his ex-girlfriend's dead bodies, the American women can only look on in horror and pity while they remain securely ensconced in the resort. They maintain a blissful ignorance of the realities of life in a country they have visited year after year. What they are continually aware of, however, are their own needs, desires, and sufferings. Thus, in the end, even though Legba and his girlfriend are the ones who are murdered, Brenda and Ellen still see themselves as the victims of this crime. In the film, the irony of this situation is not lost on the detective who is investigating the crime. When Ellen suggests that they may be in danger at the resort, the detective investigating the crime responds, in Kreyol, that "tourists never die."

In *Straight Sex: Rethinking the Politics of Pleasure*, Lynne Segal proposes that claiming sexual pleasure is part and parcel of the power gains made in hard-fought battles of the feminist movement. The liberatory sexual attitudes and practices that emerged from the movement challenged attitudes that effectively denied women the space to take joy from their sexual experiences: to claim pleasure from sex and to f**k purely for pleasure. Brenda, Ellen, and Sue represent a sensibility emerging in the 1970s among white feminists, some of whom were wives and older single women, that encouraged white women to embrace their sexual freedom by enjoying the pleasure and power of f**king. Segal (1994, 318) argues,

> Sexual pleasure is far too significant in our lives and culture for women not to be seeking to express our agency through it. There is feminism and there is f**king. As I see it, they can fit together quite as smoothly (or as painfully) as feminism and any other human activity. Straight feminists, like gay men and lesbians, have everything to gain from asserting our non-coercive desire to f**k if, when, how and as we choose.

If we consider Ellen's commentary about her own sexual awakening as an embodiment of this sentiment, we might argue that, in their colonialist desires, white women have effectively taken the place of white men: they control the networks of interactions and negotiations around sex, pleasure, agency, and coercion. If one of the major gains of feminism was indeed freedom of sexual expression for gay and straight women, the question remains what might this freedom actually look like if defined and enacted through the lives of young Haitian boys and girls. Networks of interactions and negotiations around sex, pleasure, agency, and coercion are still shrouded in authoritative patriarchal discourses that emanate largely from within structures of the state. Has the feminist movement in the United States been able to overturn power structures for women across the generational, racial, and class divides that continue to frame societies globally?

Global feminists continue to question the assumption that freedom of sexual expression means the same thing for Black and white working-class and working-poor women as it does for middle- and upper-class white gay and straight women. "The Network," a short screenplay in *Heading South*, ironically brings the entire collection into focus by completely obscuring what had seemed readily visible. The stories in the first half of the collection align with Cantet's cinematic representation, in which white women seem to have the upper hand sexually. In the stories in the second half, however, the complex power negotiations that appear to be controlled by the people with money, power, and influence are slowly exposed as a network of interactions that are deeply rooted not only in Haiti's social hierarchies but also in its troubled, exploitive relationship with the United States. Laferrière's screenplay is a blueprint of the network of negotiations that occur between Black men and women around their sexuality. Fanfan states, "It's true though, that I've always been fascinated by social interactions. Power, money and sex, as my history teacher would say: that's the infernal trinity that drives all men. When you understand that gentlemen, you understand everything. Love you ask? He booms in his thunderous voice. Hey, we're only talking about serious things here" (Laferrière 2009, 10). And so, Fanfan's education begins, and from his reputation and his conquests throughout the collection, it is clear that he is a quick study and deft at his trade. But in this regard, he is not unique. Many of his friends have learned that, in the absence of material wealth, sex is not merely a commodity: it is a weapon that, when wielded carefully, gives them as much, if not more, power than enjoyed by some of the wealthiest people around them. Unfortunately, what that cannot provide them is protection, and this is where the world of the resort becomes important. In *Heading South* the resort functions as a safe space not only for the wealthy but also for Haitians who have managed to gain access to it. The country clubs and restaurants belong to the same food chain as the resort. They are so visibly opulent because their supply is assured; often they control the routes through which food, money, sex, access, and power flow. But in the poor neighborhoods of Haiti where the social and dietary pyramid are easily disrupted, there is an increased need for capital to secure access to all these goods and services. Most often, sex is the tool of choice for this task.

There is a strong connection between sexual intimacy and the consumption of food in Laferrière's novels. For Laferrière food is the glue that binds the body politic(s), desire, and pleasure. But it is also what often undoes the social and sexual pyramid because food, like sex, music, or any other import/export, is a commodity bound by powerful historical and political pathways and negotiations. In the opening passage of the story titled "A Mortal Blow" in *Heading South*:

> Lying between Missie's long, slender legs, employing the same degree of skill that Shoubou, the lead singer of Tabou Combo, devotes to his microphone, Charlie dips his tongue into the juiciest bit of fruit in Port-au-Prince. Missie never tires of this exotic but exquisitely executed caress . . . Missie's sweet pulpy body. Her sex exhales an odour of ripened fruit. She may be European on the outside, but inside she is pure Caribbean. Her slit smells of guava . . .
>
> Charlie gets up and begins to dress. Missie looks up at him in astonishment.
>
> "Where are you going?"
>
> "I'm going out to eat."
>
> Missie is still writhing and trembling on the bed.
>
> "You can't do this to me"
>
> "Do what?"
>
> "I'm hungry. It's all right for you to go on a diet for a few days. Your ancestors have been stuffing themselves for centuries . . ."
>
> "What are you talking about? It's not food I want now . . ."
>
> "Your hunger can wait, mine can't."
>
> "Why are you bringing all of this up now. It's not fair."
>
> "I don't have time to philosophize with you . . . I need to eat . . . Anyway, maybe we can do both at the same." (Laferrière 2009, 180–181)

Across Laferrière's collected works there is the continuous juxtaposing of sexual desire and physical hunger that is always couched within the complex shared histories of Haiti and the United States. These blurred lines heighten the parallels between the vexed relationship of convenience between the two countries and the revolutionary history that made Haiti a free nation-state in the Western Hemisphere. The same food, sex, power, and pleasure pyramid emerges in *How to Make Love to a Negro without Getting Tired* and in another short story from *Heading South* titled "Beach Bar." In this story, young boys gather at a bar to replenish themselves with food and drink before they return to the work of sexually servicing several women, all of whom are over sixty. Much is made of the stamina of these older women as the boys complain about their various demands and sexual idiosyncrasies—none of which I will list here.

We should not think for a moment, however, that white women are the only women with power in the social worlds of Laferrière's novels. He is careful to implicate every protagonist in the inequitable power dynamics that are complicated by other social constructs. Virtually all the social classes, gender constructs, sexual orientations, and even racial categorizations are upended in one way or another. But very often, the racial identity of many of the Haitian women in the collection is curiously ambiguous, which leads us to wonder whether Laferrière is inviting us to expand the way we imagine Haitians in Haitian society. In other words, do white Haitians wield power and privilege any less conspicuously than Black Haitians? Or do the class positions of Black Haitians influence how they exercise power and influence differently from white Haitians, tourists, or political officials? What is certain is that all the women are conscious of their positions in the social pyramid at work at every level of interaction.

Laferrière goes to great lengths to destabilize how we understand women as sociosexual beings. Rather than simply fixing "woman" as a category of engagement and performance, he shows them effectively occupying many of the same roles as men, not merely in the way they wield power among other women but also in their relationships with both Black and white men. However, it is the sexual relationships among (and between) women that tell us the most about how they understand their agency and their vulnerability. Near the end of *Heading South*, we discover that Tanya, who was once Fanfan's love interest but is now merely his occasional bed partner, is herself quite the power broker in her relationships with powerful white men and virtually all the young women in the book. Despite her representation throughout the collection as dependent and needy, Tanya's relationship with Fanfan is very different from what we might expect, given her seeming inability to pull herself out of his orbit. But we learn later that Tanya exercises power in her own right: she chooses to use her status "on top" primarily in her sexual relationships with women:

> "He's just a man Simone. Nothing more, nothing less. He's available when I feel like a f**k, that's all."
>
> I don't believe you Tanya. That guy has driven you nuts. Ever since you met him you haven't been the same. I think it's very simple what you do. You sleep with us, and by 'us' I mean Minouche, Carole, Mari-Flore, even Alta, but you really only give yourself to men. You play with us, but it's only men who can hurt you."
>
> "What do you mean by that?" . . .
>
> "You get on top for us, but you go down on your back for a man. Even I can see that Tanya. So you see, everyone knows what's up with you."
>
> A long silence.
>
> "It's true that sometimes I feel like a man."
>
> "With us Tanya. But whenever there's a man in the house, you turn into the worst kind of woman."
>
> "You've noticed that?"
>
> "A child could see that, Tanya."

> "There is no man in the house now, Simone . . ."
> Tanya leans over Simone and kisses her long and skillfully.
> "Oh, Tanya . . . Do what you like with me." (Laferrière 2009, 152–153)

This passage richly complicates Lynne Segal's statement about f**king and feminism by highlighting the ways in which performing straightness and gayness, and indeed masculinity, relies not only on sexual desire but also on factors such as social mobility and, in the absence of actual power, access to the avenues through which power operates. Even while performing various gendered and classed roles in these relationships, each protagonist is represented as being acutely aware of the very tenuous freedom each occupies in the social and political hierarchies in Haiti. In all of Laferrière's writing, but particularly in *Heading South* and *Dining with the Dictator*, he is very aware of the politics of positionality among and between the young women and boys. That they are having sex is not *all* that matters. Being distracted by the sex act causes readers to miss an invaluable opportunity to think more critically about how pleasure is negotiated based on who is in the most advantageous position at any given time. Although Simone has an insightful critique of the way Tanya plays her "position" in relation to men in power, she seems powerless to extend this same critical lens to her own interactions with Tanya. Yes, f**king is important, but pleasure is not guaranteed. One certainly hopes that the experience will culminate in sexual satisfaction for both parties, but whether it will or not relies on an equitable desire to ensure that each partner's needs are tended to; at times this might well mean relinquishing a particularly gratifying position.

Every one of Laferrière's narratives is concerned with how colonial relationships between empires and colonies are reproduced through global circuits and commodities, with how our own desires, expectations, and positions within these circuits reproduce equally destructive, inequitable dynamics. More important, however, is this proposition, one of the more difficult concepts to consider: in the face of newly emerging systems of exploitation, agency and even resistance need to be reimagined and redeployed through the framework of staying "on top." Laferrière's discursive and poetic engagement with sex and food consumption suggests that "tops" can indeed *choose* to be "on their backs" when it serves their desires and aims, particularly if they are members of exploited communities for whom basic survival and security are foremost in their minds. At the same time, however, this construction begs the question: If the choice that remains is deciding to stay in relationships that are, by their very nature, exploitive, is this really choice or is it coercion dressed in the finery of postmodern "progress"?

4

"Fashion ova Style"

The Art of Self-Fashioning in Jamaican Pop Culture

I begin with two seemingly disparate images: one an eighteenth-century oil painting of an unnamed Black boy dressed in a bright red jacket, gold collar, and a padlock about his neck, and the other, that of the flamboyantly clad stylistic maverick hip-hop artist Andre 3000. Can the depiction of the enslaved boy, whose life was defined by service to an eighteenth-century gentleman, reveal anything about the magnetic appeal of this contemporary celebrity, known for his leadership of the African American Gentlemen's Movement, a recent fashion trend? It is this transformation in Black style—from costumed object designed to trumpet the wealth, status, and power of white masters to self-styling subjects who use immaculate clothing, arch wit, and pointed gesture to announce their often controversial presence—that this book seeks to elucidate.

> In "What is Art?" James describes the Black athlete as embodying a poetics in motion that facilitates, relationally and interpersonally, what Massumi calls the "movement-vision" of the spectator: "a kind of vision that grasps exactly and exclusively what the mirror-vision misses: the movement, only the movement ('walking, standing, moving normally through a room')."

The historical scope of this epigraph reflects the increasing critical attention to mapping the ways Blackness has been produced, performed, and consumed by a range of global consumers. Like Monica Miller, I am interested in a deeper analysis of what clothing, fashion, and style have come to signify in Black transatlantic popular culture, with a focus on the different ways in which Caribbean Blackness has been interpolated into transnational popular culture through an increasingly malleable vision of Blackness in dancehall and hip-hop culture. The phrase "fashan ova style" is commonly used to explain the value of certain aesthetic practices in Jamaican popular culture (e.g., skin bleaching, hair styles, clothing, and other modes of body modification). In this chapter I examine the dancehall mega star and cultural icon Vybz Kartel, whose deployment of vernacular aesthetics challenges how we interpret both Blackness and Caribbeanness in the popular imaginary of the global consumer. I am interested in why and how he rose to such popularity globally and what his prominence suggests about the complex ways in which Blackness "mutates" as a commodity in the global marketplace. I want to consider how Kartel's "mediated Blackness" can be read as a form of contemporary minstrelsy that pits "style" against "fashan" to create a kind of queer visual dissonance around Blackness and sexuality. I am evoking the term "queer" as belonging to the tradition not only of American critical theory but also of contemporary critical theory in the Caribbean proposed by scholars such as Nadia Ellis (2011, 11) and Omise'eke Natasha Tinsley, a tradition that draws on the conception of queer as a "term of unstable and shifting signification" (Ellis 2011, 11).

Kartel's verbal affinity for describing female genitalia and his countless homages to it have earned him the title of the "pum-pum laureate" of Jamaican dancehall music. This newfound interest in the "lower regions" of women suggests a lyrical turn from the anxieties expressed earlier by dancehall artists; however, this is not the case. Kartel's lyrical turn reflects an effort to reestablish the order of things in the dancehall not only in a discursive style but in terms of fashion. Kartel's musical prowess was overshadowed when he appeared in public several shades lighter after bleaching his skin, a practice most certainly not often attributed to men. For decades women have sought to "even out" their skin tone, as the popular skin crème from the 1970s, Ambi, promised to do for women of color. To be clear, I am not interested in making a case in favor of Kartel's skin bleaching as an aesthetic preference. What I am interested in, however, is a critical consideration of how body art, modification, and fashion aim to reinscribe Black bodies in a way that makes them at once very accessible to commodity fetishism while also obscuring the personal modes of self-fashioning that are integral to their performances of subjectivity.

I want to begin, however, by decentralizing the Caribbean to magnify the extent to which Black masculine performance is deeply embedded in a complex set of historical and political investments in imagining Blackness as difference, first and foremost, and then as visible in a compromised fashion weighed down by racial and racist meanings. Just as social environments can deeply influence which fashion trends take hold, the same is also true of political and social trends. In 2013 we witnessed the inauguration of Barack Obama to his second presidential term, a definitive moment in the political climate of the United States. If Obama's initial victory in the 2008 elections evoked a wave of enthusiastic optimism, his election to a second term sent an even stronger surge of enthusiasm through the country, but with a healthy dose of white anxiety that would make itself resoundingly clear in the 2016 elections. These watershed moments in political history in the United States are linked together in my analysis if only because of the optics of Black leadership on an international level. In the United States, an unabashed surge in the rhetoric of "post-Blackness" was ushered in on the heels of these political gains, a rhetoric that I suggest quickly met its limitations in the period leading up to Obama's anticipated departure from the office of the presidency in 2017. Once more, the heightened awareness of the state-sponsored violence of police officers against Black citizens served as a brutal reminder that any notions of a "post" where race and racism were concerned in the United States were not well founded. By my estimation, it will take another generation or two to penetrate the psyche of a country that has its roots in a long history of racism and prejudice. I continue to assert that the most likely driver of this shift will be the realm of popular culture.

Several critics have analyzed the complex relationship between the general public and Black artists and athletes, who are both the subject and object of the sign of "Blackness" in all its complex and terrified imaginings. Recently, in *Skin Acts: Race, Psychoanalysis, and the Black Male Performer*, Michelle Stephens widens the critical lens for thinking about the meteoric rise of Black male performers as icons in twentieth-century America. Her book is particularly important because it enters the landscape of critical discourses on race at a prescient moment in global popular culture when the performance of Blackness and Black masculinity have taken center stage across the globe. Stephens maps the politics of performance for Black actors and political leaders and seems to forecast the growing anxieties and the backlash (now commonly referred to as the whitelash) in response to a two-term African American President. *Skin Acts* is not the first text of its kind to postulate on the extent to which Black skin poses a peculiar kind of "problem" for viewers and, for this analysis, consumers of Black skin and Black culture. This critical conversation is decades in the making and of a piece with Stuart Hall's seminal essay, "What Is this 'Black' in Black Popular Culture?" Hall (1993, 106) notes the critical importance of mapping and engaging shifts in both the desire and fetishization of Black skin in popular culture:

> Michelle Wallace (1990:39–50) was quite right, in her seminal essay "Modernism, Postmodernism, and the Problem of the Visual in Afro-American Culture," to ask whether this reappearance of a proliferation of difference, of a certain kind of ascent of the global postmodern, isn't a repeat of that "now you see it, now you don't" game that modernism once played with primitivism, to ask whether it is not once again achieved at the expense of the vast silencing about the West's fascination with the bodies of black men and women of other ethnicities. And we must ask about that continuing silence within postmodernism's shifting terrain, about whether the forms of licensing of the gaze that this proliferation of difference invites and allows, at the same time as it disavows, is not really, along with Benetton and the mixed male models of the face, a kind of difference that doesn't make a difference of any kind.

I quote Hall's essay at length here because his concerns, like the questions posed by Wallace, are at the center of Stephens's critique nearly thirty years later. There is an overexposure of Black skin in the twenty-first century; yet it is this visibility that has authorized and even initiated a new era of devaluation of Black subjects precisely because of their difference, as marked by their skin color. This "difference" is exactly what many imagined the first African American president of the United States of America would make in the lives of Black citizens world over. But what was this imagined difference? What literal and figurative difference would Barack Obama's presidency usher into the landscape of race relations and representations of race in the global landscape?

Presidential power aside, the difference (imagined and otherwise) was supposed to mark progress in American society, proof positive that the United States had finally moved beyond its long history of racial discrimination and prejudice. Yet the nature of this difference and whether it rises to an aesthetic are still open for debate. Obama's difference has been chronicled in two significant discourses on difference: his mixed-race ethnic identity and his charisma. In other words, the "now you see it, now you don't" tradition of visualizing Blackness is tied very closely to modes of performing Blackness, both physically and discursively. One of the more recent global discursive performances of Blackness occurred during Obama's first presidential campaign: on March 18, 2008, Obama stepped to the podium of the National Constitutional Center in Philadelphia to address the nation and undoubtedly the world about the role that race played in his presidential campaign. He began with an account of his genealogy:

> I am the son of a black man from Kenya and a white woman from Kansas. I was raised with the help of a white grandfather who survived a Depression to serve in Patton's Army during World War II and a white grandmother who worked on a bomber assembly line at Fort Leavenworth while he was overseas. I've gone to some of the best schools in America and lived in one of the world's poorest nations. I am married to a black American who carries within her the blood of slaves and slaveowners—an inheritance we pass on to our two precious daughters. I have brothers, sisters, nieces, nephews, uncles and cousins of every race and every hue, scattered across three continents, and for as long as I live, I will never forget that in no other country on Earth is my story even possible.
>
> It's a story that hasn't made me the most conventional of candidates. But it is a story that has seared into my genetic makeup the idea that this nation is more than the sum of its parts—that out of many, we are truly one.[1]

The semantic emphasis on the historical past that brought "the Senator from Illinois" and arguably, most of those listening to that contemporary moment in history is critical because it makes every effort to bring the experiences of the entire Americas into focus in the face of the man on our television screens. Obama begins with his African ancestry in an act of insisting that viewers abroad, U.S. voters (those who voted for him in the past and those who did not), and those who did (or could) not participate in the democratic process contend simultaneously with his Blackness and his Africanness. His mother's whiteness is filtered not only through her skin color but also through what would seem to be an exotic path of adventure that led her from Kansas to Hawaii, and then to Indonesia, the place where she would meet his father. But the period in U.S. history that made possible Barack Obama's election saw tremendous gains for Blacks within the worlds of arts, music, and letters, so the excitement was not only understandable but also expected: the wait, as so many had noted, had been so long. However, in the midst of the euphoria, there were several cultural indicators of caution that were either ignored or went unnoticed; these indicators pointed to the coming cultural clashes between the hope and expectations of a "post-Black" era and the lived realities of entrenched racism that would not be so easily changed. Curiously, fashion and style in popular culture were one of the earliest indicators of this tug of war.

But there is a counterbalance to the narrative of the "more perfect union" vision of Black identity in the American landscape. According to one of Black America's more vocal cultural critics, Michael Eric Dyson, the advent of post-Black aesthetics in American popular culture allowed Black people to embrace the joy of their racial and cultural identity. Yet this is not to suggest that this view of Blackness is void of a political or social agenda—quite the contrary. In his foreword to Kwame Touré's book, *Who's Afraid of Post-Blackness: What It Means to Be Black*, Dyson (2012, xvi) writes,

> If Black folk are ever to enjoy the sublime and raucous joys of Blackness, we've got to step into the sunshine of disobedient and complicated Blackness.
>
> That's why I'm so glad that ingenious Black folk like Touré exist. He's free to be black the way he sees it, and he feels no need to apologize for who he is or what he says or thinks. Ever see him on television? He's a riot of complicated Blackness: his handsome, chiseled face all aglow with mischievous ideas about the world we live in, delivered in an over-the-top style that dares the stereotype of the loud black man to darken his reputation even as his mind races to put pop culture and politics into intelligent perspective.

At the heart of both Eric Dyson's and Touré's ideas is a larger concern about the marketability of Blackness as a commodity in global consumer cultures, by which I mean the capacity and interest by investors in "buying into" Black art, Black athletes (and the brands they are associated with or represent), and Black popular culture. Dyson's foreword to Touré's book suggests that it is a playbook of sorts, akin to a "Lonely Planet's Guide to Buying into the Selling Power of Blackness." A glance at the list of contributors to this edited collection suggests that the battlegrounds for transformation to this new approach to "post-Blackness" are television, music, art, and, unfortunately, academia. Touré's book uses a peculiar application of the phrase "post-Black," coined by art curator and historian Thelma Golden, to describe the vantage point and critical processes of the emerging African American artists (including Glen Ligon, Kara Walker, Rashid Johnson, Laylah Ali, Mark Bradford, and Adler Guierre) featured in a 2001 exhibition at the Studio Museum in Harlem titled *Freestyle*. In her review, "Is There a "Post-Black" Art? Investigating the Legacy of the "Freestyle" Show," Cathy Byrd (2019, 39) describes Golden's evocation of the phrase in the following way:

> Golden's definition of "post-black" centered largely on art with ideological concerns. In the exhibition catalogue, she described "post-black" as "a clarifying term that had ideological and chronological dimensions and repercussions," writing that the new genre was "characterized by artists who were adamant about not being labeled as 'black' artists, though their work was steeped, in fact deeply interested, in redefining complex notions of blackness."
>
> "In the beginning," Golden writes, "there were only a few marked instances of such an outlook, but at the end of the 1990s, it seemed that post-black has fully entered into the art world's consciousness. Post-black was the new black."

Golden's use of the term is different from how it is deployed in Touré's *Who's Afraid of Post-Blackness*. For Dyson and Touré, the concept of "touring"

Blackness suggests that there are identifiable degrees of Blackness and that it also has a spectacular element that one can indeed stop and take note of. Taking Blackness "on the road" suggests that race is a cultural commodity that circulates in the same way that bands, sports teams, fashion shows, and food fairs move about different parts of the world. In other words, Blackness is very much a part of performance culture, and these performances carry different valences depending on audience and cultural context. Golden's concept of post-Black seems less concerned with the performance of certain notions of Blackness, and more on an effort to create new modalities of Black expression. For the artists and the curator of *Freestyle*, post-Black is an aesthetic founded on the practice of improvisation, something that is by no means "new" for Black people in any part of the African diaspora.

Monica Miller's *Slaves to Fashion* (2009) offers another point of entry into how we read, engage, and interpret Black transatlantic popular culture. This is not to say that the "fashioning" of Blackness is in any way free from the same global market forces to which Touré's text is responding. Yet Miller's critical engagement with fashion invites us to enter what I call the "intimacies of the fashion" that underlie certain practices of Black popular culture through clothing and its sometimes overlooked and misunderstood close cousin, body art—or what I refer to as the "indelible narratives" of body refashioning. As Miller suggests, the practice of fashioning through clothing is by no means a new concept for Black transatlantic subjects: there is a long and complex history of the extent to which fashion and, indeed, style have come into conflict with institutional power structures around race and representation. In fact, the phenomena she outlines in her book became the basis for a well-placed article in the *Chronicle of Higher Education* on Black academics and their sense of style in relation to their professions. Acknowledging the extent to which clothing is indeed part of the conversation about race and identity, Hasan Kwame Jeffries, an associate professor of history at Ohio State University, notes that "a black dandy . . . conveys a professional swagger in the face of racial stereotypes about place and profession," whereas Sharon Holland, associate professor of African and African American studies at Duke University and the only woman featured in the article, comments on the aesthetic and affect that are a part of self-fashioning: "Truthfully, when I'm done dressing and have tried all manner of combinations, it's all about being OK with feeling sexy in a piece of fine cloth. Dressing up is art and love, pure and simple" (Patton 2013, B10–B11). Despite the small number of Black academicians, their presence as educators in traditionally white institutions of power gives them an outsized influence. The *Chronicle of Higher Education* article was indeed an effort to raise the profile and visibility of Black educators through a conversation about how and why clothing and fashion complicate what their Blackness may mean to students and university administrators who interact with them. It seems, therefore, that Black popular culture critic and connoisseur Touré's assertion about academics moving into the dandy limelight alongside other luminaries like Andre 3000, Lebron James, and Dwayne Wade, all of whom are part of the cutting edge of this refashioning of Blackness, is correct, not only from the standpoint of sartorial styles and fashions, but also based on the burgeoning interest and investment in African American art, literature, music, and film by Black popular culture icons. Touré seems to have a finger on the pulse of the arena of arts and culture that had historically preoccupied the Black intelligentsia and which had become a preoccupation of popular culture icons and athletes alike, just as the world of haute couture, not typically seen in academic circles, had also crossed over.[2]

Nowhere is the work of refashioning Blackness more literal and more prominent than in one of the most lucrative enterprises in American culture, the National Basketball League; ironically, it was one of the first major sports institutions to implement a strict dress code aimed at disciplining modes of expression that had long been part of Black diaspora culture. The meteoric rise of NBA fashion icons occurred in an industry that, at times, seemed to be obsessed with ensuring the uniformity of its players' clothes and most certainly its brand. With African American or African diaspora players comprising more than 76 percent of NBA players, the desire for "uniformity" among its players may well have been achieved had Blackness been the only sign of "sameness" that mattered. In response to athletes in the 1990s wearing braids, over-sized jeans and T-shirts, and baseball caps—all cultural markers of the hip-hop generation whom NBA executives sought to attract to boost the sales of team jerseys and of tickets to fill arenas—implemented sweeping changes and a dress code in 2005. While NBA officials wanted to attract the hip-hop generation, they wanted to do so from a distance and with some control over "the look" of the National Basketball Association. Yes, it was a predominantly Black sports league, but the kind of Blackness being expressed through clothing seemed to run contrary to what the NBA wanted to convey about its brand. After all, the Jerry West iconic NBA logo symbolized a league that was predominantly white, less flashy in its style of play, and certainly not from the urban centers of the United States. This version of the NBA no longer existed. The league was decidedly Black, urban, international, and infused with hip-hop culture, and increasingly so was its fan base. This demographic of the newly emerging NBA on court presence was crucial to diversifying its brand globally. However, the challenge for basketball executives was condensing this panoply of difference into a unified brand on and off the court. The commissioner argued that first and foremost it would have to be "professional," and this meant the players needed to look like management when they were not on the basketball court, and look like each other when they were on the basketball court. In other words, the singularity of style made famous in Black American culture needed to be vacated from the sport in favor of uniformity.

It was fine for the fans to dress in baggy jeans, big gold pendants, and baseball caps; after all, this was the fashion being lauded in the songs that blared through the arenas during time outs and at half-time shows. But NBA executives wanted to draw a clear line between its industry and its consumers. As Allen Iverson famously put it, "I dress like the guys from my neighborhood. I couldn't believe they were making a big fuss about the whole thing. You want to market the guy, but not who he is. I took the ass whooping for guys to be who they really are."[3] The following is a list of items that players are not allowed to wear at any time while on team or league business:

> Sleeveless shirts; Shorts; T-shirts; jerseys; or sports apparel (unless appropriate for the event (e.g., a basketball clinic), team-identified, and approved by the team); Headgear of any kind while a player is sitting on the bench or in the stands at a game, during media interviews, or during a team or league event or appearance (unless appropriate for the event or appearance, team-identified, and approved by the team); Chains, pendants, or medallions worn over the player's clothes; Sunglasses while indoors; and Headphones (other than on the team bus or plane, or in the team locker room).[4]

Two things should stand out here: (1) the very specific nature of the restrictions on iconic symbols of hip-hop culture in America and (2) the special attention to the way public, private, and professional spaces—the bench, the plane, the locker room, press conferences—are demarcated in these policies. Unlike the masking effect that fashion and clothing once played as a "dressing-up ritual to disguise the subaltern and the transgressive," clothing in the NBA became a means of controlling the power of the subaltern Black subject to signify his transgressive desires or tendencies (Archer 2010).

Clearly, the fashion choices made by NBA players before imposition of a dress code were deeply influenced by hip-hop culture and the social and political circumstances that hip-hop sought to bring into the view of mainstream consumers. The dress code, implemented on October 17, 2005, is now commonly referred to as the Allen Iverson Rule (A.I. Rule) because many attribute the league's clamping down to his unique, unapologetic style of dressing, which included the "bling" of large diamond necklaces, bracelets, and earrings; sagging pants; do-rags that covered his signature braids; and baseball caps that often represented Major League Baseball (MLB) or National Football League (NFL) teams, rather than the team he played for, the Philadelphia 76ers. Since the code's imposition, several athletes have decided to push the envelope by violating it as far in the opposite direction as possible: rather than wearing baggy jeans, they are now wearing skinny capri pants. One sports fan who called into a radio show the day after the Miami Heat's resounding win (88–65) over the Chicago Bulls in Game 4 of the 2013 NBA Playoffs expounded,

> This stuff is getting out of hand and I think Commissioner Stern is being hypocritical by letting these athletes get away with it. Tell me what is so

> professional and business-like about a dude wearing skinny jeans or a Capri pants suit, like Dwyane Wade just did recently. Then again, maybe I should look at the perception of the attire these athletes are wearing, similar to what Stern and his other cronies are promoting. Besides, it is a lot more intimidating seeing a guy wearing some baggy jeans, a jersey and a Jesus piece, than it is a guy who is wearing some skinny jeans and Capri pants.[5]

The dandies of academia are a far cry in terms of privilege and compensation from NBA athletes—though there is a connection to be made between them: whether in the hallowed halls of academia or the hardwood courts and packed arenas of the NBA, the link between clothing and the performance of power is undeniable. The professors and the players are on opposite ends of the spectrum in considering how fashion shapes the ability of Black subjects to occupy some public spaces and not others. We only need to think about Trayvon Martin's killing as one such instance. The increasing market power of hip-hop, dancehall, and R&B culture and its influence of mainstream cultural fashion signals the degree to which fashion can reflect the social realities of sports and academia while being totally divorced from them simultaneously.

"Clean" Skin Tun' Up: Yuh done know, "fashion ova style same way!"

Fashion and music are fleeting indicators of particular social moments in history, and I am more interested in the permanent markers, particularly those that penetrate the skin and yet give us only a glimpse of what they contain. It is those permanent markers that bring me to my discussion of the Jamaican dancehall deejay Vybz Kartel and his unexpected June 16, 2011, appearance on the front page of the *New York Times* music section in a feature article headed "Managing a Brand He Made Himself." Though Kartel was already a dancehall star of prominence long before his skin bleaching took center stage, I am more interested in the possibilities and problematics that his marketing prowess presents for interpreting popular culture.

This was not Kartel's first appearance in the *New York Times*, however; a 2006 piece was titled "A Reggae Star Forged in the Dancehall Furnace." But the more recent *Times* article suggests a new moment in conversations about "branding" in Black transatlantic popular culture. As the headline "Managing a Brand He Made Himself" implies, pop culture marketing has evolved, and artists are no longer satisfied with being spokespersons for popular or luxury brands. Many are investing their time and resources into (re)branding themselves, literally and metaphorically. However, the suggestion that Kartel has indeed turned himself into a brand is a curious one.

Kartel's growing prominence in the dancehall industry marks a notable shift in the power dynamics of the business; this change is both generational and grounded in the changing economy of popular culture in the African diaspora. The emergence of the "Gully" Alliance and the "Gaza" Empire has shifted how talent is located, developed, and marketed in Jamaican dancehall music.[6] The Gaza Empire is an offshoot of the Gully Alliance, founded in 2003 by the iconic dancehall deejay Bounty Killer as a collective (some would say a gang) of artists who included Elephant Man, Busy Signal, Mavado, Wayne Marshall, Bling Dawg, and, once upon a time, Vybz Kartel. Gaza is the nickname of the Empire's home community of Waterford, Portmore, whereas Gully(side) is the nickname of archrival Mavado's home community, Cassava Piece. Vybz Kartel departed the Alliance after an internal feud with Bounty Killer and in 2006 launched the Portmore Empire, now known as Gaza, which once included an impressive stable of dancehall artistes such as Popcaan, Blak Rhyno, Tommy Lee Sparta, Lisa Hype, Craig Dennis, Aidonia, Baby Doll, and Nuclear.[7] The Gully Alliance, led by the "Gully God," Mavado, also features its own robust list of artistes: Busy Signal, Savage, Safhya, Tyrical, Stacious, and Slimmaz, among many others.[8]

What initially began as an effort to consolidate and control a burgeoning industry soon mutated into a nationwide feud with supporters on both sides prepared, at times, to resort to violence to defend their honor. The clash reached beyond Jamaica and into other parts of the Caribbean where dancehall music was part of the popular landscape. In a 2010 *Village Voice* article titled "Reggae's Civil War," Baz Dreisinger commented that he had

> traversed four Caribbean islands in the past two months and spied one common denominator: graffiti. Scrawled precipitously on a cliff suspended above the lush mountains of Saint Lucia, on the aluminum siding of a rum shop in French Saint Martin, on the concrete walls of a Trinidad office park, on accessible surfaces covering urban and rural landscapes across Jamaica, one of two words made its inevitable appearance: "Gully" or "Gaza."

Although many claim that the feud was largely a publicity stunt to boost the appeal of both collectives in the music business in Jamaica, the emergence of "dis tracks" from both sides fueled the rivalry, making it more and more personal and more dangerous. Many began to compare the feud to the East Coast versus West Coast rivalry between Biggie Smalls and Tupac Shakur. Kartel initiated a public diatribe dissing Mavado, calling him "a pseudo-gangsta," dubbing him "Mafraudo," and claiming to have had sex with his mother. Mavado retorted that Kartel was, among many other things, a "battyman" (a gay slur in a country that takes such accusations very seriously), a skin bleacher, and an atheist"(Dreisinger 2010).

The feud finally reached significant enough proportions that in December 2009 government officials intervened to try to mediate a truce and gain a commitment to a peaceful resolution:

> Prime Minister Bruce Golding requested a meeting with the two artists. . . . The real peace decree, though, came just before the meeting, when the two DJs took the stage together at a Kingston concert and Kartel called Mavado "my brother." The performance was, by all reliable accounts, coordinated by so-called community leader Christopher Coke, a/k/a "Dudus": current target of a U.S. extradition request on drug- and weapons-trafficking charges and the son of gangster icon Jim Brown, who was the founder of the legendary Shower Posse gang that ran much of Jamaica, New York, and Miami in the '80s. (Dreisinger 2010)

Although this elaborate drama was homegrown, it moved beyond the small impoverished communities of Jamaica to spread across the region into Caribbean strongholds in the diaspora such as New York and Washington, DC. In those cities, the feud continued, with deejays being mindful not to spin too many Mavado or Kartel tunes, lest they be branded as "Gully" or "Gaza" because "Once they're branded, they'll have problems . . . getting what they need from Jamaican artists—dubplates, for instance" (Dreisinger 2010).

As Stuart Hall eloquently argues, "within the black repertoire, *style*—which mainstream cultural critics often believe to be the mere husk, the wrapping, the sugar coating on the pill—has become *itself* the subject of what is going on" (Hall 1993, 27). This admonishment is poignant considering the controversy around Vybz Kartel's skin bleaching. Kartel's public embrace of skin bleaching is an opportunity for cultural critics to consider the efficacy of body modification as a means of reimagining conversations about race and color in Caribbean popular culture. Hall invites us, in a most provocative fashion, to think again about the particular ways the black body is utilized by black subjects by highlighting that black diaspora cultures "have used the body—as if it was, and often it was, the only cultural capital we had. We have worked on ourselves as the canvases of representation" (Hall 1993, 27). Given the persistent practice of skin bleaching (and other forms of body modification) in Jamaican popular culture, why was there such a public outcry when Kartel admitted to bleaching his skin, allegedly with cake soap? Did the outcry occur because this form of body modification was not in keeping with the traditional notions of masculinity within dancehall culture? Did it go against the grain of bleaching being seen as a "private" practice that usually carried with it significant communal shaming if and when such information was made public? Or did this new assertion of the skin as canvas/coloring book signal a new moment in Caribbean popular culture, in which body modification transgresses the boundaries not only of respectability but also of interpretability, even within the secular realm of the dancehall? Although critics like Mimi Sheller have commented on the impact of mobility on how Black bodies perform and are (in)vested with meaning, as well as the mechanisms through which "bodily self-fashioning" has emerged in Black transatlantic popular culture, not enough attention has been paid to how these shifting mobilities have necessitated new modalities for expressing personhood and subjectivity. Even though critics have examined in detail the lyrics, dance, and fashion historically deployed by Black subjects to "fashion" new identities, the recent controversy about Kartel's bleaching is useful because of what his skin reveals—his tattoos.

The furor began after Vybz Kartel accepted an invitation by the University of the West Indies (UWI), Mona campus, to discuss his life and his work on March 10, 2011. In the question-and-answer period after the speech, he was asked a question about his skin bleaching and replied, "My life is my art, my art is my life. Life is a colorless coloring book, and we all have the crayons to make it as colorful as we want. Everything I do from controversial lyrics, bleaching, etc. precisely is orchestrated to achieve a desired response. My skin alteration has nothing to do with self-hate; bleaching now is just a style. I bask in its controversy, wid cake soap as my suntan."[9] These comments might easily be read as a flippant response to a question seeking a more thoughtful reflection of Kartel's personal politics in a society where light skin has historically been highly favored. But given the overwhelming influence the media has on how Blackness is both produced and consumed, and indeed commodified, we might begin to consider the possibility of interpreting body modification such as bleaching as a tool for intervening in the "overdetermined" nature of Black skin in the media. Yet skin bleaching is not a trend unique to Jamaica or the Caribbean, and its aesthetics have mutated to mean different things to different people depending on their social and cultural beliefs and practices.

Take, for example, one of the most prominent baseball stars from Latin America, Dominican right-fielder Sammy Sosa, who played Major League Baseball (MLB) for nearly a decade and a half, most prominently and successfully for the Chicago Cubs. Even after retiring from the game, Sosa's post-baseball lifestyle has kept him in the limelight. After leaving the game under a cloud of accusations about his alleged use of performance-enhancing drugs (PEDs), Sosa returned to his native Dominican Republic, where he gained success as a businessman and part-time diplomat. But neither of these post-baseball careers is responsible for Sosa's repeated appearances on the cover of magazines, tabloids, and special interest television shows. The drastic change in Sammy Sosa's appearance—from a dark-skinned person to an individual who is at least four shades lighter—unleashed tremendous criticism from baseball fans in the Dominican Republic and the United States. Sosa has faced it in the most stoic fashion, never denying his skin modification but never feeling the need to explain it other than as an expression of his own aesthetic preferences. On the ESPN show *E:60* which aired on June 28, 2018, Sammy Sosa sat down for a long interview with Jeremy Schaap. After a heated, uncomfortable exchange in which Schaap pressed Sosa about his PED use, Sosa got up, abruptly announced that the interview was over, and walked off the set. About thirty minutes later he returned and apologized to Schaap, noting that his intent was not to disrespect him but that he also did not want to be disrespected.

When the conversation turned to the public's response to the change in his appearance, Sosa was unapologetic in his defense of lightening his skin. His responses to Schaap's questions about his skin bleaching suggest that he was painfully aware of the way his Black skin belied a narrative about what and who he is in the Dominican Republic. The power of this inscription is so significant that it could override his successes and the wealth he had acquired as a major league baseball player.

SCHAAP: One of the big topics on social media has been the way you look, the fact that your complexion has lightened over the years. What do you have to say about all that?

SOSA: You know, a lot of people been mentioning that. But you know because I have a little lotion that I put on my face but it's not like I'm, you know . . .

SCHAAP: Why do you put the lotion on?

SOSA: I dunno . . . I put it on 'cause I like to have my skin clean. That's it. For me, I do what Sammy Sosa wanted to do. It's my life. It's Sammy Sosa's life and I'm entitled with my life to do whatever I want. . . . I do it because I'm going to be fifty but I look seventeen, and that's why I do it. It's simple as that. I feel happy with myself.[10]

The responses to Sosa's skin lightening have been wide-ranging, varying depending on the sector of the sport or entertainment industry. Sports pundit and media personality Stephen A. Smith argues that Sosa's skin bleaching is proof of his PED use; musicians and other entertainers—most notably, rapper TI—have gone on record describing it as an act of "self-hate."[11] Although most interpretations of his bleaching point to Sosa as a flawed subject with an identifiable neurosis about his Black skin, we need to be reminded of the historical constructions of Black skin and of how Blackness is interpreted visually and discursively. Skin color carries a wide range of social consequences based on how those in power interpret and "translate" Blackness. As Stuart Hall reminds us,

> When Frantz Fanon, in *Black Skin, White Masks*, who as you know was transfixed by this inscription of racial difference on the surface of the black body itself. What he called the dark and unarguable evidence of his own blackness. "I am a slave," he said, "not of an idea that others have of me, but of my own appearance, I am fixed by it." Well, what indeed, of course, what can people be transfixed by other than that which is so palpably evidentially concrete, undeniable, there. A racial difference which writes itself indelibly on the script of the body. . . . When you say race is a signifier. No it is not! See the folks out there they are different! You can tell they are different. Well, that very obviousness, the very obviousness of

> the visibility of race is what persuades me that it functions because it is signifying something; it is a text, which we can read. (Hall and Taylor 1997)

There has been a recent shift in attitudes among bleaching practitioners not only about the politics of their aesthetic choices but also about the way in which their successes and failures are interpreted in relation to changes in their complexion. Sosa's description of his skin as "clean" is consistent with how many in the bleaching community describe the end product of their effort. In his interviews Sosa has also consistently linked the changes in his appearance to his successes in his professional life after baseball.

Thus, body modification and fashion may be understood as a mode of gendered and racial performance within popular culture. These modalities of performance, I argue, are aimed at reinscribing Black bodies in a way that makes them very accessible to commodity fetishism while also obscuring the personal (resistant) modes of self-fashioning that are integral to their performances. In other words, what might be gained from reading the rise in skin bleaching, tattooing, and other body modification techniques as an aesthetic, but one that aims to cause viewing audiences to "look" on these bodies in a more engaging and empathetic manner? This notion of visibility is bound up with an understanding of how "being seen" matters socially and politically in Black diaspora centers of the world. In *Shine: The Visual Economy of Light in African Diasporic Practice*, Krista Thompson (2105, 114–115) succinctly connects the issue of visibility with social justice by arguing that skin bleaching and media technology are often understood as pathways for underprivileged citizens who have been erased from sight to gain visibility:

> Bleached skin, the body's surface that is permanently "lit up," may be understood as a contemporary manifestation of long-standing efforts by Jamaica's urban classes to have their rights as citizens recognized through appeals to the camera. Since at least the 1970s, protesters from the island's black communities have often sought redress by taking up residence at local televisions stations, where they have waited for cameramen to enable them to air their grievances. Indeed, I suggest that public visibility through visual media—through one's appearance on-screen—has become a sought-after way of asserting one's rights as a citizen.

Sosa and Vybz Kartel, like many other performers and practitioners, are keenly aware of the extent to which the appearance (or visibility of Black skin) is met with a notably indifferent, if not prejudicial, gaze in the social, political, and certainly judicial spheres. They understand fully how Blackness is easily vacated from spaces of influence through visual erasure and manipulation. Bleaching is, among other things, one mode of interrupting the ease with which these kinds of erasures are made.

On June 19, 2013, Television Jamaica's talk show, *All Angles*, aired a forty-five-minute episode hosted by Dionne Jackson Miller, a well-known news personality in Jamaica. It presented Jamaicans who bleached—many of whom appeared to be working-class people—for the first time in the full glare of the media, a phenomenon that many of the practitioners referred to as "fashion ova' style." I use this phrase in the title of this chapter because it is an example of the shift in how Blackness is performed and mediated in Black popular culture. During the episode, Dionne Jackson Miller conducted interviews with a wide range of people, including cultural critics, medical professionals, and social workers, all of whom shared their perspectives not only on the practice of skin bleaching itself but also on its relevance in the new global marketplace where Black diaspora culture is a hot commodity.

According to Donna Hope, a cultural studies critic at the University of the West Indies, Mona, visibility is key:

> Being in the video light in dancehall is a big thing, you know. Video light shines your presence into many spaces that you can't take plane and go because you don't have a visa. People see you. People have been in videos and people request them to come and take part in their stage shows and parties all over the world. Video light becomes very important, it's a way of sending yourself into different places . . . you're famous. The television and the media industry help us to understand that if you're on TV, something ah happen fi you. People want to be made visible in that way, especially when they live their lives locked in all these little boxes that we have created in Jamaica called the inner cities, ghettos and poor communities.[12]

And it is this latter point made by Donna Hope that brings me back to the Jamaican dancehall deejay and his public discussion of his skin bleaching. When asked by an audience member at UWI about his skin bleaching, he replied that his "skin is like a canvas." Envisioning the skin as a canvas, or a blank page, on which the subject can construct their own narrative in ink, effectively recasts the overdetermined meaning of Black skin. In fact, this conceptualization of the skin as canvas also highlights the constructed nature of what Black skin has come to symbolize. This intervention in the narrative process illustrates Stuart Hall's assertion that "the sugar coating on the pill—has become *itself* the subject of what is going on . . . think of how these cultures have used the body—as if it was, and often it was, the only cultural capital we had." (1993, 27).

If it is indeed the case that the "sugar coating" of racial constructions—notably Black skin and, indeed, Blackness—has now become a sought-after commodity, all the while being despised, discriminated against, and weaponized, what would it look like for poor, working-class, Black, and brown people to stake a claim in and through their bodies? Can we consider the practices of body modification efforts to shield Black athletes and entertainers from hypervisibility a byproduct of cultural commodification? One of Kartel's most popular post-bleaching songs provides a valuable perspective on the aesthetics and market value of tattooing in Jamaican dancehall culture:

> When di ink load up and di needle ah jook,
> Tattoo sell off, everybody haffi look.
> Gyal say mi pretty like a coloring book,
> She say mi skin pretty like a coloring book.
> Gyal say dem waan find where mi live ah Norbrook,
> She ask if it hot like rice whe just cook . . .
> Look pon mi skin, tattoo like dirt, mi no wear shirt.
> Gaza ink inna concert, Phillip haffi work til mi mark up like schoolbook,
> Ah di new look, gyal ah say di flava shook, police sey mi fava crook.
> Mi ink up like di *Gleaner* and *Observer*,
> Brando di ink surgeon wid di serger.
> Skin paint up like Berger 404
> Omar from Waterford so him ah lock down Portmore.
> Styles. Push di needle thru di epidermis,
> Hottah dan a makka, burn you like ah furnace,
> Pretty when it finish but it hot when it ah service.

Kartel's song, "Coloring Book," serves as a companion text to his indelibly marked and modified body. Once more, his lyrics highlight the incongruent perspectives of his reading/viewing audiences who see the contradictions in the aesthetic and cultural value of his bodily gestures. The list of official institutions to which he compares his body are worthy of note because, as Donna Hope mentions, the power of the media—in this case print newspapers—to fix and therefore overdetermine what Black bodies mean socially is significant. The criminalization of Black bodies is also part of Kartel's counter-narrative, particularly when read in relation to the favorable attention he receives from girls who admire his bodily adornment. The lyrics of "Coloring Book" provide a partial index of some of his tattoos, particularly the most easily recognized ones for consumers of Black popular culture, such as the teardrops.[13] Although teardrop tattoos are often associated with gang and prison culture, they are also memorials in ink to loved ones who have died. Kartel's teardrops are in memory of several members of the dancehall fraternity: Craig Dennis, Tweety Bird, Masicka, and Cappo.

The now ubiquitous "THUG" emblazoned on his left hand (an acronym for "The Hate U Give," a tattoo made famous by the late Tupac Shakur[14]) and "GAZA," the small community in Portmore once known as "the Borderline," both reflect the extent to which the Black body is a territorial space that is hotly contested, even when it is not in plain sight. The name "Gaza" is borrowed from the Palestinian region of the Middle East that has been the site of several wars with Israeli forces. But the importation of this name into the Jamaican lexicon also speaks to the uncomfortable relationship between masculinity and homosexuality in Jamaican popular culture. The adoption of the name "Gaza" by the community once known as the Borderline was spearheaded by none other than Vybz Kartel, and the legend of the name change was chronicled by one of Jamaica's best-known cultural critics, Annie Paul (2012), in her blog, *Active Voice*:

> The induction of the name "Gaza" into the Jamaican firmament came about because in the very first insanely popular Stages Production, Bashment Granny, there is a scene where a policeman confronts the sinuous Shebada asking "Yu a man or yu a woman?" "Mi deh pon di borderline" declares Shebada unabashedly, emphasizing his retort with an exaggerated wag of his hips. The phrase became so popular in the context of discussions about sexuality that Vybz Kartel decided that the name of his community "Borderline" had been irrevocably contaminated by association. He therefore adopted the name of the most violent place he could think of at the time—Gaza in Palestine.

The remarkable power of naming in formerly colonized spaces is on display here, as is the continuously precarious nature of the relationship between the nation-state and its citizens, particularly if they appear queer. That Vybz Kartel had the power to rename his community because of an association with a popular stage character, Shebada, speaks to the symbolism that is implicit in performances of identity. Ironically, part of Shebada's stage persona's "costume" is an excessively bleached face that stands out starkly from his lips, legs, and other parts of his body. Naturally, Shebada's bleaching and claim that "he deh pon di borderline" quickly became synonymous with Kartel's bleached body and social location, despite his own "badman" persona in song and deed.

In fact, Shebada's own "badman" antics in his stage performance, combined with his appearing openly and flamboyantly queer, represented an emerging social culture among Jamaica's gay population who—having been forced "outta door" or thrown out of their homes by family and out of their communities by the church and the state—were also laying claim to their own "man ah bad man" postures when attacked by the police or citizens intent on physically harming them because they were gay. The willingness of the gay men who dwell in the "gully," also known as the "Gully Queens," to speak the language of violence when confronted by violence marked a turning point in Jamaican popular culture. The bravado of heterosexual men in popular culture, typically displayed through violence and sexual innuendo, no longer marked them as more "manly" than gay men because, as we see with Shebada's stage performances, queer men in Jamaica no longer fear the police and are prepared to meet violence with violence when they are under threat.

But Kartel's index of tattoos stops far short of engaging some of the most controversial symbols etched into his skin. During the Q&A portion of Kartel's

2011 presentation at UWI Mona, a number of students inquired about "whether or not he had sold his soul to the devil in order to be a successful artiste." In response, Kartel pointed out that similar charges have been thrown at other contemporary pop icons, such as Beyoncé, Jay-Z, LeBron James, and Rihanna. The highly visible "Eye of Providence"—the all-seeing eye of God—inked on the left side of his chest near his shoulder is one of the primary sources of anxiety for many detractors of Black pop icons, even in Jamaica. This emblem and the variations of the pyramid often flashed by Jay-Z the ROC, Spike Lee, and a host of other Black pop icons have taken on a remarkable power globally. My aim here is not to debate the valence of the "illuminati" in Black popular culture; countless websites are dedicated to this debate, dutifully deciphering every music video by pop icons to uncover the illuminati references and symbols. However, the strategic silence around these images by Black pop icons is interesting precisely because it denies that which consumers are most keen to claim ownership of and lay claim to: intimate knowledge of their Black bodies and indeed Blackness as a commodity. I am similarly interested in how Kartel's tattoos and his appropriation of Freemason imagery might function as a layer of obfuscation for Black subjects that are highly visible, and, at the same time, untranslatable.

Reading Kartel's plethora of tattoos as part of an emerging style of body modification deployed by Black pop icons and of a larger preoccupation with body art adopted by young Black men (and women) globally takes us back to twentieth-century moments in Black Atlantic history when Black people turned to fashion as "a way of operating" in cultural contexts that sought effectively to erase both their presence and their humanity. Can or should we read these moments, these practices/performances—both historical and contemporary ones—as modes of relief from systemic domination? Can they be considered as viable interventions aimed at disrupting the seeming fungibility of Blackness, historically speaking? I would argue that these contemporary practices in popular culture are similar to what Saidiya Hartman (1997, 50) refers to as "transient zones of freedom and re-elaborating innocent amusements [that were] central features of everyday practice" deployed by slaves. Drawing on de Certeau's definition of practice Hartman writes,

> Practice is, to use Michel de Certeau's phrase, "a way of operating" defined by "the non-autonomy of its field of action," internal manipulations of the established order, and ephemeral victories. The tactics that comprise the everyday practices of the dominated have neither the means to secure a territory outside the space of domination nor the power to keep or maintain what is won in fleeting, surreptitious, and necessarily incomplete victories. (50)

A closer consideration of the textual signs that inform the practice of body art among Black popular cultural figures is revealing, more for what it tells us about the power of certain narratives and mythologies surrounding "Black progress" than their social, political, or religious practices. In this vein, we have to consider whether the assertions made about these Black pop icons are any different from those I mentioned earlier, made by Pat Robertson shortly after the earthquake that struck Haiti a few years ago. The notion that Black progress and, indeed, Black freedom, regardless of its expression, can only (or even best) be understood as "unnatural" has a long history that rests as much in mythology as it does historical facts.

However, many Black pop icons seem to be fully cognizant of the historical contexts from which these narratives about Black progress emerge. In fact, artists like Vybz Kartel, Jay-Z, and Kanye West have all acknowledged, typically through their art forms and at times through their bodily expressions, that they are not above exploiting these long-held notions about their success as once-poor Black people. As Stuart Hall (1993) suggests, although the Black body may indeed have once been the only capital that Black people had, today's Black pop icons have marked out several complex ways of representing their selves and their bodies to capitalize on the potential for commoditizing these new ways of being "Black" in the global marketplace. These practices are not, in and of themselves, performances of "total freedom": they still function within the systems of domination (Hartman 1997). Yet, these bodily interventions have the capacity to provide a space of refuge (if only momentarily), enabling other possibilities for self-fashioning for Black subjectivity to emerge.

The increasing power of rhythm and blues, hip-hop, and dancehall culture to strongly influence mainstream cultural fashion is unusual. In a very provocative essay, "Accessories/Accessaries; or, What's in Your Closet," historian and exhibition curator Petrine Archer describes an incident that occurred in 2010 when a team of art historians from the Yale Center for British Art who were researching material for a large-scale exhibition marking the two hundredth anniversary of the abolition of slavery visited her in Jamaica:

> While dining, a last-minute nighttime excursion was planned to visit Kingston's infamous *passa passa*, a weekly street dance where locals and their *dons* gather in their blingiest finery to pose and hang out until daybreak . . . Our trip was a moment of détente; it was another scouting downtown with ubiquitous historical precedents stretching back to Belisario's time, our middle-class intellectual voyeurism now displacing the painter's panoptic gaze. As gatekeepers, we guided these British visitors so that they could experience first-hand the legacy of a culture that had also once been theirs. It was an opportunity to consider the historical origins and peculiar aesthetics of Jamaican street life—its crude cultural dissonances, its ambivalent male posturing, and its violent outpourings—as part of a larger discussion about performance, masking and subaltern identities. (2010, 95–96)

For many years the dancehall has been known as a space of excess: excess sexuality, excess masculinity, excess braggadocio, and, some would argue, excessive expressions of violence and homophobia. Despite the keen interest in the weekly street parties that populate the social calendars of downtown people in Kingston and in other seemingly forgotten political garrisons like Tivoli Gardens, Mango Valley, and Waterhouse, until recently those who resided "uptown" had no desire to partake of the cultural practices often denigrated as "slackness." These same communities are barely noticed except for references to political violence, crime, or civil unrest provoked by a lack of the most basic services (housing, water, electricity, good roads) that the government is supposed to provide for all citizens.

However, as dancehall music has begun to gain international notoriety (in both good and bad ways), not only have those living "uptown" begun to venture into the "lower regions" usually castigated as "unholy" and "unwholesome" but also scholars and artists have returned to the culture of the "folk" and the working poor as a source of inspiration. Moreover, never far behind in the quest to connect economies (both formal and informal) to one another, several global corporate entities such as Hennessy and Moët, as well as governmental icons like Bruce Golding, have sought to elbow their way into Passa Passa, Bembe Thursday, and Weddy Weddy due largely to the sheer power of dance to attract consumers and voters alike.

Yet, several aspects of dancehall music—more specifically, dancehall aesthetics—have not been able to bridge the class divide in Jamaica. The two main aspects are dancehall fashion, which features a plethora of modes of adornment for both men and women ("accessories," in Archer's essay), and skin bleaching (or accessorizing), which has long been a politically charged topic within Jamaican society.[15] Traditional debates about the practice often characterize it as symptomatic of a contempt for Blackness or dark skin among the urban poor and as a sign of the cultural and social disintegration of the political efficacy of race-based nationalism in the 1960s, 1970s, and even the late 1980s. However, near the end of the twentieth century there was a marked shift in the terms and locational politics of these conversations: they moved out of the parlors and pulpits of the middle classes and other locations of respectability to the streets and sidewalks of Kingston—to the beauty salons, barber shops, and homes of the fashion industry and informal economies of dancehall.

The practice of consuming fashion has long been a means of expressing the desire for upward mobility and respectability and its entrapments. The precarious nature of Black artists is that they are both a representation and a representative of "Black performance" in discourses on identity formation. If we have learned anything about the relationship between clothing, style, fashion, and identity, we know that clothes and accessories mean very different things depending on the subjects who don the fabrics, fashions, and finery. As Miller's title, *Slaves to Fashion*, suggests, historical and discursive transitions in fashion and style often correspond to "crucial moments in which Black sartorial style can be read as an index of changing notions of racial identity and the other identities in which race is constructed, performed and lived—namely, gender, sexuality, class, and nation" (Miller, 2009, 19–20). Miller examines nineteenth-century America where "black people negotiate the transition from slavery to freedom" (21). This period saw a tremendous explosion of theorizing about Black dandyism and race politics, focusing on DuBois and his "talented tenth" through to the Harlem Renaissance, and James Weldon Johnson and Wallace Thurman's debates about imagining Blackness (and certainly Black men) beyond prescribed tropes of both American exceptionalism (nation) and the New Negro movement (race). It would be easy to anticipate the slow demise of the Black dandy, which is certainly part of the underlying narrative in Miller's analysis. However, rather than interpreting the increasing inability of the Black dandy to "define or embody black modernity as a failure for the Harlem movement," Miller defines it as a singular moment of success that points to multiple, and sometimes conflicting, potentialities of modern Black identity (Miller, 2009, 23). According to Miller, this shift from fashioning Black identity through clothing to fashioning the body in other ways provides an increasingly complex register of ways of being for Black diaspora subjects.

Praise Songs for "Tun Up" Pum-Pum: Queering Aesthetic Practices in Dancehall Culture

> Yuh p***y comin like bible when it open up
> Mi see heaven, yuh punnany blessed my angel
> Loving yuh, loving yuh, like Rachael
> Yuh p***y comin like bible
> A parable of some great sex
> From yuh born till now that stay bless
> Never never fraid a di AIDS test
> [Chorus:]
> Yuh have di ever blessed pum-pum
> Ah God ah go wid yuh
> And am in love with yuh like woah
> The ever blessed pum-pum
> God ah go wid yuh
> And am in love with yuh like woah
> The ever blessed pumspum
>
> —"Ever Blessed"

The critical phrase "perverse modernities" is an apt description for the collisions of ideologies, performances, bodies, desires, histories, economies, and institutions in critical conversations about popular culture in Jamaica. Jamaican popular culture, particularly reggae and dancehall music, shares some of the equally problematic ideological foundations that inform the ironic, contradictory nature of secular and sacred traditions. This irony is most visible in the overlapping anxieties about sexuality felt by religious, national, and popular cultural institutions. The aesthetic and discursive landscapes of Jamaican popular culture have accelerated the need for more theoretically sophisticated ways to engage with the changes that are underway. Though these unholy alliances remain unencumbered by emergent critical discourses, the turns in the aesthetics of Jamaican popular culture suggest that the boundaries I outlined earlier are no longer simply being "fused." Rather, they are being queered such that a completely new aesthetic that borrows liberally from both "camps" (i.e., "gunman" and "batty man," "don/politician," "whore/sex tourism") rests un/comfortably outside both these realms.

Vybz Kartel's song, "Ever Blessed," is an excellent example of the "queering" phenomenon, and Leasho Johnson's work shown in figure 1 reflects this aesthetic in productive, provocative ways. If David's Rudder's "High Mas" left the church-going community at odds with his appropriation of traditional liturgy for street mas, one can only wonder what church officials, and even the dancehall faithful make of Vybz Kartel's praise song to pum-pum. I have long argued with several friends and colleagues that, in light of Jamaica's long tradition of exceptional (formal and informal) poets and the recent naming of the country's newest poet laureate in 2014, there should be something of a similar order for recognition for the laureates of dancehall culture. Quite naturally, there would have to be different categories of dancehall laureates. I venture to say that, of all the dancehall artistes, Vybz Kartel would undoubtedly be a finalist for the "pum-pum laureate" of Jamaica. This is not to suggest that he is the first dancehall deejay to be preoccupied with female sexuality, sexual expression, and genitalia; dancehall music has always been a referendum on sexual appetites, proclivities, positions, and politics; the "run di place red," "slammin' in de bed," "stabbing up di meat" tunes have always populated the playlists in every dancehall session. But "spread out inna bed" songs and, indeed, this aesthetic, are distinctly different: there is a newfound reverence for pum-pum, spearheaded in music by Vybz Kartel and chronicled wonderfully in Johnson's series of modified liquor bottles that features terms and phrases that have come to embody/represent this newfound "love affair" with pum-pum in a most succinct fashion (figure 1).

According to Johnson, these repurposed, reimagined alcohol bottles are part of "a series of experiments about Caribbean identity as a by-product of colonial commerce. It's a comment on a lost identity transformed (or bottled) for the sake of commercial gain."[16] Somewhere around 2010, as the titles in Johnson's series highlight, "Pum-pum tun up," and pum-pum became an overt focus of dancehall culture (figures 2 and 3). In Jamaican parlance, the phrase "pum-pum tun-up" connotes p***y that is of high quality, has exceptional stature or power, or (in the interest of not overstating the obvious) is extraordinary, as two of Johnson's titles "Gumtion" and "The Good Hole" indicate (figures 4 and 5). The fundamental difference between the "pum-pum tun-up" aesthetic and the previous "spread out inna bed" representations seems to be a matter of agency. The implication here is akin to what is expressed in Kartel's song, "Ever Blessed."

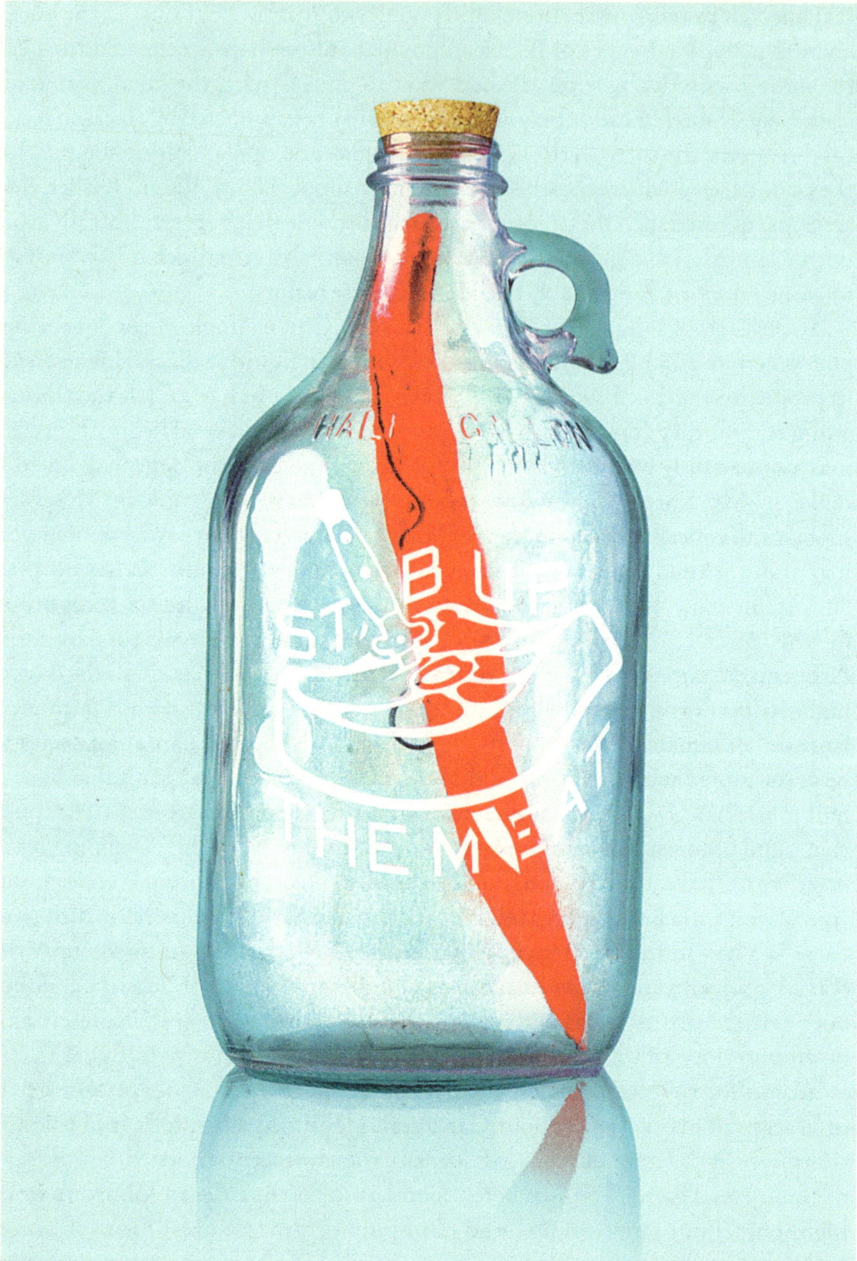

FIG. 1 Leasho Johnson, *Stab-up the Meat*, 2014. Bottled "ratchet" knife with white cut-out label, 4.4 × 11.5 in. Courtesy of the artist.

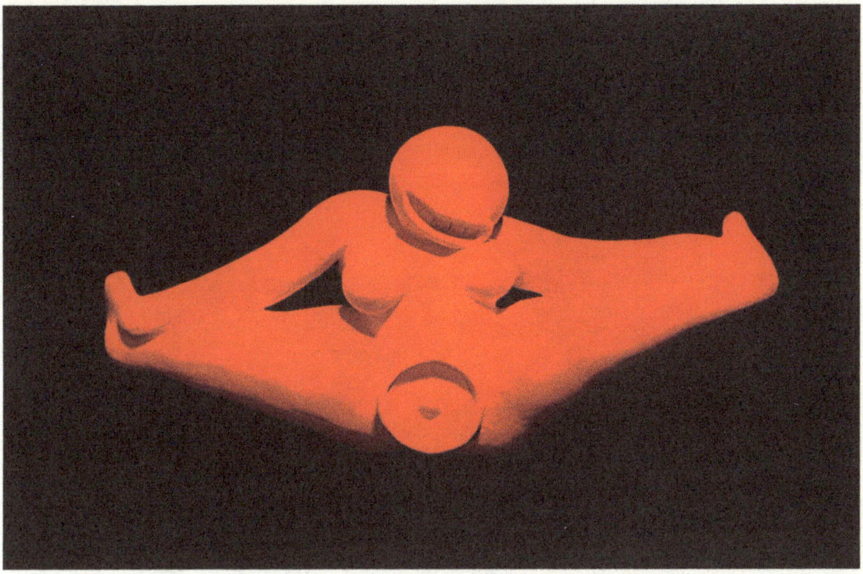

FIG. 2 Leasho Johnson, *Pum-Pum Tun-Up East and West*, 2012. Earthenware, 12 × 8 × 5 in. Courtesy of the artist.

Pum-pum was no longer simply to be mash' up and "dashed whe" ("spread out"). The advent of "tun-up" pum-pum marks a shift in its aesthetic and value in Jamaican popular culture. In fact, this cultural moment also marked a decidedly feminist turn in pum-pums political symbolism as well.

Suddenly, female genitalia went from a supporting role in dancehall culture to that of the star to headlining in more than one genre of Jamaican popular culture. What makes Kartel's songs unique (and there are a wide array of them, including "Benz Punaany," "Happy Pum-Pum," "Pum-pum Paradise," and "Ever Blessed") is the unabashed manner in which each song expresses its reverence for pum-pum. As the lyrics suggest, the perversity is not coincidental, nor is it necessarily contradictory in its origins. In fact, Johnson's "Pum-Pum Tun-Up Heaven Bound" (figure 6) is a direct descendant of the same ambiguity that novelist Michael Thelwell captures in one of the iconic scenes in his 1980 novel, *The Harder They Come*. The scene in which Ivan enters a bar for the first time and encounters Miss Ida is narrated in terms that seem wholly spiritual; however, readers realize quickly that the godly subject of adoration is not the heavenly father but Miss Ida herself. The reverence shown to Miss Ida by the men in her bar is drawn in parallel to the dedication exhibited by supplicants of the church when they are in a holy space. The only thing that prevents this scene from being sacrilegious is the thin layer of respectability that cloaks the descriptions of how she walks and how her body moves the men in the bar. Miss Ida represents the very thin line between the ecstasy expressed in "Ever Blessed" and the ecstasy

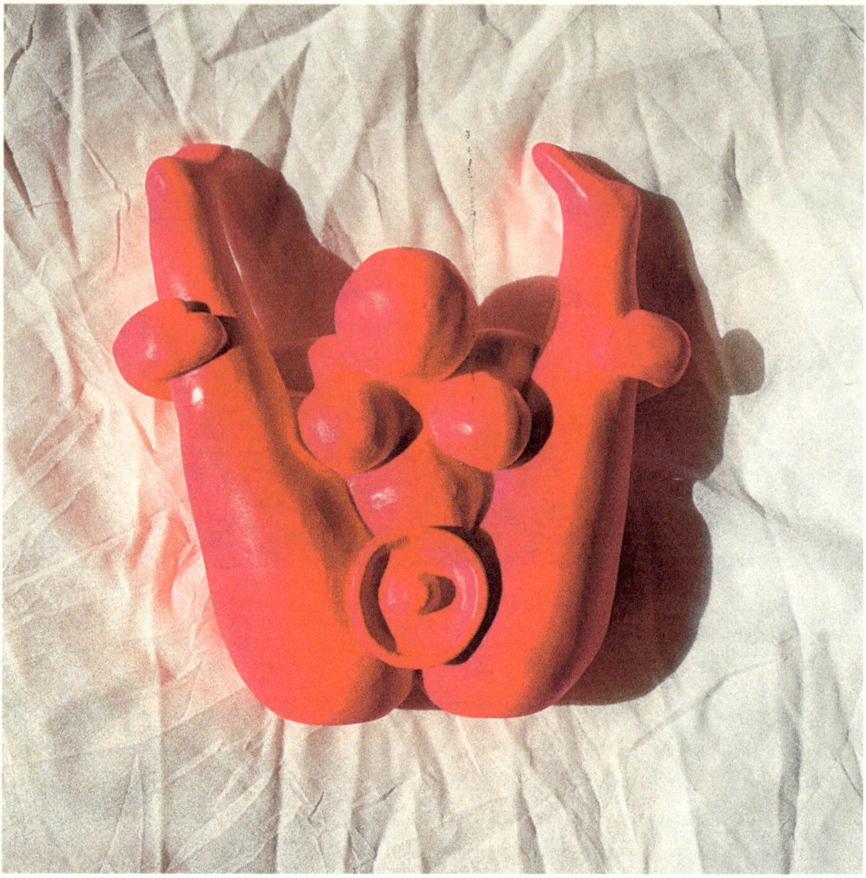

FIG. 3 Leasho Johnson, *Pum-Pum Tun-Up North and South*, 2012. Earthenware, 12 × 8 × 5 in. Courtesy of the artist.

of catching the holy spirit: both are God made and heaven sent in these iconic cultural representations.

In these recent representations of female genitalia, the layer of respectability is still there (in a manner of speaking), but not at all in the ways we imagine. Quite naturally, several questions come to mind in response to this current trend. How should we account for this shift in the representation of Black women's bodies in dancehall culture? Can we understand this shift as corresponding to a heightened awareness of the failures in the rhetoric of respectability, particularly in the face of increasing demands to brand Jamaica for consumption? Or is this shift a kind of performance that functions similarly to the "consecration" of the dancehall space that opens up new terms of engagement for performances and practices that are not traditionally welcomed in the dancehall?

Increasingly, there is an interest among contemporary Jamaican artists to do more than simply reproduce the aesthetic of the dancehall in their work. They

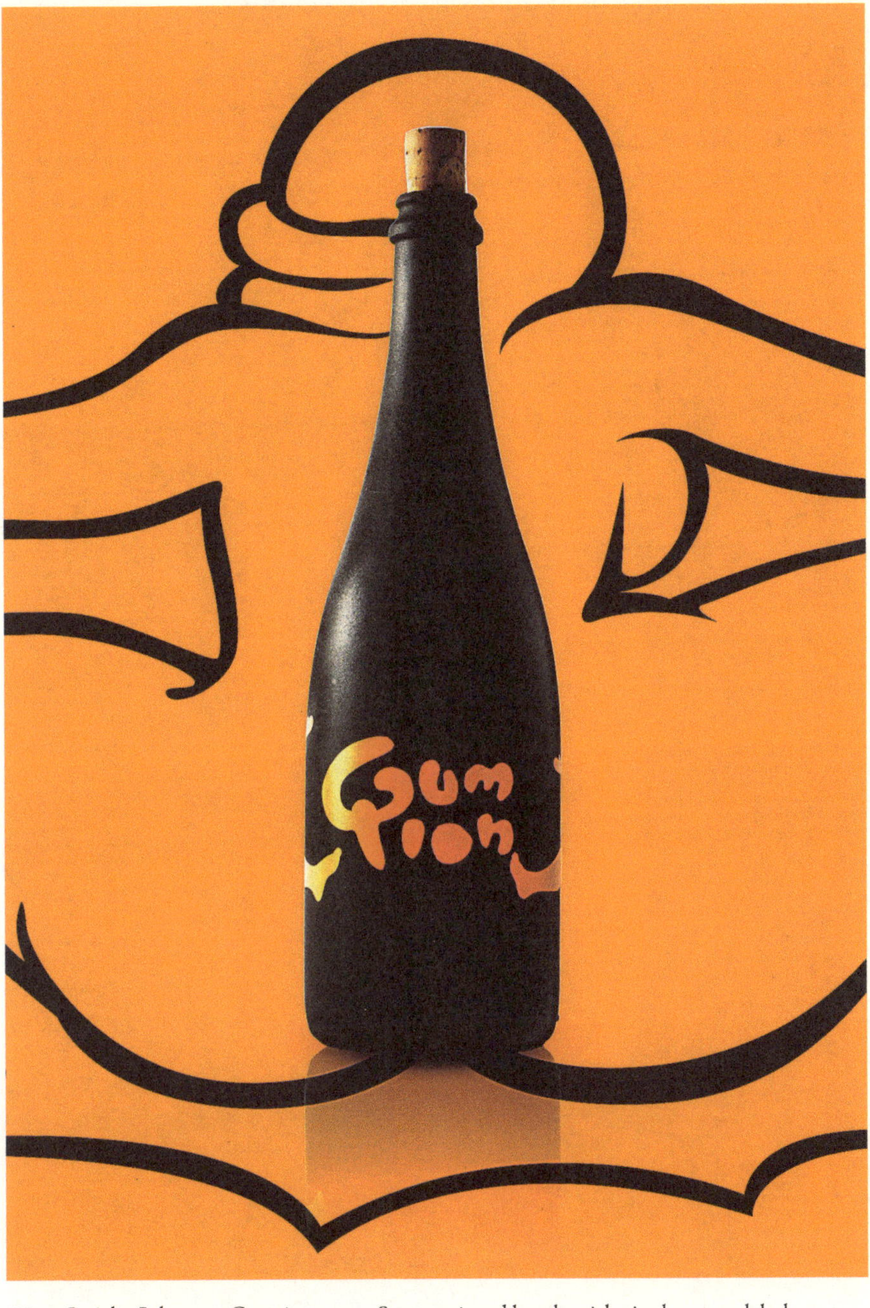

FIG. 4 Leasho Johnson, *Gumtion*, 2014. Spray-painted bottle with vinyl cut-out label, 3.5 × 13 in. Courtesy of the artist.

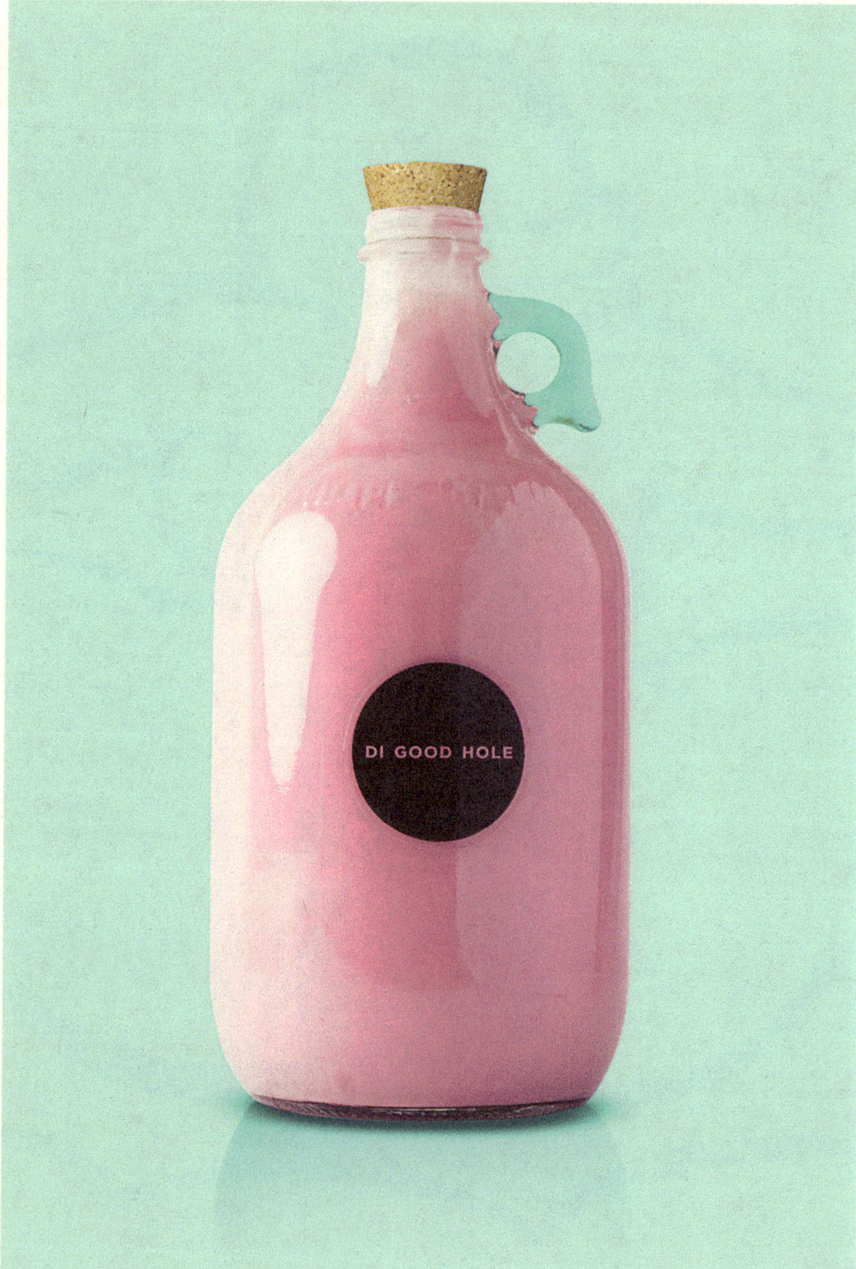

FIG. 5 Leasho Johnson, *Di Good Hole*, 2014. Bottled pink paint with clear vinyl printed label, 4.5 × 11.5 in. Courtesy of the artist.

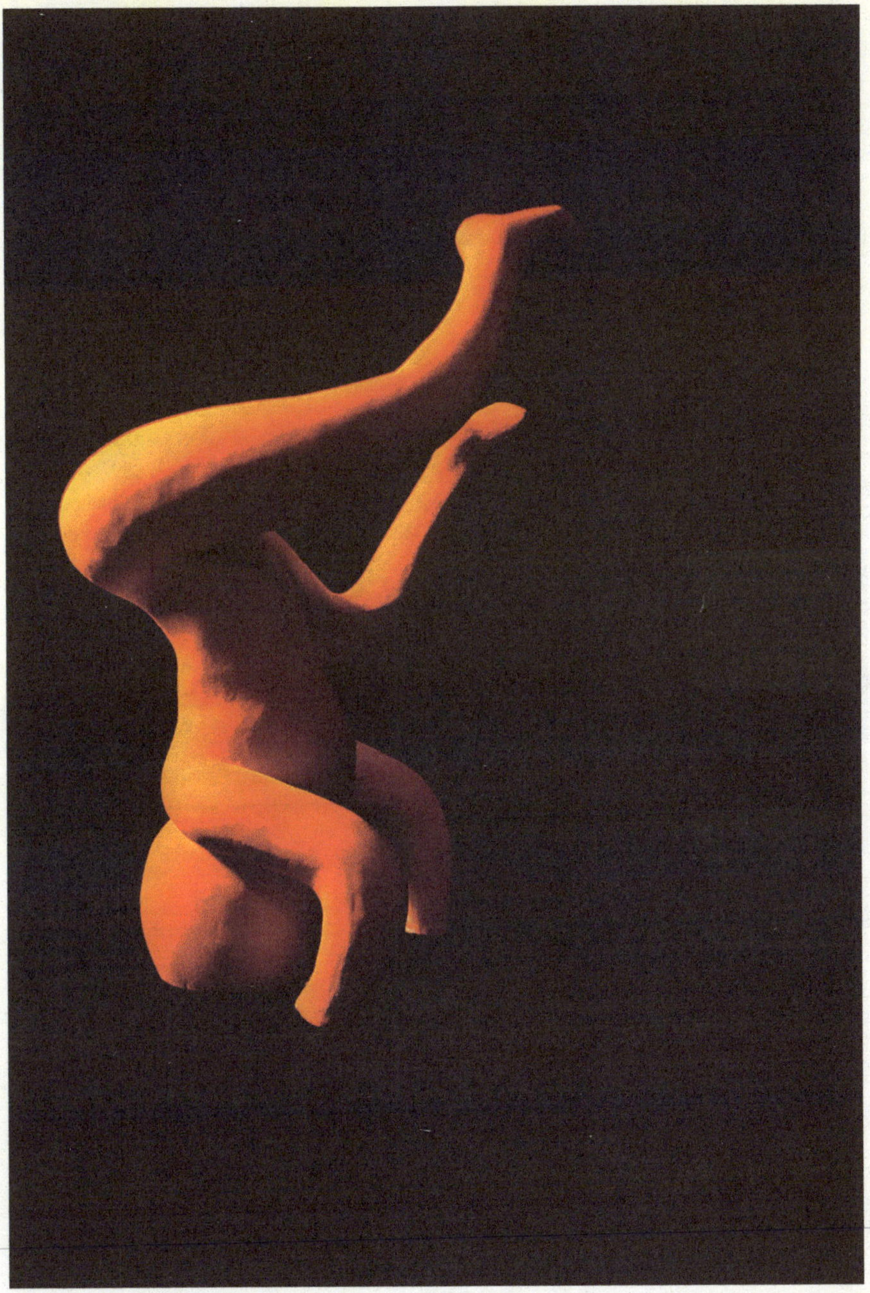

FIG. 6 Leasho Johnson, *Pum-Pum Tun-Up Heaven Bound*, 2012. Earthenware, 4.5 × 5 × 9 in. Courtesy of the artist.

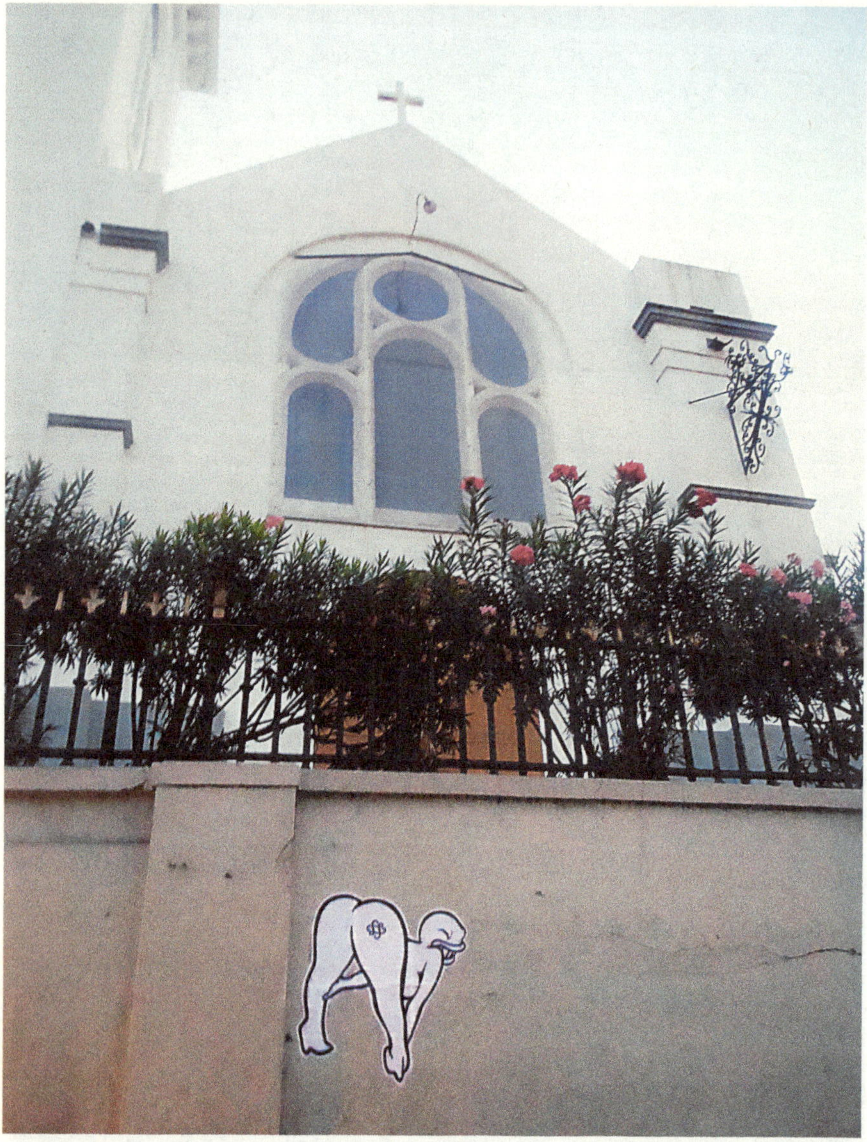

FIG. 7 Leasho Johnson, *6:30*, 2014. Paper and yeast paste on wall, approximately 30 × 30 in. Kingston Parish Church. Photograph by Randall Island.

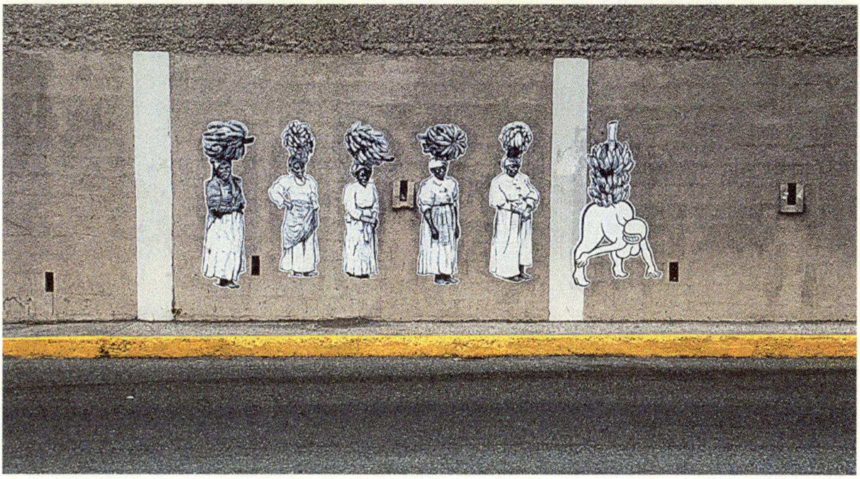

FIG. 8 Leasho Johnson, *Back-fi-a-bend*, 2015. Paper and yeast paste on wall, Kingston. The work was installed for Labour Day and removed after three days by the apartment authorities. Photograph by the artist.

seek to detail the social and political changes taking place in Jamaica by paying closer critical attention to fashion, style, and modes of performance; for instance, through his liquor bottles, Johnson has the ability to queer traditionally stable boundaries that have effectively demarcated who has a right to be seen, in what venues, and for what purposes. He has sought to engage Jamaicans by repurposing colonial/tropical and postcolonial/popular iconic images and installing them in public spaces to highlight the circuits of consumption that affect Black subjects whose lives, labor, and struggles continue to be castigated by the state and the church (figures 7 and 8). His approach is markedly different from other contemporary artists, but his critical interests mark him as one who understands the power of the popular and the public sphere. Johnson's representation of dancehall performances questions the relationship between secular rituals and performances by juxtaposing them directly against religious and political institutions that have castigated these modes of expression as vulgarity dressed in the vices of excess. Of course, the deep irony in re/cycling the "disposable" elements of Jamaican popular cultural expression and consumption is that it highlights an engagement with the politics of class and identity formation in Jamaica, which makes Johnson's work across the range of media (paintings, ceramics, public art/ graffiti and graphic art) all the more insightful.

5

"Outta Order" or "Outta Door"?

Caribbean Women Performing Power, Politics, and Sexuality

> In what I call "Afro-alienation acts," the condition of alterity converts into cultural expressiveness and the specific strategy of cultural performance. . . . Afro-alienation acts draw from what Hortense Spillers describes as the "dehumanizing, engendering, and defacing" conditions that African peoples encountered in the New World. Having little access to the culture of property, to the culture of naming, or to patriarchal wealth, the mythically rendered black body—and the black female body in particular—was scripted by dominant paradigms to have no movement in a field of signification." Born out of diasporic plight and subject to pornotroping, this body has countenanced a "powerful stillness."

Public performances carry with them a tremendous amount of semiotic value in Black diaspora communities, particularly when women enact them. To fully appreciate the extent to which gender informs both how and where "unscripted" performances are consumed, critiques of women's performances must consider how women constantly negotiate embodied realities personally and professionally. Music, dance, fashion, sports, and other bodily expressions have always been crafted into forms of resistance in Black diaspora communities across the globe. In the past musicians, athletes, and performers were once content to have their art speak on their behalf. But recently, they have raised the stakes by using performance to transform their bodies into tools of intervention.

Bodily performances translate into practices of "style," and for Black male subjects, what C. L. R. James refers to as the "line of vision" in cricket allows viewers to grasp *movement*, which is essential to how Black male bodies occupy social spaces. The *movement* to which James refers might be understood as the antithesis of the "powerful stillness" that Daphne Brooks describes as part of the reality experienced by Black women as they move through social and political spaces. However, in the interest of not thinking in binaristic terms, Uri McMillan proposes another possibility that encapsulates what these new modes of consumption might mean for Black diaspora subjectivity in the twenty-first century. He argues that Black female performers have provocatively transformed themselves or, more precisely, their bodies, into objects through acts of "self-objectification" to adopt a third option that parallels the two possibilities offered by James and Brooks. Before we explore this third option, it is crucial that we understand the ontological stakes at work between the two perspectives outlined by these two cultural theorists. For James, movement is the modality through which Black male bodies occupy space and, as Brooks notes, women have been forced into stillness by longstanding patriarchal structures in which they are "scripted by dominant paradigms to have no movement in a field of signification" (Brooks, 2006, 5). These two perspectives outline the implausibility of freedom within the parameters often available to Black citizens in the twenty-first century. Somewhere sandwiched between the immobility imposed by immigration, incarceration, and institutional racism, new ways of imagining and performing freedom emerged out of necessity.

For Black subjects, the practice of carrying oneself "as though you come from somewhere" was traditionally accomplished through clothing, profession, and positions of respectability within African diaspora communities. All of these ways of fashioning the self were in the service of assuring the world that who you and your family were was enough for you to carry yourself in a "certain" way. Arguably, this "nuffness" served as fertile ground for Caribbean men, but it left very little room for experimentation among the women who also had to carve out spaces for themselves and their daughters in the cultural and political landscapes of countries like Jamaica, Trinidad, and Barbados. There is a long tradition dedicated to conditioning women to police themselves in the public sphere, particularly because their conduct in that arena is understood to be a reflection of the social status of the family, the school, the church, and the community to which they belong. Male behavior in the public domain signifies very differently and is policed differently and, arguably, less frequently than that of women. Many of these distinctions date back to the post-emancipation era when colonial officials frequently sought to curb the amount of space, as well as the behaviors, taken up by Black women in the public domain.

The texts examined up to this point all provide invaluable insights into how Caribbean sexualities, in the tradition of "anancyism," mask underlying power negotiations in relationships of power (which include political, social, sexual, and romantic relationships). Thus far, these shifts, from negotiating public spaces to private spaces, have highlighted how masculine power structures are being renegotiated, albeit to a small degree. What is different about the changes women are spearheading are the mechanisms they are deploying to lay claim to cultural spaces in which they have been historically marginalized and oppressed. In these instances, discourses that traditionally frame constructions of "foreign" and "local" tastes are thrown into disarray because the intersections of mobility, location, and pleasure and desire become part of the intimacy of the conversation/performance between the artist and her audience. The stage is no longer simply a public space; it has effectively been turned into an intimate physical space similar to that of the bedroom. By making these public spaces more intimate, Lady Saw makes sexual appetite and desire a topic of conversation; by deploying lyrical outlandishness, she renders visible the ways desire is always constructed, particularly for female performers.

Writing about modern Blackness in Jamaica, Deborah Thomas reflects on the potential for dancehall culture to provide an alternative political and cultural space of resistance that functions similarly to what Daphne Brooks (2006, 4–5) calls "cultural expressiveness and the specific strategy of cultural performance." To counteract or even convert the "powerful stillness" into an embodied resistance, performers began to perform their selves in notably different ways to elicit an uneasy interaction with their audiences. Through their insistence on rejecting middle-class sensibilities about respectability, female performers level the playing field by taking the ideological underpinnings of masculine power—which often masquerade as "private moments" or "man/woman business"—and making these structures public—laying them bare, usually through humor:

> Ghetto feminism, then, is a type of what Elizabeth McAlister has called "sexualized popular laughter" (2002:61), a way in which women "read" and critique the social order. I am not suggesting here that Jamaican women have only recently begun to use these tactics to carve out spaces for their own power vis-à-vis the men within their intimate social worlds. What I am noting, however, is that dancehall has created a space for a new *public* advocacy of these tactics by women for women. Further, this is a space that exists beyond the

> realm of intimate relations, and as such it has potential to infiltrate a more general political vision. (Thomas 2004, 255–256)

Here, Thomas is referring specifically to the lyrical interventions of songs performed by female dancehall deejays Lady Saw, Tanya Stephens, and the then-emerging star, Ce'Cile. Although Saw and Stephens have had long-lasting careers, theirs has been a precarious existence within the dancehall fraternity because they always have had to rely on an industry standard that grants space very begrudgingly to female artistes, particularly when their worldviews are not in lockstep with the men who control the industry.

Although feminist critics like Carolyn Cooper have long argued for the Jamaican dancehall as a performative space of empowerment for women, performing (particularly dancing) in the dancehall is still regulated by (and for) the male gaze of male promoters, deejays, and participants. In the dancehall arena, women are constantly reminded of this through unspoken (and, though unseen, certainly enforced) rules of engagement among women, men, and their sexual/political bodies. There has been a moderate shift in these regulated norms, but this change has occurred less in the structures of power per se and more in the ways in which female performers have laid claim to these structures to diffuse the power typically exercised against them. Skirting the razor's edge, female performers have always deployed different kinds of perverse humor, a strategy that is an essential part of Caribbean culture across the region. This humor incorporates an element of anancyism that relies heavily on the cover of the "joke" for its effectiveness. In Jamaica the saying, "yuh haffi tek bad ting mek joke," refers to one of the coping mechanisms deployed by citizens in response to government corruption, violence, the exploitation of the poor, and many other social and political ills. In the popular idiom of Trinidad and Tobago, there is a similar saying: "joke is joke, but damned joke ent no fun," which includes the cautionary maxim (damned joke) about taking the joke too far. In the latter saying, the danger lies in presuming the ignorance of a person at whose expense the joke is being made. There is always an invisible line between a joke and the dangerous situation that humor glosses over to provide a viable, desperately needed outlet for the person or group against whom the joke is directed. But what does it mean to skate on that thin line, to evoke this "sexualized popular laughter" during a live stage performance? What are the risks involved in assuming that an audience will engage and participate in the joke, especially if it comes at the expense of a large segment of the community?

"Outta Order" or out in the Open? Shifting Power, Gender, and Sexuality through Performance

There are three female deejays whose performances in the dancehall arena provide us with provocative responses to the questions I just raised: the indefatigable queen of dancehall deejays, Lady Saw, whose career spans more than thirty years;

Spice, who has been an integral part of the dancehall scene for more than a decade; and Ishawna, the latest female deejay to ascend to prominence. I focus on Ishawna because she is one of the few female deejays of her generation to take up the mantle passed down by Lady Saw in her unabashed advocacy for women's sexual freedom. What makes her contribution unique is the way she appropriates the style of *vershanns* introduced to Caribbean readers in Michael Thelwell's *The Harder They Come* (1980) and later adapted as a critical tool by Evelyn O'Callaghan in *Woman Version* (1993).

One of the hallmarks of ghetto feminism is the "public affirmation of female agency, especially as this is related to sexual fulfillment" (Thomas 2004, 253). Although Lady Saw's lyrics have always been sexually explicit, earlier in her career they tended to stay within the boundaries of what could be considered "acceptable" sexual norms. Her lyrics leaned more toward the "bad gyal" persona intended to match and, at times, exceed the lyrical bravado of her male counterparts. However, Lady Saw's career has been characterized by her willingness to step outside the accepted norms of what is deemed appropriate for public consumption. Most notably, her 2007 release of the single "No Less than a Woman (Infertility)" brought the issue of infertility and the social stigma associated with it out of the shroud of secrecy, shame, gossip, and innuendo cloaking women who could not conceive. It also openly addressed adoption and the social stigma associated with women raising children who are not biologically theirs, two issues that are only now being discussed in less hushed tones across the region.

Yet one of Saw's most indelible contributions to dancehall music and its strained, contentious relationship to Black female sexuality is her upending of the order of things as a performer. She has always used the stage as an unscripted space for subverting narratives of conformity aimed at patrolling sexual desire. She blazed a path for her contemporaries, such as artists Ce'Cile and Tanya Stephens, both of whom also successfully crafted spaces in the dancehall landscape through their own lyrical expressions of female desire and sexual pleasure. Although heteronormative discourses are found in the lyrics of recorded music, who wrote those lyrics is only revealed to listeners in the liner notes of CDs and albums. Given the fact that many of the songs performed by dancehall artists are not produced under the same stringent regulations that govern the music industry in other parts of the world, it is even more unlikely that this "inside information" is available to consumers. Because these "hidden transcripts" remain unseen, audiences are encouraged to believe that the perspectives expressed in the songs are those of the performer. This kind of opacity has particular consequences when female performers are singing songs that express perspectives about female sexual desires. On stage these voices and perspectives often appear seamless.

Lady Saw's performances and lyrics draw heavily on anancyism and in so doing leave space for her performances to publicly expose what I define as "extranational" configurations of sexual freedom and desire that are more easily characterized as part of the landscape of "foreign" consumers, even when the audiences are Caribbean people living abroad. In these instances, discourses that traditionally frame constructions of "foreign" and "local" tastes are thrown into disarray because the intersections of mobility, location, and pleasure and desire become part of intimacy of the conversation/performance between the artist and her audience.

Lady Saw's performances convert the public state into an intimate physical space similar to that of the bedroom. But as we all know, the bedroom has always been a public space, constantly under surveillance and heavily legislated by the state, the church, and the nation. By making these public spaces more intimate, Lady Saw makes sexual appetite and desire a topic of conversation by deploying lyrical bravado and humor to make the constructed nature of desire more visible to her audiences. During a 2004 performance at Sting that I attended in Miami, I watched Lady Saw come onto the stage and, less than one minute into the show, stop to sit down and take off her shoes, something she seems to do with some regularity during her stage shows. I mention this here because such an act is usually reserved for spaces of comfort and hominess: the removal of one's shoes effectively consecrates the stage as a private space, albeit one that she is sharing with thousands of people in the audience.

After removing her shoes, she remains seated on the stage, inviting her audience to participate in this segment of the show. This mode of call-and-response is a staple in most stage shows in the Caribbean, as audience members are asked to put lighters, flags, rags, and hands in the air to indicate their approval or participation in some aspect of the performance. She asks members of the audience to raise their hands if they (the men) "know seh dem no nyamm no punaany bout here" and then poses a similar invitation to the women: raise your hand if you "nah nyaam no hood boy deh." After the men and women raise their hands, she calls to the men again, saying, "Nuff ah unna ah liard to raas claat, and you and I know that… Cause nuff ah dem man here tell lie more time hear baby, so no watch no face, you and I know what they like… and I like it, so… big up the man who ah lie."

Later in the set, she calls on the women in the audience to recognize the value of what they have sexually, admonishing them not to "gi it weh for free:"

> You know why we no gi it weh free? Cause we have di pink ting!
> We pink like flowers, healthy and pink.
> Whey di woman dem wid di pink, me no talk no white business!
> You know when you visit your gynecologist,
> Him seh boy it look healthy, pink and bloom like a flowas.
> Tight oh right oh, blind boy sigh oh,
> Mi no want no boy whe ah taste an ah buy oh
> Pink, pink, pink me no carry not ah white oh
> Not for sale mi no hustle it ah night tho'
> Rest it, me no stress it this here tightness for life oh.

Same time mi have mi kriss car ah drive oh
Ring pon mi p***y just a glisten in di light oh!
Aye Jamaica no see yuh coulda bright so,
P***y like this haffi mek mi turn wife oh
Tight oh right oh, blind boy sigh oh,
Mi no want no boy whe ah taste and ah buy oh
Dem haffi . . .

Stopping rather abruptly, Lady Saw then instructs the selector (the deejay who selects which songs to play during a stage show) to "hold on deh man! Ah Spragga write dat lyrics dey gimme ya know! 'Mi no want no boy whe ah taste an ah bite oh.' But dat ah lie cause me like it sometime!" She then proceeds to perform a song that expresses (in graphic detail) a female perspective that is quite contrary to that conveyed in Spragga's song. She moves on to express her own ghetto feminist perspective not only on oral sex but also on extramarital or non-monogamous relationships.

The man inna mi house neva go down low,
But di bwoy outta road nuff tings him haffi do like
Kiss up mi catty and suck off mi toe,
All mi bright bulb him haffi blow.
The man inna mi house give me raw born sex, oh yes
Also di hickie pon breast
But before ah next boy try tear off mi dress,
Mi p***y tongue him haffi wet!

In Saw's hierarchy, her full-time, live-in partner has the privilege of sex that does not include oral sex; her partner on the side, however, needs to perform kinkier sex acts (i.e., toe sucking and cunnilingus). Her lyrics provide a curious moment of elision that allows the reference to vaginal piercing (in Spragga Benz's song) to appear in lockstep with her lyrics about cunnilingus, because, after all, why else would one acquire such a piercing? But there are other aspects of Lady Saw's lyrics that are worthy of attention, most notably her invitation to the women in the audience to listen to her talking about vaginal health. Given the overwhelming preoccupation with female genitalia in dancehall music, her positioning of the otherwise private matter of gynecological visits into the conversation about erotic desire and female sexual pleasure is particularly productive. This lyrical construction moves these once "intimate matters" from the bedroom, the home, and personal health "outta door" and into the public sphere in the tone of advocacy presented in a very woman-centered fashion. Ironically, as we all know, female genitalia have *always* been a public subject in Jamaican popular culture, but not in a way that allows for this kind "*public* advocacy of these tactics for women, by women" (Thomas 2004, 256).

In fact, despite the sexually charged atmosphere of the performance, the men in the audience are noticeably uncomfortable during this segment of the concert. Many join in the laughter but it is an uncomfortable laughter: women are waving their hands in the air while the men are standing by, trying their best to look unaffected by the sight of the women waving their hands. Thus, the "sexualized popular laughter" that fills the audience has as much to do with a response to Lady Saw's outlandishness as with the truth she is revealing (Thomas 2004, 253). Recognizing the uneasiness of the crowd, Saw poses a rhetorical question before moving on to the next set: "Yuh think is a joke ting? I'm plain and straight." Her question lingers in the air while many of the women respond with approving applause and hands in the air, seeming, at least for the moment, to be "in on the joke."

In "Change the Joke, Slip the Yoke," Ralph Ellison (1958, 55) describes this phenomenon through the paradigm of masking:

> Very often, however, the Negro's masking is motivated not so much by fear as by a profound rejection of the image created to usurp this identity. Sometimes it is for the sheer joy of the joke; sometimes to challenge those who presume, across the psychological distance created by race manners, to know his identity. . . . America is a land of joking maskers. . . . The motives hidden behind the mask are as numerous as the ambiguities the mask conceals.

Ellison's critical insight about masking, humor, and Black identity is particularly useful for this critique of Black women's sexual identities and how they are performed publicly and privately. But it is also insightful because of what it tells us about how humor can be used to destabilize systems of knowledge that have constructed female desire and sexuality. Lady Saw's performance is aimed at disrupting the audience's assumption that the performing body always speaks the body politic of the performer. By stepping "outta door," outside of Jamaica and out of character, to announce that which is never discussed on stage—that she is singing songs that someone else wrote for her; that the words of the song are contrary to her personal/political preference; and that possibly her performance itself is a fiction, but one worthy of consideration—she lays bare the systems of masking that are an integral part of the masculinist narratives that shape popular conceptions of female desire and pleasure. Lady Saw's candidness has made her a force to reckon with in the dancehall industry.

Few, if any, male deejays have challenged her lyrical content and the ideologies expressed in her music: her longevity in the industry has earned her "real big ooman/woman" status. This has enabled her to collaborate with male deejays but always on an equal basis. This is evident even in the music videos. Her collaborations with Beenie Man on "Healing" and again with Beenie Man and Sean Paul on "Bossman" are performances in which she brings as much to the table as her male collaborators and, at times, even more because of her following. That she appears on Beenie's single titled "Bossman" alongside two of the more successful crossover artists is significant. At the same time, there is an undeniable amount of goodwill among and between Lady Saw and many of the male deejays in the business: Sean Paul is the love interest in the original release of "Heels On," whereas Beenie Man, Bounty Killer, and Pitbull all make cameos in "Summer Love," one of her summer party songs.

The next generation of women who have come up in the industry since Lady Saw was crowned the dancehall queen have had to navigate an even more tumultuous landscape: the terrain of the dancehall has changed significantly, arguably becoming even more masculinist in the music produced and in dancehall performances. Spice (aka Grace Latoya Hamilton), like Lady Saw, has achieved success and longevity in the dancehall industry. Her emergence in the dancehall occurred through skillful manipulation of masculinist norms and expectations, but her breakthrough came when she was featured in "Romping Shop" and "Conjugal Visit" alongside Vybz Kartel. These collaborations were wildly popular because of their explicit lyrics and sparring style, with the two lyricists exchanging braggadocious comments about their sexual abilities and preferences. Like Lady Saw, Spice met and often exceeded her male counterparts in lyrical skills and sexual bravado. In addition, her music accomplished this end through a brand of sensuality that put "women on top," particularly in songs like "With My Heels On." Before her breakthrough collaborations with Vybz Kartel, she was positioned next to male deejays, who were the focus of the performances while she danced in a sexually suggestive manner that buttressed and elevated the sexual appeal of their songs. However, since she has emerged as a talented lyricist and performer, Spice has tackled other socially and politically relevant issues in her music.

Spice, who is a member of the Gaza Empire, has gained a solid foothold in the industry through her dancehall collaborations with Vybz Kartel. Her newfound status within the Empire and the industry gave her the power to experiment and begin to formulate her own brand. She recently released an eyebrow-raising single that put the inequities of the dancehall music industry "outta door" with a slamming, sexually explicit track titled "Like A Man." The backstory for the song and the music video is that they are her answer to this question posed to her during a radio interview: "We all know that it is a male-dominated business. As a top female artist, do you think that females get the ratings they deserve in this industry?" The video features Spice made up in a somewhat comical fashion as a male performer: first in a formal suit and then in the ubiquitous "wife beater" undershirt and jeans with a plethora of tattoos on her arms.

> Suppose me start get x-rated and raw
> Gyal suck hood if you waan cause ah your four jaw
> Bore yuh tongue, ah your own do what you waan do yah
> Any gal nuh like it tell dem suck dem madda

If me deejay like Kartel and ah spit nuff rhyme
Get bad like Bounty and Ninja one time
Bleach out, tattoo mi eye like Alkaline
Den answer mi, make mi sing back the punch line.
Chorus:
You think dem woulda rate me more?
If me was a man and a drop it hardcore, eeehhnn
If me do a couple badness and a say skull fi bore, eeehhnn
You think dem woulda rate me more?
If me say you gyal go f**k pon the floor, eeehhnn
You think dem woulda rate me more?
You think dem woulda rate me more?
If me was a man me woulda be ah ole gyallis
Mi gal woulda haffi stay home, her man fren woulda haffi vanish
Her phone her iPad everything woulda abolish
And she couldn't cook me food and have on nail polish
Gal whine up yuh body show yuh flexibility
You have the capability fi get man instantly
Yuh nuh dead, yuh p***y never send no man ah cemetery
Skin out if you wah dweet it explicitly.
Dem say a male dominate the industry
But ah nuff ah dem male dem nuh bad like me
No versatility nuh have no creativity
The only difference is dat me have breast and p***y.

Ironically though, she makes no effort to hide her breasts while wearing this costume, as if to drive home the point she articulates near the end of the song. Lyrically, "Like a Man" is a double-edged sword because it chronicles Spice's entry and ascendance into the dancehall industry while also highlighting the centrality of the male-centered gaze in dancehall aesthetics. There is certainly room for a meta-critique of the song, because it belongs to the same discursive and performative community of most of Spice's other releases and of songs released by Kartel. Although the lyrics of the song clearly highlight the tradition of misogyny in dancehall music, there is also a recognition on her part that a double standard keeps this tradition in place. Spice's crossover appeal, from music to television entertainment, really took off when she was added to the cast of Season 7 of VH1's hit reality television series, *Love and Hip Hop: Atlanta*; this required her to make the major transition from dancehall music to hip-hop music and culture. Many wondered how she would "translate" as a Jamaican woman in the context of Black American popular culture, despite the fact that other cast members have a Caribbean heritage or connections. Like her close friend and mentor, Vybz Kartel, her prowess as a hustler with serious standing in the marketing arena became very evident during Season 8 when she appeared looking at least three shades lighter than she had in the previous season. Cast members were shocked, horrified, and angry when Spice introduced them to the new version of herself, explaining that colorism has been a real limitation to her professionally. She initially took to social media sporting the new look, having deleted all her earlier posts featuring a "darker" Spice. Many questioned the impulse behind her apparent skin bleaching; the Twitterverse exploded with comments from both members of the African American community who were introduced to her on *Love and Hip Hop: Atlanta* and from Jamaicans who felt that she was embarrassing her country to gain ratings in the U.S. television market.

She reappeared later on social media to inform her followers and friends that her new mixed tape[1] "Black Hypocrisy" would be released soon—and, by the way, she was returning to her original skin tone. On the eve of the release of "Black Hypocrisy," Spice took to Instagram and Twitter to explain that she had not actually bleached her skin, but she took pains to insist that it was not a "publicity stunt." Instead, she explained, "I wanted to create awareness to 'colorism,' and it was more so done to intentionally create shock value so that I could have the world's undivided attention to deliver the message in my music."[2]

The music video opens with Spice delivering a modified version of Martin Luther King's "I Have a Dream" speech to a group of women, one that stresses "black women supporting each other rather than bashing each other" and ends with her saying she is "black without apology." She then begins the song by acknowledging that what she is saying is unpopular but is also a reflection of the colorism and preference for "brown" skin in Jamaican society:

> It's not what you expect me to say, but I'mma go ahead and say it anyway.
> I was told I would reach further, if the color of my skin was lighter.
> And I was made to feel inferior, 'cause society says brown girls prettier.
> Mi love the way mi look, mi love pretty black skin.
> Respect due to mi strong melanin.
> Proud of mi color, love the skin that I'm in
> Bun racism, demolish colorism . . .
> Chorus:
> Them say mi black 'til mi shine and mi look dirty
> And it's the only line in life that would ever hurt me
> Because it never come from a Caucasian trust me
> This black colorism big hypocrisy
> So if I wake up tomorrow, look like a brownin'
> Automatically mi woulda carry the swing
> Nuff ah oonu not gwaan like this song mi ah sing
> Because nuff ah onnu guilty fi di same damn ting . . .

In the new visual regime of social media, appearance seems to mean as much as, if not more than, what is said, and this reality has shaped much of the aesthetic in dancehall music today, particularly for women. In *Bodies in Dissent* Daphne Brooks examines performances by nineteenth-century African American women artists in the public sphere. Her analysis of the Black body in movement highlights the specificity of performances or what she also refers to as Black women "doing" their bodies differently to provoke their audiences into moments of discomfort. This "doing" of the body is not simply about how women contort themselves visually as performers. Much of what Brooks says about physical performances is applicable to the ways in which women perform their own bodies discursively. The efficacy of "private" lies told publicly depends largely on the frequency with which these public performances "out" those lies. In other words, as is the case with most "inside jokes," the more they are heard and told, the less taboo and arguably more humorous they become, because those on the "inside" now outnumber those who are outside. In the long run, this makes for unimaginably powerful moments of political advocacy.

Talk and Taste Yuh Tongue: Dancehall Dissidence in Unsavory Political Times

The recent release of Ishawna's hit song "Equal Rights and Justice," which went viral on the internet and in almost every chat room dedicated to Jamaican popular culture, was one such moment. That Ishawna borrows her title from another hit song, Peter Tosh's "Equal Rights," while also sampling from Ed Sheeran's "Shape of You," highlights her investment in explicitly linking women's rights with sexual freedom and sexual expression. In her essay "Dub Versioning Ishawna's 'Equal Rights,': From Chanting down to Louding Up," Isis Semaj-Hall (2018, 31) argues, "By using the phrase 'equal rights and justice,' and titling the song as 'Equal Rights,' Ishawna generationally links her song to Peter Tosh's original or master song. But because of the focused gender perspective of Ishawna's lyrics, she inadvertently opens up Tosh's song to gendered critique." This observation is critical because Ishawna's song appeared on the Jamaican dancehall scene at a politically auspicious moment in Caribbean feminist history. Responding to the alarming rate of women and girls who were kidnapped, raped, and brutally murdered, or murdered by their partners or spouses at home, the Tambourine Army was formed under the leadership of LGBTQ activist Latoya Nugent. Thus, Ishawna's "Equal Rights" both marked a confluence of political crises at the center of Jamaican society and had immediate relevance to Ishawna's own experience with domestic abuse, as shown later in the chapter. Her appropriation of Tosh's 1977 call to political action, in addition to opening Tosh's song to a gendered critique, links the social and political climate of the late 1970s, when women were very susceptible to physical violence and domestic abuse, to 2017, the year her song was released when the abuse and violence had not abated.

Rather than seeing her song primarily as a link to Tosh's "master song," we might consider it a historically located and politically situated "daughta vershaan" similar to Michael Thelwell's rendering of the range of social and political vantage points involved in telling Ivan's story in his 1980 novel, *The Harder They Come*, which was published three years after the release of Tosh's song. Ivan's troubles multiply and finally culminate in the penultimate chapter titled "Pressah Drop," which is also the title of a song recorded by Toots Hibbert and released in 1970.

Ishawna's song emerges during the bourgeoning women's rights movement in the Caribbean generally and in Jamaica more specifically. Semaj-Hall (2018, 31) astutely notes,

> Capital and common "Equal Rights" were politically and provocatively re-gendered in 2017. When fourteen women quietly entered a rural Moravian church in January of that year to rally support for a young victim of rape,[3] these women who sat silently in the congregation, effectively applied a dub treatment to the previous master record of sexual abuse in Jamaica. . . . This new, amplified *version* of equal rights is marked in Latoya Nugent's words to the UK's *Guardian*: "We [Jamaican women] want to change the culture [Jamaicans] have of assigning blame and shame to survivors . . . We want to place it at the feet of perpetrators and change the current narrative."

Although Semaj-Hall rightfully acknowledges the confluence of social and political forces that ushered in the arrival of both the Tambourine Army and Ishawna's "Equal Rights," continuing to insist that it takes its cue from a "master record" obfuscates the long history of women's political movements in Jamaica and the wider Caribbean region. Beginning with the labor riots that took place in 1934 in Belize, Trinidad, Guyana, and Jamaica and that slowly but assiduously spread across the entire region, women were on the frontlines of these social and political movements. Elma Francois and Daisy Crick in Trinidad and Amy Garvey from Jamaica cut their political teeth as members of Marcus Garvey's United Negro Improvement Association (UNIA) and later went on to become leaders in the Negro Welfare Cultural and Social Association (NWCSA). This is to say nothing of the global impact of Claudia Jones, who demanded that gender equity in labor and society remain at the center of the Communist Party Platform and leftist, Marxist politics on the whole. In fact, as Rhonda Reddock (1994, 111) notes, "In both the mass-based Garvey movement and the vanguard type NWCSA, women were able to hold leadership positions. Little is known of the particular situations that facilitated this or the struggles that ensued around these questions. Clearly, however, at this time male leaders realized the importance of organizing women as part of their broader struggle."

Thus, Semaj-Hall's (2018, 31) assertion that "this new gender-inclusive *dub version* is what undergirds the now outrageous lyrics of Ishawna's single" neglects the fact that the Black nationalist politics to which Tosh's song belonged, while certainly revolutionary in their anticolonial stance, was in fact quite retrograde in its inability to recognize the constitutive nature of women's rights in the struggle against anticolonialism. Far from creating a generational link to Tosh's generation, I argue that Ishawna's song, like the Tambourine Army and the other women's movements that are unifying women across the region, belongs to a well-established feminist genealogy routed/rooted in the local, urban ghettos among the working poor and those aspiring to become working class. The phrase "ghetto feminism" highlights the centrality of Black women's understanding that their sexuality is an integral part of their political power. But it is not a recent development in gender politics in Jamaica; it has always been a part of social and political consciousness of working poor and working-class women. In fact, Thomas (2004, 251–252) tells us, "Peggy Antrobus has remarked that while she was working as the first director of the Jamaican government's Women's Bureau during the mid-1970s, she discovered that black lower-class women identified sexuality (as distinct from sex) as one of two primary sources of power in their lives (personal communication)."[4]

Thus, in the spirit of the discussion of dub versions and remixes, I want to instantiate a rewind, or PUULL UUP, so as to redirect the rhythmic and lyrical trajectory to the beginning of the genealogy to which Ishawna's song belongs. Just as Ce'Celie's song "Do It to Me," Tanya Stephens's "Yuh Nuh Ready," and Lady Saw's Sting performance implore men in earshot of the dancehall session to embrace their inner freak and "stop watch face," Ishawna's recent release takes up the torch and blazes out the call for men to step up to the plate politically and sexually to meet women's expectations as desiring subjects in the enterprise of sexual gratification. Although Vybz Kartel's celebration and praise songs for "pum-pum" certainly rise above the kind of vitriol expressed toward female sexuality and female pleasure during the 1990s, his songs often situate men as the primary desiring subjects for sexual gratification. Saw's stage performances helped create a space for other female recording artists to inhabit public sexual landscapes by priming audiences to participate in the public pronouncements that threatened the usual order of things in the dancehall. But the curious twist in Ishawna's song hinges on her public breakup with Foota Hype, one of Jamaica's well-known sound selectors. That the song was personal set it on course to become an even more relevant moment in Jamaican popular culture because its impact reached far beyond the dancehall:

> I just got started
> Wha' you think one round can do?
> Bumper to your forehead
> Show me wha' your tongue can do
> If you nuh have it inna waist, you better have it inna face
> Bright enough fi a look gyal fi shine you . . .
> And you nuh waan taste?
> [Chorus]

You have a clean mouth and your lips dem sexy
Treat me like a bottle of Pepsi
Yuh back nuh have no use and yuh face look cute
Deal wid mi like a bag juice.
Mi say equal rights and justice
Nuff ignorant people ah go cuss dis
Mi p***y tight, cut up your cocky like cutlass
But if you waan head, my youth, you haffi suck this.
[Verse 2]
Boy, me nah go compromise
Me waan feel how your head feels between mi thighs
Me waan look inna your dreamy eyes
When you a chew pon mi pum pum like french fries
You never hear 'bout foreplay?
A modern times now, boy, relax . . . it's ok
If me ever bring it up inna the group chat
You get the threesome for your birthday.
[Verse 3]
Mi love it when di man dem brave up
Cause nuff man have dem good tongue ah save up
That mi like when you eat mi right
When you do it mi go long outrageous . . .

When "Equal Rights" hit the airwaves in Jamaica it became an instant flashpoint not only because of its lyrics but also because it was released at a time when the continued social and political inequities between men and women in Jamaica were receiving renewed public scrutiny and when the question of social justice and equity under the law was very much up for debate, particularly in the media. It also attained notoriety because of Ishawna's public breakup with Foota Hype. According to several accounts, Ishawna released a barrage of "diss-songs" about her ex-boyfriend when their nine-year relationship ended abruptly. In response to the songs, Foota took to the national airways to denounce her as an opportunist and a sexually deviant woman. In a 2014 interview with Winford Williams on the popular entertainment talk show *On Stage*, Foota Hype gives this explanation for why he ended his engagement and relationship with Ishawna: "She wanted oral sex and threesomes and mi no inna dat!" Foota goes on to admit, "We have had physical encounters, yes mi cheat, mi ah star. Mi ah one ugly boy get rich and have likkle money and mi have likkle swag. Mi ah goh have a next girl, ah so it go."[5] The host never presses Foota on his "less than perfect" status, even though he admitted in a roundabout way that he abused his fiancée and cheated on her. What does pique Williams's interest, however, is the charge that Ishawna had an affair with another label mate and had "deviant" sexual desires. In all of this, the irony seems lost on Foota Hype who proclaims at the end of the interview that "Jamaica is a moral country, morals work here, and mi is a moral yute."

What is most interesting about the whole narrative between Foota Hype and Ishawna is the extent to which the media machinery never really questioned his account of events and treated her not as generously when she appeared on the talk show a few weeks later to refute Foota's charges. She is asked repeatedly to justify her decision to leave her relationship, and after disclosing that she was in an abusive relationship for nine years, the host asks her, "Why did you stay with him?"[6] We know this to be a common question posed to women who decide to stay in abusive relationships, and Ishawna, like many other women, goes on to explain that he held the financial power in the relationship, that he was able to manipulate her because he knew that she had no family in Jamaica, and that he told her he was the reason she had a music career. In fact, the reasons Ishawna lists for not leaving are among the same reasons Foota cites during his interview as proof of Ishawna's ungratefulness: the store he opened for her, the opportunities he gave her to work with other artists like Wyclef Jean, the music studio time he gave her to record some of her music, and the list went on. Ishawna admits finally that the price she had to pay behind closed doors for her "success" was too great, and so she decided to leave. The final straw according to Ishawna was Foota beating her in front of their young son.

Foota Hype's public assertions about Ishawna's moral decay seem drawn from the 1990s handbook on sexual conduct for women, not only in the dancehall sphere but also in Jamaica in general—despite the rapidly increasing presence of queerness in dancehall that I discuss in the previous chapter. Knowing the power of the moral argument about the "freaky things" condoned by people in the United States, Foota clearly intended the charge of deviant sexual behavior to derail any career possibilities for Ishawna and for her to be diminished in the public eye. This expectation makes her complete embrace (in song) of the charges singularly ghetto feminist, in Thomas's sense of the word. Furthermore, her disclosure of the circuitous process of securing a restraining order against Foota Hype undoubtedly spoke to hundreds of women who have had to go through this process but were not fortunate enough to have the backing of a record label and the protection of the national media. She disclosed publicly that Foota threatened to kill her and then himself, if she ever left him. Although Foota denied these allegations, the story is a familiar one, and not just in the Caribbean region. According to Ishawna, her release of the song "Restraining Order," was intended to be a kind of insurance policy: "Me neva want Foota come hurt me and nutten nah come out of it. So, mi ah decide to mek Jamaica know seh that mi ah been stalked, and mi ah goh get a restraining order, so if ah pin touch Ishawna, you know seh fi find Foota."[7] Even for a high-profile artist like Ishawna, her lack of faith in the ability of the judicial system to protect women from violence is unequivocal, and by using her craft to draw attention to her plight, she gained an instant fan base.

The dancehall fraternity, however, was far less enthusiastic about embracing Ishawna's brand of braggadocio, particularly coming from a young, very attractive, brown woman. The outrage was immediate and took the usual form of threatening behavior by male artists who were booked to perform with Ishawna. As long as Ishawna was singing songs like "Mi Belly," "Everybody Needs Someone," and "Slippery When Wet"—all songs that promoted the "bedroom bully" fantasy—her male fan base was locked in. But the moment she shifted gears to focus on female sexual gratification, that abruptly changed. When she took the stage during Dream Weekend's Xtreme Wet N Wild at the Kool Runnings Water Park one hot July weekend in 2017, she was greeted by male attendees with extra-large water guns who took aim at her and sought to wash her off the stage when she began performing "Equal Rights." The streams of water damaged the sound equipment, and things threatened to get out of hand before dancehall selector and icon Tony Matterhorn took the stage and warned the patrons that they were destroying his property and preventing other people from enjoying the show. While the sound guys attempted to find another mic for Ishawna, she continued to dance to the "Shape of You" remix rhythm while hundreds of women came to the front of the stage and began singing the chorus of her song loudly, in defiance of the earlier efforts to silence her.

Most famously, however, the Warlord, or Bounty Killer, when told he would be performing with Ishawna at the Bikini Flossing and Food (B.F.F.) Labour Day celebration in Portland, took to Instagram to voice his displeasure, stating, "@mslegendary cyaah sing da song deh at this show, else mi a go rush har. Nuh kitten or catfish can nuh bloodclaat bother come because that cyah sing, else she cannot be on no more shows with me." This post may have been just a way to boost attendance at the show, but Bounty's sentiment reflected a growing sentiment among men in the dancehall industry, as well as her male fan base. In response to Bounty's Instagram message, Ishawna responded, "This festive bad. Mi never know me and Killa a guh war dung a Portland next week? Bring it on Rodney! #equalrights." As if to return to Lady Saw's onstage "outta door" secrets, the last verse of "Equal Rights" evokes a very "plain talk, bad manners" approach to the public outcry from some of her detractors:

Mhmm
Me nuh 'fraid ah nobody
And when me talk, me nuh care who nuh like me
Me shave up mi body
Mi drink mi pineapple juice nightly
Me take care of mi body
So him supposed to nyaam me nightly
Me nuh 'fraid ah nobody
Who nuh like me, dem fi bite me!

When Ishawna took the stage at the B.F.F. Labor Day before Bounty Killer, she began her set with her songs that implored men to "rate/respect women." But what made her concert set so effective was not only her performance of the song itself but also the salvos of education and advice she intermittently proffered to her audience. As is usually the case, Ishawna implored the sound system to "pull up" on more than one occasion before she launched into "Equal Rights" fully. The performance was punctuated with several digressions filled with advice to women, the most notable and scandalous of which was her advice to women about how to "test" men to ensure they get their "equal rights":

> Lemme tell oonu ladies how fi get yuh equal rights. Ladies, yuh know when you and yuh man ah deh at home, and him start wid some foreplay? Yuh know him like fi kiss up oonu neck, and rub up oonu tits and slap oonu ass and ting? Lemme tell yuh what fi do fi test di man now. Yuh see when yuh rub up oonu p***y and ting, put yuh hand down dey pon yuh clit, touch yuh clit yuh know. And then just wipe it inna him mouth so! When yuh do dat . . . yuh ah bruk him out![8]

The women's response to this advice was a combination of raucous laughter and scandalous screams. The host for the evening, who was on stage with Ishawna, began jumping up and down while waving her hands in a performative gesture that was eerily reminiscent of women catching the spirit during church service. By the time she came to her signature song, which was the closing number, crowds of women rushed to the front of the stage and began to sing along with her. In fact, there were moments when the audience was much louder than the singer on stage as they sang the refrain with a deeply felt enthusiasm. The energy was palpable, and the performance lived up to the hype and expectations of the women in the audience.

Most of the men in the audience had retreated from the front of the stage, the message having been delivered: this space and set were woman centered, women occupied, and unapologetically aimed at women's sexual empowerment. In this last regard, Ishawna had torn a page from Peter Tosh's call for equal rights and justice in his song by the same name but had used it to create another social and political watershed moment in Jamaican popular culture.

When Bounty took the stage, he paid tribute to all the tourists who come out to this event in Portland, and he reminded them and the members of the audience that "Jamaica is the land of HOOD (with an extended crotch-grabbing gesture) and water,"[9] which ironically is one of the most prolific stereotypes that attracts both Black and white men and women to the country. He continued his set with a few of his signature pieces; "Me Cyaan Believe Mi Eyes" and "Look into My Eyes," were among those that drew the greatest response from the audience. However, just before launching into the latter song, he implored the selector to

"PUULL UUP" so he could deliver this admonition to Ishawna's fans in the audience: "A long time no artist put them career pon de line again. Listen me! Unno fi know what unno ah sing. Yuh see the real equal rights? It's when poor people and rich people can buy rice/rights. That is the real equal rights in a suffering country like Jamaica."[10] Just a few minutes later, after abruptly ending a segment of "Look into My Eyes," he returned to the topic of Ishawna's song lyrics. As if to assure his audience that he distributed his allotment of scorn equitably, he reminded them, "Me slaughter Kartel for singing bout freaky gyal; when Gage come and sing about down in a throat, me murder him too; and when dutty Alkaline come and talk about batty wash, me done him too. So, if Ishawna think she as go come here and talk about bumpa pon forehead, you ah go let Ishawna tell unno bout bumpa to badman forehead? No bumper to badman forehead!"[11] He then launched into one of his more gangsta anthems, "No Cream to Mi Face," but not before returning to the topic of Ishawna again to remind the audience that Ishawna is "mi daughter and mi love her, but we need fi guide her." He then called out Prince Pin to address Ishawna as her peer, because as a father figure, he could not go to war with her; he launched into a diss track, recorded to the "Shape of You" remix. The lyrics to the diss track are less important here than the fact that Bounty Killer, a veteran of the dancehall industry and the founding member of Alliance, which has launched the careers of several leading artists in the industry, was so undone by the fact that he had to perform on the same stage on which Ishawna had sung "Equal Rights" that it totally derailed his entire performance. As was the case in 1990s when the spate of "nah bow" songs commanded the most rotations in the dancehall sessions, Bounty could not believe his eyes or ears. But Ishawna's sentiment and song had captured the imagination of many of the dancehall faithful.

So, what does it mean to remix and reroute Ishawna's song through Miss Mando's and Elsa's genealogies in *The Harder They Come*, rather than Peter Tosh's? Recall that it is only at Miss Mando's funeral that both Ivan and the reader learn of her high rank and status in the Garveyite movement. Before that we knew her primarily as a surrogate mother to Ivan and as a desexualized partner to Mass Nettie. And we know of Elsa primarily as "Ivan's girl," who follows him out of the preacher's yard and fully into Babylon. But we cannot forget Elsa's lament before she is forced into her final decision to turn Ivan over to the authorities: "every game whe' I play I lose" (Thelwell [1980] 1988, 382). And yet, she is able to manipulate the police officer into sending an ambulance, and once again to cajole the driver to allow her to ride with Man-I to the hospital before her final seduction of Precha, who in exchange for "what [he] has always wanted," is told to sign a document agreeing to provide care and an education for Man-I (387). Elsa is a literary and political descendant of several generations of women who understood that, although they might not control the game, they were certainly capable of advocating for themselves, even under the least ideal circumstances.

In the same tradition as Lady Saw and other female deejays in dancehall, Ishawna brings the notions of consuming women's body into focus in a way that reminds women that sex is a social contract between consenting parties who are *both* invested in the outcome. As she tells her love interest in the song, "A modern times now, boy, relax . . . it's ok / If me ever bring it up inna the group chat / You ah get the threesome for your birthday." Whether the desired outcome is an orgasm or "a threesome" is less important than the idea and implementation of equity "inna house" and "outta door" in the same way. In other words, the struggles for social and political equity have their parallel in equity in sexual desire and gratification. By drawing this debate out of its "private" domestic sphere, the conversation is relieved of some of the baggage of respectability and, in the era of the Tambourine Army, the shame that threatened to suffocate the conversations publicly. In so doing, it left open a significant space for the possibility of public advocacy for women, by women (Thomas 2004, 253).

6

Gardening in the Garrisons

(Un)Visibility in Contemporary Caribbean Art

> At three in the afternoon
> you landed here at El Dorado
> (for heat engenders gold and
> fires the brain)
> Had I known I would have
> brewed you up some yellow fever-grass
> and arsenic
> but we were peaceful then
> child-like in the yellow dawn of our
>   innocence

Vibrant color has always been one of the most prominent features of the physical landscape in the Caribbean, whether the blues of the ocean or the yellows, reds, and greens of the flora and fauna. For colonial explorers, the beauty of the landscape was matched only by the implicit threat that lay in wait, just behind the excessive lushness of the landscape, to impose its will on foreign intruders. Mr. Rochester, one of Jean Rhys's protagonists in *Wide Sargasso Sea*, describes the Jamaican landscape surrounding his Coulibri estate as "menacing." He surveys the landscape and finds his surroundings excessive: "too much blue, too much purple, too much green. The flowers too red, the mountains too high, the hills too near" (1969, 89–90). Yet, as early as the nineteenth century, colonial travelers began to consider the Caribbean region an "exotic" place filled with amazing fruits, flowers, and vistas. This shift in perspective from dangerous to beautiful led to the region becoming a sought-after location, initially for wealthy businessmen and then later also for working-class people seeking the status that comes with vacationing in "exotic" locations. Although this beauty is part of the inheritance of the region, contemporary artists have deployed this idea of landscape as "menace" in myriad ways to argue that the trademark "exotic beauty" of the region blinds visitors and audiences to the individual tragedies and inequities that lie just underneath the dazzling colors, bright sunshine, and the ocean.

This chapter borrows its title from Olive Senior's collection of poetry, *Gardening in the Tropics*.[1] Senior's recognition and appreciation of the beauty and the menace entangled just beneath the surface of Caribbean landscapes are particularly useful as a framework for thinking critically about how contemporary Caribbean artists appropriate neocolonial tropes of landscape in their aesthetic practices. Caribbean landscapes have long provided the backdrop for slave revolts, labor riots, romances, fantasies, and nightmares in a wide range of Caribbean art.[2] Senior returns to the metaphor of the garden to highlight the historical lessons that are buried in Caribbean flora and fauna, making the garden a pedagogical space. Her "gardens" are neither simply nor purely ornamental; they include sugarcane fields and plantations, jungles filled with life-sustaining weeds and plants, and large trees that provide both shelter and weapons of resistance. Moreover, the diverse landscapes of the region have always been as critical to literacy in the Caribbean as any textbook, political treatise, or newspaper. Artists have a keen sense of what the landscape yields, what it withholds, its healing powers, legacies, and, most importantly, its metaphorical terrain for mapping political and social changes.

In *Gardening in the Tropics* (Senior 2005), colors that once drew colonial explorers to these islands five hundred years ago are now reimagined through the eyes of native and transplanted inhabitants with the benefit of hindsight. Senior's poem "Meditation on Yellow" is introduced with an epigraph by Gabriel García Márquez that reads, "The yellow of the Caribbean seen from Jamaica at three in the afternoon" (11). Picking up the thread of Marquez's meditation on the tone and temperament of the color as seen by those *in* Jamaica, Senior infuses that vantage point with the perspective of several generations of Jamaicans beginning with the indigenous Indians (then), New World transplants, and their descendants (now). Each poem appropriates colonial discourses of servility and colors them with a similarly complex imagining from *within* the country. In so doing, these imaginings paint the landscape in sinister ways, removing some of the "shine" we have come to expect of/in the Caribbean. These meditations touch on Columbus's arrival and the insatiable desire for gold; the slow but certain destruction of indigenous peoples and their lands; the extraction of coffee, bananas, sugar, and cocoa pods; and, finally, the arrival of tourists in search of service with a smile, sunshine every day, and an escape from their inhibitions. Hindsight gives way to regret and even to a taste for revenge in many of the poems in this collection, which moves readers away from the idea of gardening as a relaxing enterprise and implicates them as consumers, in one way or another.

The constant refrain, "gardening in the tropics, you never know what you'll find," encourages a degree of trepidation each time we dig into the rich soils and colors of the tropics. Then Senior turns our eyes toward the ugliness in the color yellow: "But it was gold / on your mind / gold the light / in your eyes / gold the crown / of the Queen of Spain" (2005, 14). Like a painter modifying shades of yellow as the crops and historical context shift, she broadens and narrows her palette: "I've been dallying on the docks / loading your bananas / I've been toiling in orange groves / for your marmalade / I've been peeling ginger / for your relish / I've been chopping cocoa pods / for your chocolate bars / I've been mining aluminum / for your foil." This literary strategy is particularly effective because it parallels the aesthetic expressed by other contemporary artists such as Christopher Cozier and Hew Locke, who produce shifting visual and discursive representations and interpretations of the Caribbean. Color is indeed intended to pull us in, all the while insisting that we do more than just look, in our uninterested way, without actually seeing.

In this regard, Ebony G. Patterson's work has an affinity with two generations of Caribbean artists who are concerned not only with the social and political landscapes of the Caribbean but also with different modes of literacy available within the region and its diaspora outposts. Representing three generations among them, Olive Senior (b. 1941), Trinidadian artist and curator Christopher Cozier (b. 1959), and Jamaican artist Ebony G. Patterson (b. 1981) share unique perspectives on the troubled and yet wonderfully complex, contradictory space that is the Caribbean. I am not suggesting that these artists are preoccupied by Caribbean landscapes in the same manner as are Caribbean writers. Rather, I am interested in those moments in Caribbean art that create a rare opportunity for intertextual engagement that stretches across the borders of form and cultural geography. My first interactions with Patterson's work left me with a clear topography of Kingston's dancehall culture: its popular movements, its sounds, and the textures of "town" landscapes. Senior's archaeological project begins with the uncultivated lands of the indigenous people of Xaymaca, continues with the forced labor that transformed these lands into the plantations on which the British relied for their power and wealth, and then excavates the next wave of colonialism: the tourist resort. In topographical terms, Christopher Cozier's *Tropical Night* seems less committed to the country or the town. His work is more of an excursion into the terrain of independence, one that imagines the "country" as the nation, a landscape that (in his youth) had been excavated very recently. Each of these artists is engaged in extensive archaeological projects invested in laying bare, shining light on, and exposing what lies buried beneath the structures of power.

This chapter focuses on the work of Ebony G. Patterson, but it is crucial to situate her work within a broader tradition of critical interventions in Caribbean arts and letters that spans several generations. She provides us with the unique opportunity to map the trajectory of these conversations across generations and political landscapes, as well as technologies of representation and oppression. Despite the differences in their aesthetic and generational inheritances, Senior, Cozier, and Patterson have not only captured the contemporary social and political landscape of the Caribbean region but have also managed to challenge, in fundamental ways, the cartography in such a way as to make viewers wonder seriously if they have actually been *seeing* the Caribbean beyond the conventional tropes of the exotic vacation destination filled with sun, sand, and blue waters. Each artist, drawing from the unique cultural and political contexts of his or her respective countries, movements through the diaspora, and distinctly different historical watersheds in Caribbean history, incorporates aspects of one another's aesthetic practices to engage pertinent issues in the Caribbean region.

Through its size, scale, and muted use of color, Cozier's *Tropical Night* series seems to work actively against the typical standards of the beautiful landscapes so commonly attributed to the region. Nicholas Laughlin (2007) describes the use of color—in this case, brown—in several of the images in this series as disruptive because it diverges from the typical representations of the Caribbean in the popular imagination.[3] These representations of the Caribbean region are deeply influenced by Cozier's experiences coming of age in the shadow of newly minted independence in Trinidad and Tobago. This is most evident in his appropriation of tools from the era of (post)colonial education such as the textbook, the *Nelson Reader*, and daily newspapers:

> "Afro-Ophelia" makes a link between the Neo-Raphaelite image of Ophelia in my Nelson Reader, the book through which formal English was conveyed to me as a child, and the front page images of the dailies which showed the dead body of a young woman who was part of a political group called NUFF in the 70s. I often feel that this moment to which we have developed an astonishing blind spot may explain something of our current social predicament. (Cozier 2007).

Ironically, the reading primer and contemporary newspapers are aimed at educating two different generations of Trinidadians: those born under colonial rule and those coming of age after independence. One would imagine that the educational aims for the post-independence generation would be different; bolder, aimed at building new social and cultural institutions in the wake of the new horizons independence would bring. Caribbean students have always been taught "book learning," while being warned about the painful lessons of being "a smart man." The *Nelson Reader* is intended to educate the next generation of civil servants, who were trained to many of the same British strictures that allowed power to stay in the hands of the few, while the masses worked diligently to emulate respectability, adherence to authority, and above all else, knowledge of "their place" in the other of things. The daily newspapers sought to disseminate similar values and, when necessary, to provide visual reminders about the deadly consequences of not adhering to these lessons, particularly for women. The political narratives undergirding these images manage to shine through despite the largely dull colors in which they are rendered.

"Afro-Ophelia" (figure 9) is an image of a Black woman drawn onto the landscape in charcoal in the same browns and muted greens as military fatigues. The landscape fuses seamlessly into her hairline and large Afro; the muted colors mimic camouflage, the fabric of choice for the military designed to give soldiers the advantage of being undetectable outdoors. Describing the inspiration for this piece, Cozier recalls seeing, as a young boy, a photograph on the front page of the daily newspaper of a young woman who had been shot to death. The photo was of Beverly Jones, a child of seventeen years, who had joined the militant group NUFF (National United Freedom Fighters) and was killed by the military in a battle at Caura. This organization was made up largely of young people between the ages of fifteen and twenty-five who, on the heels of the small gains of the Black Power movement in Trinidad and Tobago, saw armed conflict against the state as the most viable option to change their social conditions. The provocative gesture of discursively linking the image of a slain young woman to the *Nelson Reader*, and ultimately to the political landscape in crisis, is an explicit effort to highlight the disciplining structures of patriarchal power in post-independence Trinidad and Tobago.

In much the same way that the *Nelson Reader* instructs students in the rules of grammar, daily newspapers effectively remind their readers of the rules of political and social engagement, as well as the consequences of breaking these rules. The second image in the *Tropical Night* series, "see-through body" (figure 10), is also inspired by an image on the front page of a newspaper that Cozier saw as a child: it had a similar impact on his imaginative landscape, but for very different reasons.[4] Ironically, by pairing these two images, the artist is creating a grammatical relationship between these two figures: both are dead, killed by the state (one by the military, the other by the police). By presenting them in their "youth," whether real or imagined, the artist reminds viewers that there are disciplinary forces at work, and their purpose is to punish disobedient citizens regardless of age, class, or gender. More than anything else, institutions of the state rely on the grammar of visual literacy to discipline citizens.

Just prior to the fiftieth anniversaries of independence in Jamaica and Trinidad and Tobago, Ebony G. Patterson's 2011 multimedia installation, "Of 72," presented a monument to the lives of the seventy-two men and one woman who went "missing" during a military incursion into the Tivoli Gardens community in the summer of 2010.[5] The military action was allegedly prompted by a request from the United States to extradite Jamaican drug lord Christopher Lloyd Coke

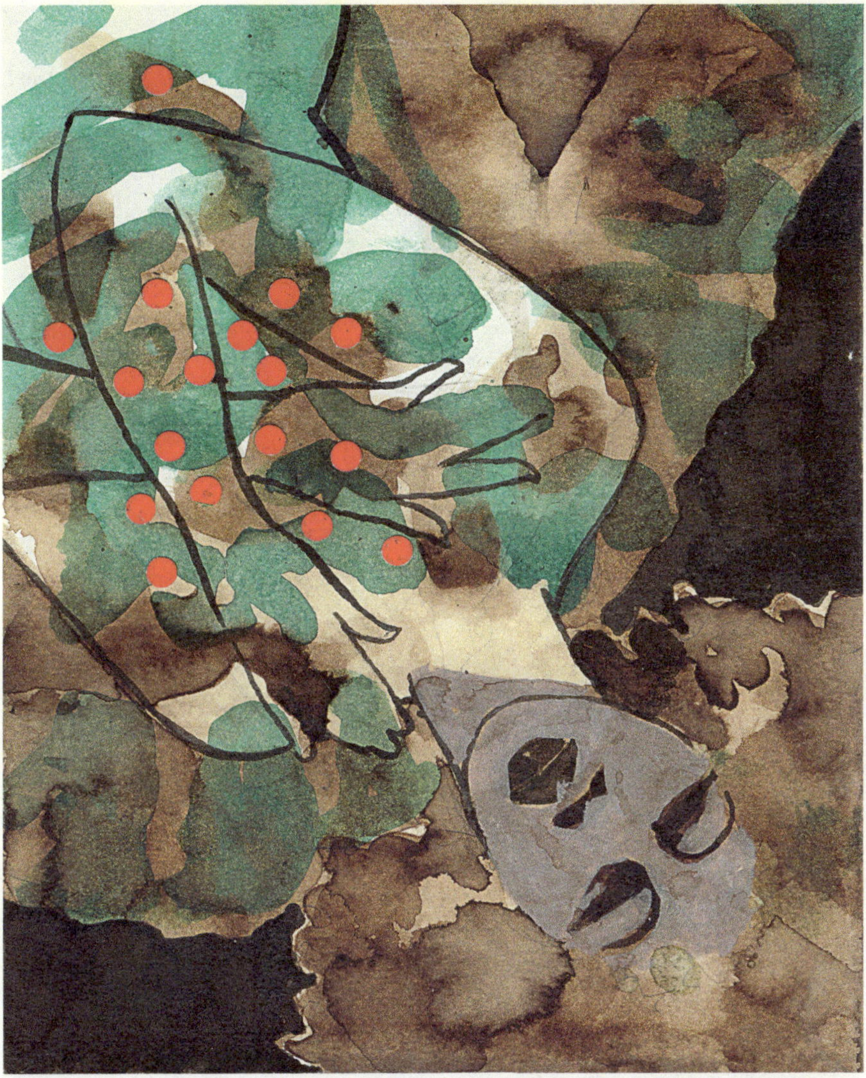

FIG. 9 Christopher Cozier, detail from the *Tropical Night* series, *Afro-Ophelia*, 2006–ongoing, 9 × 7 inches each; ink, rubber stamps, and graphite on paper. Image courtesy of the artist.

(also known as Dudus), who, according to Jamaican government officials, was being given refuge in Tivoli Gardens, an area said to be his base of support. Patterson created this installation to give a face to each of the individuals from Tivoli Gardens who were missing, unaccounted for, and presumed dead (figures 11 and 12). This project was a way to remember and mourn those whose very presence was erased and risked being forgotten. "Of 72" was a memorial aimed at

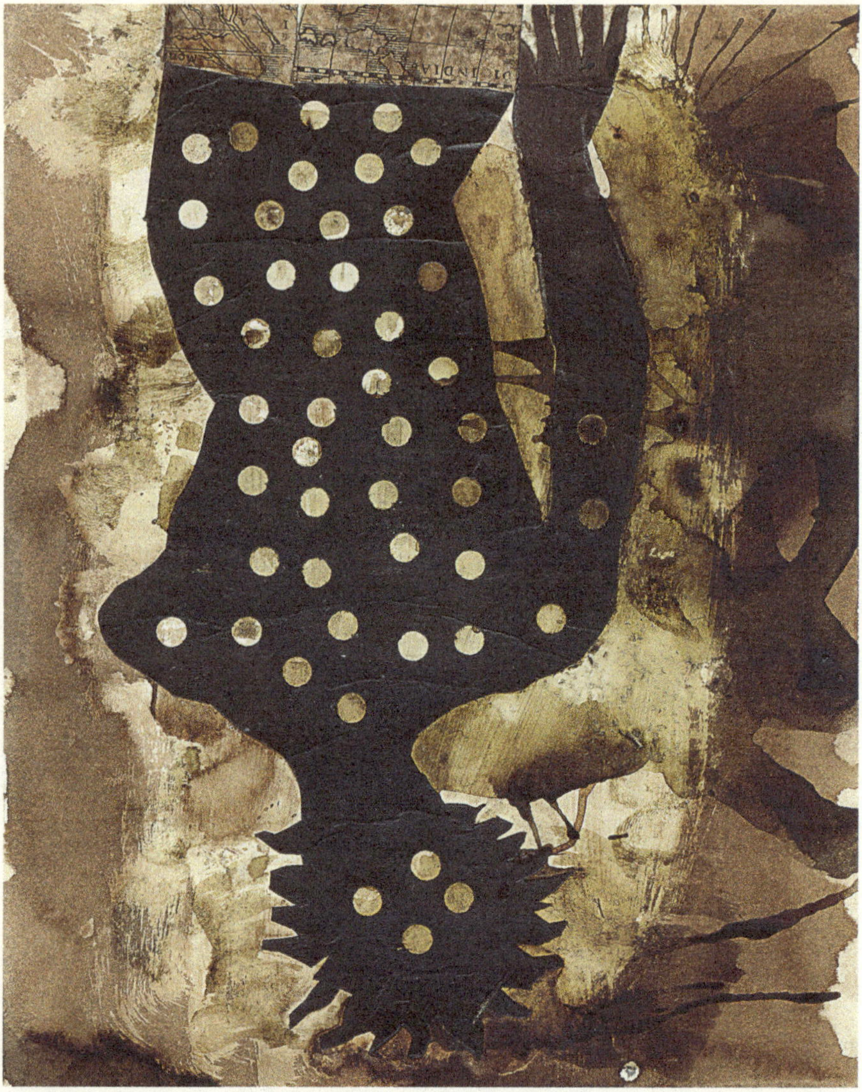

FIG. 10 Christopher Cozier, details from the *Tropical Night* series, *see-through body*, 2006–ongoing, 9 × 7 inches each; ink, rubber stamps, and graphite on paper. Image courtesy of the artist.

answering questions that the Jamaican government did not care enough to consider, questions that treated these individuals as more than statistics:

> What happens when seventy-two men (72) and one (1) woman dies [sic] and no one knows who they are?[6] Who were these men and this woman who were killed during the incursion of May 2010? Did they have children? Did they have a mother? Father? Did they have brothers or sisters? How old were they? What did

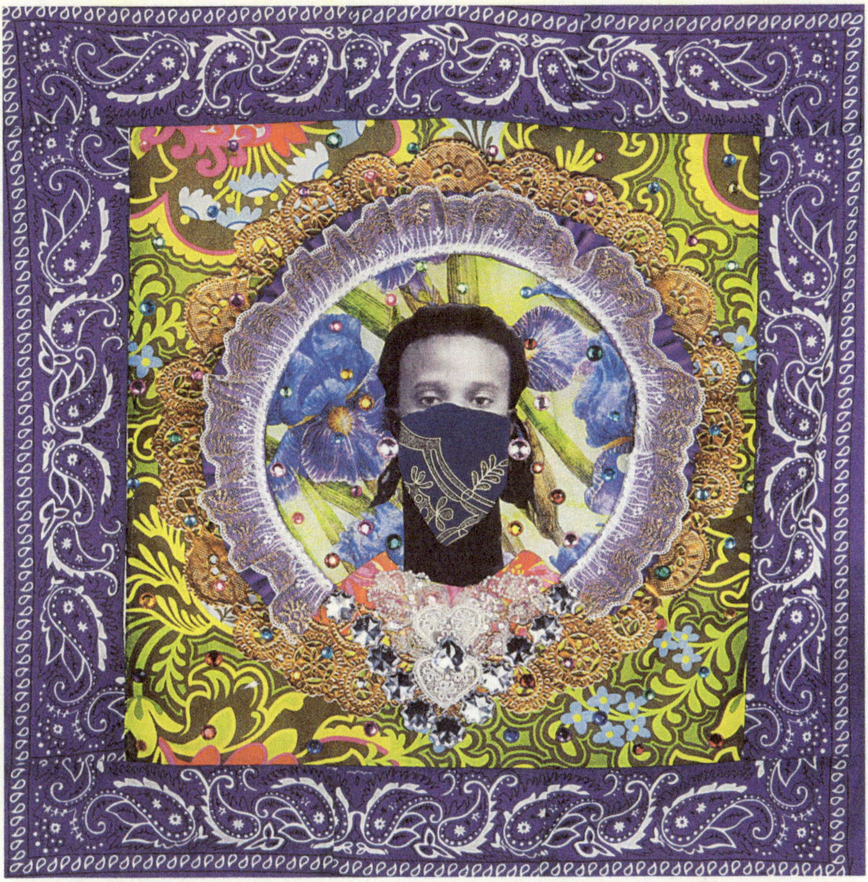

FIG. 11 Ebony G. Patterson, *Of 72* project (detail), 2012, digital prints on hand-embellished bandanas, 73 bandanas, 21 × 21 inches each. Commissioned by *Small Axe Magazine* and the Andy Warhol Foundation for the Arts Grants. Image courtesy of the artist and Monique Meloche Gallery, Chicago.

> they like to do on the weekends? Were they employed? Where did they work? If they weren't employed . . . what did they do? Were they young . . . were they old? Did they like Beenie Man, Bounty Killer, Vybz Kartel, Movado [sic], Beres Hammond or Bob? What was their favorite colour? What did they like to eat for breakfast, lunch or dinner? What did their voice sound like? . . . Who were they???[7]

These questions remain unanswered, but social activists and members of the community continue to demand answers. For Patterson, "as long as the identities of these people remain masked its [sic] going to be quite easy for us to just carry on . . . you know continue—It's the least I can do as a concerned citizen, to kind of etch this episode into history, so that these people are not forgotten" (Paul, "Hung out to Dry," 2012).

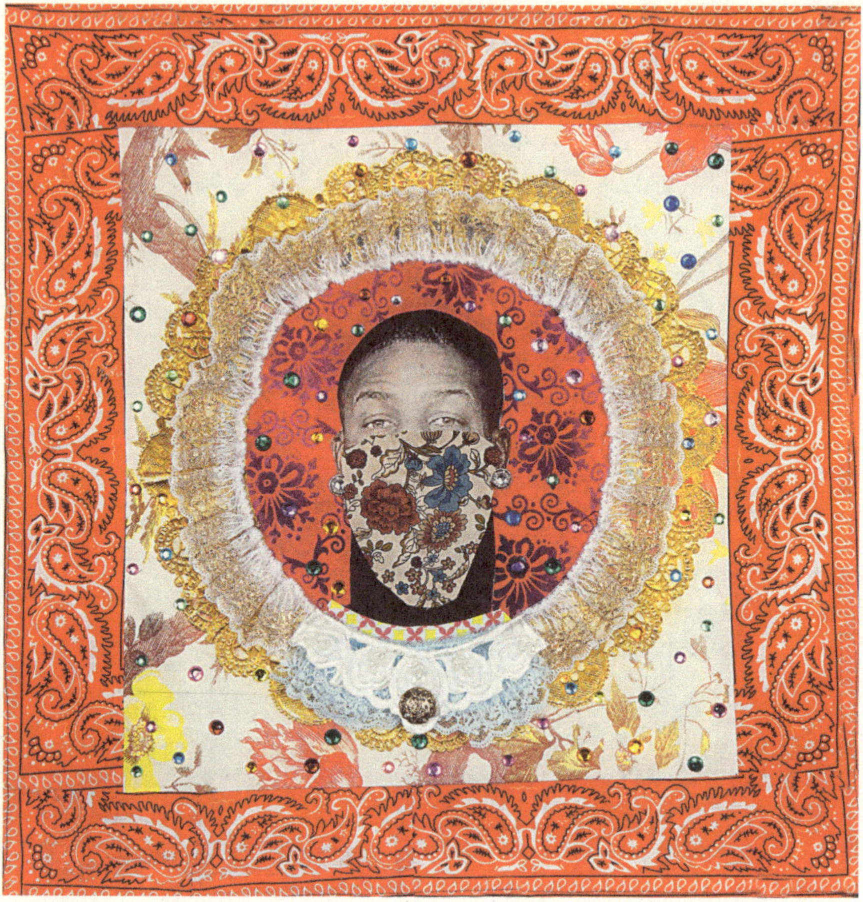

FIG. 12 Ebony G. Patterson, *Of 72* project (detail), 2012, digital prints on hand-embellished bandanas, 73 bandanas, 21 × 21 inches each. Commissioned by *Small Axe Magazine* and the Andy Warhol Foundation for the Arts Grants. Image courtesy of the artist and Monique Meloche Gallery, Chicago.

There was no formal vigil held for those who were missing, disappeared, and presumed dead. Many wondered about the resounding absence of the community's poets, songstresses, singers, and performers. One blogger, @cucumberjuice, commented, "An entire week of bloodletting yet nothing's come out of Jamaica's prolific music establishment? Nothing from our Reggae stalwarts or up-and-comers? The silence seems so opposite of our musical and cultural traditions that I'm surprised I haven't noticed this before."[8] In the face of this seemingly muted response, Patterson's impromptu elegy to the seventy-three missing persons came in the dark of night, not unlike the forces that arose, took the lives of these young people, and then disappeared in plain sight. The display, as Annie Paul notes in her blog, was "a special, one of a kind event." Responding to the one-night installation, which was staged outdoors, a viewer commented,

> The first reaction is that by sort of replicating the number of people that died it has an impact—you realize right away it's PLENTY people. You know when you see the news and people get killed every day it's very easy to become desensitized to it but when you see 73 different images and you see 73 different ways of treating them you realize the number of them and that each one is individual . . . The other thing that also occurs to me because half of the faces are covered is the sense that when young people die, you don't know what you've lost, you don't know the potential.[9]

Brief Lives: Invi(z)ibility in Kingston's Urban Landscapez

> Gardening in the Tropics you never know
> what you'll turn up. Quite often, bones.
> In some places they say when volcanoes
> erupt, they spew out dense and monumental
> as stones the skulls of *desaparecidos*
> —the disappeared ones . . .

Although Ebony Patterson draws heavily on the colorful palette common to Caribbean aesthetic practices, her work contains few, if any, direct references to or representations of traditional images of the Caribbean as Edenic. In fact, her Caribbean landscape imagery could be described as the antithesis of the idyllic, domesticated landscapes that surrounded colonial plantations in the past and in all-inclusive resorts today. Some argue that Patterson's use of landscape imagery is, for all its beauty, a reminder that the seeds of Jamaica's colonial inheritance have blossomed into an invasive species that has grown so dense that it threatens to block out the light needed for shrubs, flowers, and trees to grow. The abundant grass, plants, and flowers that inhabit Patterson's artwork are decidedly untamed, disorderly, explosive—all while being remarkably attractive and even inviting to the eye. It should come as no surprise then, that her evocative visual reimagining of the Jamaican landscape is paralleled by a discursive urbani(z)ation of this space that captures the harsh realities of those who reside in the ghettos, garrisons, and gullies. Blades, trees, and shrubs are transformed into *bladez*, *treez*, and *shrubz*, reflecting the edgy, precarious existence of the communities who inhabit these seemingly forgotten areas of the country's landscapes.

With titles like "*. . . two birds-beyond the bladez,*" "*. . . in di grass-beyond the bladez,*" and "*where we found them,*" Patterson's recent body of work, featured during the New Orleans Prospect 3: Notes for Now art festival held in 2014–2015, powerfully engages similar social and political terrain to that of Senior and Cozier, but with a singularly precarious and even impetuous rendering of urban landscapes in Jamaica (figure 13). Gardening in the tropics takes on a postmodern turn through her use of a wide range of mixed media materials, her embrace of Kingston's dancehall culture and, most certainly, the strong critique of social inequities that lie buried—some beneath monuments and layer upon layer of delicate fabric, brocade, and glitter, others lying just beneath bladez of grass, shrubz, and rosez (figure 14).

The insanely profuse colors and textures of Patterson's tapestries produce a dissonance that could best be described as similar to the intensity of movement, visual stimuli, sounds, smells, histories, communities, and epistemologies that one would experience when standing in Half Way Tree, Kingston (St. Andrew), one of Kingston's busiest crossroads (figure 13). The intersection, however, is not simply marked by vehicular and pedestrian traffic; it is also home to a "looming clock tower built as a memorial to King Edward VII in 1813" (Howard 2005, 103).

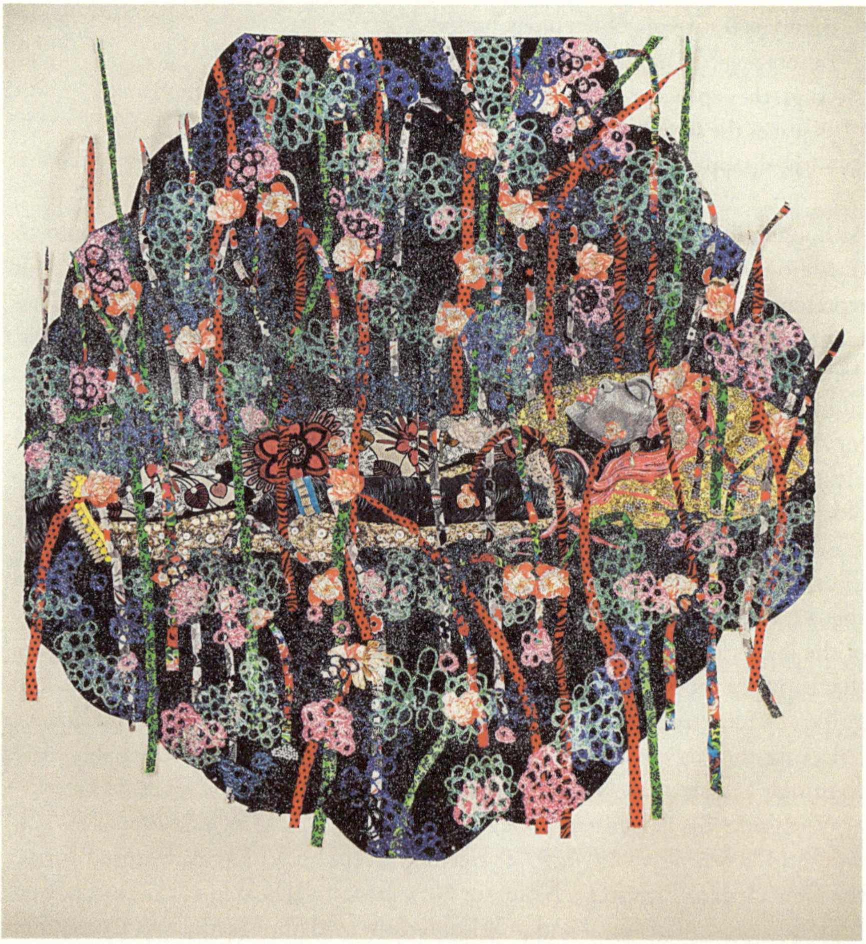

FIG. 13 Ebony G. Patterson, . . . *two birds-beyond the bladez*, 2014. Mixed media on paper, 90 × 89 in. (2 parts: 90 × 43 in.; 90 × 46 in.). Image courtesy of the artist and Monique Meloche Gallery, Chicago.

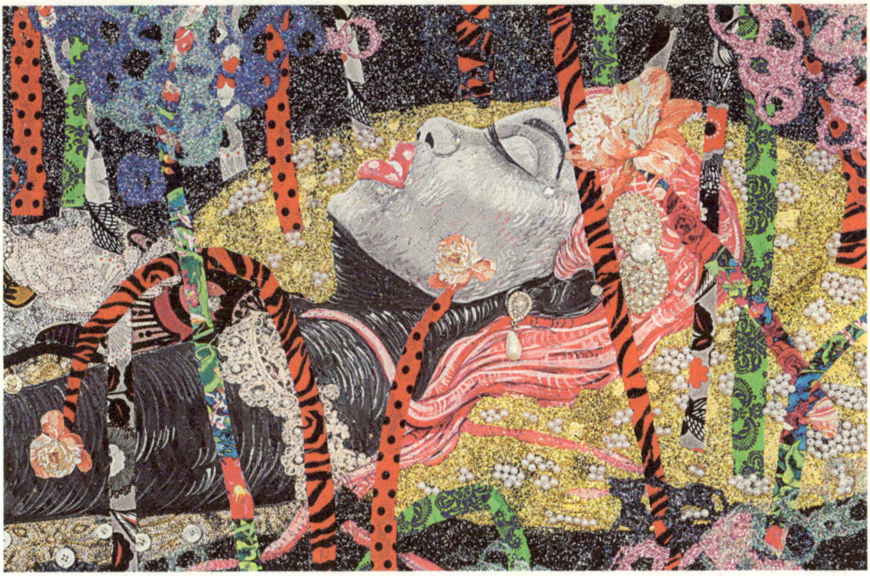

FIG. 14 Ebony G. Patterson, . . . *two birds-beyond the bladez* (detail), 2014. Mixed media on paper, 90 × 89 in. (2 parts: 90 × 43 in.; 90 × 46 in.). Image courtesy of the artist and Monique Meloche, Gallery, Chicago.

The crossroads was named after a cotton tree that stood for centuries at the junction of the four roads; it was first written about in 1696, which suggests that the tree predated the conquest of the island in 1655. It was a landmark halfway between two places: Greenwich in the St. Andrew Hills, where the English soldiers had their military camp, and the fort near Spanish Town. The soldiers always rested at this spot before proceeding to the fort. Although the tree met its demise in 1866—some say from old age (Higman 1995,146), this provides a point of connection between Patterson's work and Kingston's urban landscapes. For all its busyness, there is a beauty in the chaos that belies a larger history of the lines that divide the haves from the have-nots, a history that is as complex as the wide range of people and history that met at this intersection and the bricolage of fabrics, textures, objects, and icons that compose Patterson's massive tapestry titled, . . . *in di grass beyond the bladez* (figure 15).

The density of foliage in this mixed media installation nearly completely obfuscates the facial features of the subject that lies behind the rich colors in the bladez of grass. On first viewing this piece at Tulane University's Newcomb Gallery, I was struck by the composition of colors that replicate the iconic colors of an inverted Rastafarian flag. On closer examination, however, the textures and range of materials—gold, green, red, and silver glitter; floral fabrics; and the knitted doily pattern that appears to adorn the waist of the subject—push back against any inclination to confine the piece to the category of

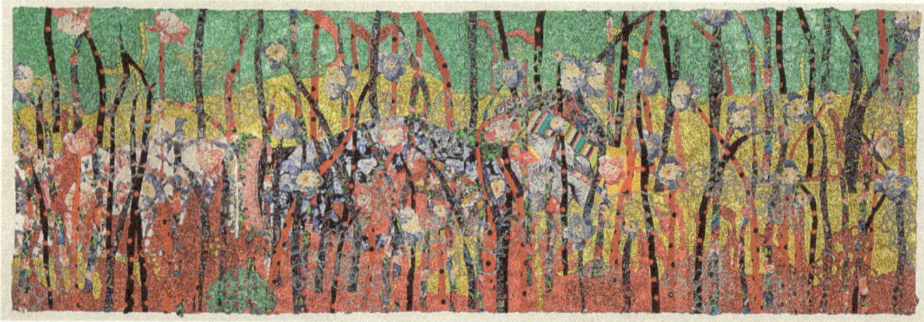

FIG. 15 Ebony G. Patterson, . . . *in di grass-beyond the bladez*, 2014. Mixed media on paper, 40 × 120 in. (4 parts: 40 × 30 inches each). Image courtesy of the artist and Monique Meloche Gallery, Chicago.

iconography. But in the final analysis we are left to wonder: Is it merely a coincidence that the backdrop mimics those colors? Is there a relationship between the background and the barrage of colors that occupy the forefront of the work? What of the subject in/of this work of art: Is this person a male or female? Does gender matter in this instance? What is the life story that lies hidden here, behind the bladez?

The textures invite us to run our eyes along the well-shined double-edged sword of tropical gardens, these insurgent landscapes that have sprung up in the unlikeliest of places: the urban garrisons, ghettos, and gullies of Jamaica (figures 13 and 15). Patterson's body of work engages in complex ways with (un) visibility in an age of hyper-exposure and the political erasures of urban landscapes and the communities of people who dwell in them. The work of keeping informed, once met by small local newspapers, is now done by social media platforms such as Facebook, Twitter, and Instagram. However, as we now know, these sources contribute, intentionally and unintentionally, to the production of large swaths of misinformation. Social media inform, teach, and show us the world to which we belong—and yet *what* this act of consumption actually transmits or renders *visible* is uncertain—and this seems to be what continues to preoccupy Patterson, Senior, and Cozier. Reflecting on the multiple layers that inspire her work and her vision, Patterson recalls a moment that gave her pause:

> An image was circulating on social media of a three-year-old who was murdered in a tenement housing project. Bystanders took pictures and shared them with the intent to raise awareness—that this photo was so disturbing that it would get attention. I think there is something very strange that happens with people who choose to share images like that. We no longer think about the individual, it's not a person, it's an image, it's an object. With this new body of work, I started thinking a lot about visibility and the internet in terms of the bee-and-flower syndrome. The bee is attracted to the flower because of its

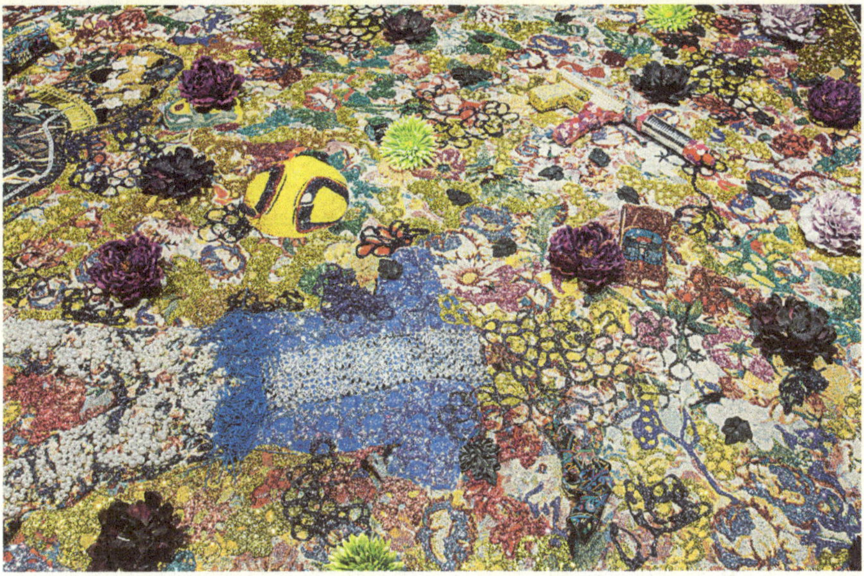

FIG. 16 Ebony G. Patterson, *Shrubz* (detail), 2014. Hand-embellished jacquard-weaved tapestry with fabric flowers and hand-embellished plastic guns, 106 × 82 in. Image courtesy of the artist and Monique Meloche Gallery, Chicago.

> coloring, because of its beauty, and it isn't until he gets in that he discovers if the flower has the nectar that he wants. (Patterson 2015)

Images circulate globally at a pace that was heretofore unimaginable, but how often do they capture the kind of minute details about the aspirations, idiosyncrasies, talents, fears, and family histories that give form to the life of the individual represented in the photograph? Do these images actually inform audiences about what is transpiring in their communities, or do they make death so "hypervisible" that the meaning of this traumatic loss is interpreted as a cold statement of fact, a statistic, full stop? Patterson's large tapestries are usually installed on the wall; in a recent installation at the Bass Museum in Miami, one of her large installations, *shrubz* (2014), was placed on a low platform on the ground (figures 16 and 17). This positioning of the tapestry dramatically shifted the audience's perspective, creating a different spatial and visual relationship to the content, materials, and the subject being treated in the work. The degree of optical engagement changes depending on the vantage point of the viewer, and this is precisely what Patterson is referring to when we consider how the brightness of her work draws viewers to look more closely. However, with the tapestry being laid flat on the ground, the viewer is made more keenly aware of the positioning of the two bodies, one seemingly younger than the other, with the embellished toy guns and the deflated soccer ball. Among the plethora of garden glitter lies

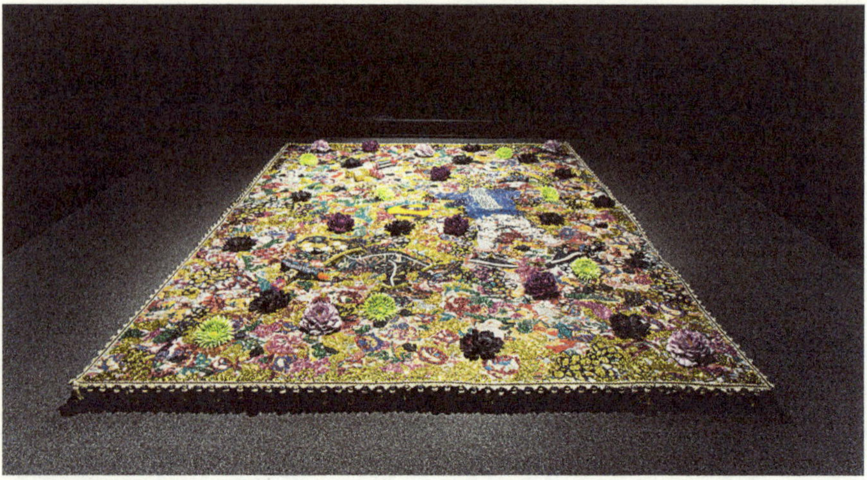

FIG. 17 Ebony G. Patterson, *Shrubz*, 2014. Hand-embellished jacquard-weaved tapestry with fabric flowers and hand-embellished plastic guns, 106 × 82 in. Installation view at the Bass Museum of Art, Miami Beach. Image courtesy of the artist and Monique Meloche Gallery, Chicago.

light green, mauve, deep burgundy, and black flowers that suggest a slow progression towards death.

Certainly, the capacity of social and print media to bestow visibility on those who seem forgotten, even discarded, can (and often does) come at the expense of overlooking their humanity, the minute details that encompass who they were, where they came from, how they lived, and, yes, ultimately the conditions under which they came to meet their sudden endz. The #blacklivesmatter and #saytheirnames social media responses to police violence and brutality against Black Americans have raised awareness and inspired social movements and marches, but the semantic value of these hashtags also highlights the extent to which these deaths have become statistical, rather than personal, losses. One of the ways in which contemporary art has been an effective tool for social justice is through its capacity to entice viewers into a more considered mode of looking. In other words, it can re/vise the grammar of visual literacy away from its disciplining model toward a mode of visual engagement that encourages more critical ways of looking that allow us to *see* the people we are looking at. How we see (socially and politically) has not necessarily improved with advances in technology (Patterson 2015). Although we can see more, this does not necessarily mean that our visual literacy or the critical perspective we require to interpret the value and meaning of what we are seeing has improved: Patterson's visual insurgency is an effective means for instigating changes in our visual literacy, which is why artists are so important.

Patterson's most recent body of work seems to respond to this challenge by emphasizing aspects of identity that may not be easily interpreted on the basis of sight alone. In a recent interview with Karen Patterson (no relation to Ebony G. Patterson) at the Michael Kohler Arts Center in Sheboygan, Wisconsin she explained her shift from highly stylized, adorned bodies: "I have been thinking about gender and objects as a way to define gender; especially since the millennium, men's fashion has shifted with this idea of metrosexuality. In thinking about how one defines gender through clothing, I wondered if we would be able to make these types of determinations if I removed the body altogether and began to include gesturing and posturing" (Saunders 2016, 123).[10] In this regard, then, Patterson's recent work invites us to consider seriously how "meaning" is performed through a range of gestures and textures that communicate different aspects of the social body. This marks a departure from some of her earlier work that chronicled other performative aspects of dancehall culture like skin bleaching, which, for many practitioners means treating the skin as an accessory no different from a hairstyle; crafting facial features (beards, eyebrows, hairlines); or wearing jewelry or a new outfit for the dancehall session. There has always been a flamboyance of fashion among women who populate Weddy Weddy, Bembe Thursdays, Passa Passa, and other dancehall sessions across Jamaica. However, as I noted earlier, in the late 1990s, these trends and aesthetic practices began to migrate across traditional gender boundaries, and young men began to openly bleach their skin and don colors and fashions once associated with women. These untraditional, "queer," or ironic sexually ambivalent styles reflect an aesthetic of color and flair emerging among male participants in dancehall culture during the last decade.

Jamaicans often use the phrase, "tun hand mek fashion," to describe their ability to make the most amazing things out of nearly nothing. This maxim is a testament not only to inventive fashion trends but also to the epistemological registers created by the poor to insist on their value in terms set out by themselves, rather than by mainstream politics and value systems. After decades of being taught to emulate respectability, understatement, modesty, and, most importantly, invisibility, the poor and the working class have rejected these tools of erasure to make their imprint on the cultural and political landscape in the shiniest, loudest, brightest colors and sounds imaginable. Where this bling did not exist, they set out to create it, using their imaginations, which, unlike their social conditions, are not limited by their bank accounts.

From the Cradle to the Grave: Bling Will Light a Path through the Valley of Darkness

> A little over a year ago I was in bondage.
> Now I'm back out here reaping the blessings,
> And getting the benefits that go along with everything
> that's out here for kings like us.
> The reason why we like this jewelry and these diamonds and stuff,

They don't understand, is because we really from Africa.
And that's from where all this stuff come from.
And we originate from kings, you know what I'm saying?

So, don't look down on these youngsters because they wanna have shiny things,
it's in our genes.
You know what I'm saying?
We all just don't all know our history so . . .

—Pimp C, Introduction to F*ckwithmeyouknowigotit, *Magna Carta*

Of course, the issue of visibility is neither unique to Jamaican nor, for that matter, the Caribbean. Despite being painfully ingrained in the hyper-visibility of mainstream media markets, Black subjectivity has historically been under the threat of erasure from the social and political fabric of citizenship since emancipation. As was the case with her analysis of skin bleaching and media visibility, Krista Thompson's aptly titled 2015 book, *Shine: The Visual Economy of Light in African Diasporic Aesthetic Practice*, is particularly useful for thinking through the intricate processes and technologies in African diaspora art that speak to these acts of invention intended to preserve and document Black presence. Black subjects were denied access to the pathways to citizenship (education, housing, security) for so long that they have created divergent structures to perform and enact their citizenship. The "art" (or what Pimp C refers to as the "stuff") of Black self-fashioning is a mode of performance developed during slavery and extended and continuously perfected through modernism into the postmodern era in remarkably similar ways. Although fashions may change across historical periods and cultural venues, two elements have remained the same: the continuous threat of erasure of the self and the denial of dignity, humanity, and citizenship for Black subjects globally. In the face of these threats, Black subjects have been forced to perform their selfhood in fraught, complex ways (for a more extensive analysis of this aspect of race and performance, see Stephens 2014). The centrality of performance has always framed how race is understood.

Although the origins of Black self-fashioning are debatable, in *Slaves to Fashion: Black Dandyism and the Styling of Black Diaspora Identity*, Monica Miller offers a vantage point that stops well short of rapper Pimp C's assertion that the desire for "stuff" (jewelry, clothes, shoes, etc.) is a genetic predisposition. She traces it back to the arrival of African slaves on American soil, noting that "the discourse on race, the definitions and meaning of Blackness have been intricately tied to issues of theater and performance. Definitions of race, like the processes of theater, fundamentally depend on the relationship between the seen and the unseen, between the visibly marked and unmarked, between the 'real' and illusionary" (Elam 2000, 4). Whether the "benefits that go along with everything that's out there for kings like us" are real or imaginary is irrelevant. What matters for Black subjects is that, in the Jamaican parlance, they "tun up" (they are turned up) or (re)present themselves as kings as loudly (the bass of dancehall and rap music) and brightly (gold, diamonds, fashion) as possible: they *shine* in spite of the daily efforts to oppress and detain them in the valley of the shadow of (un)visibility (or death).

In the social landscape of Jamaica there is nothing more real than masculinity and its vagaries. This is one of the issues that have preoccupied Patterson's work in different media, particularly in *Cheap and Clean: Interrogating Masculinities Project*. The project description encapsulates the intersections between Pimp C's perspective in the section epigraph and Monica Miller's insights on the critical nature of performance for defining Blackness and, inevitably, Black masculinity:

> Given the youth-driven nature of Dancehall, the artist worked with 14 young men and explored their own ideas about masculinity through fashion. Participants were asked to design outfits based on these ideas/ideals of manhood. The artist then had the outfits made and embellished for the participants to wear and model for pictures taken in an embellished "photo studio," "posing" and/or posturing as their ideal male. The photo studio space was constructed as a dollhouse based Georgian architecture [sic], referencing both the domestic space and toys. Both object and space are important "tools" for understanding how gender roles are shaped by and react to those of an early age. The "studio" was located in downtown Kingston, Jamaica. All participants were able to keep their hand-embellished tailored outfits along with a photograph of themselves in said outfit.
>
> Participants were documented in both clothing and space, not only photographically but also in video. The recording of the project was viewed live, virally projected to linked public spaces in Jamaica, Trinidad, Barbados, Bermuda, the Bahamas, United States and the web, via Facebook, on March 10th, 2012.[11]

Patterson's tapestries and mixed media installations find their social and political strength in this project because it engages young men in contemporary manifestations of the history that Pimp C reminds us "we don't all know." Its multimedia scope gives these young men access to the power of the "video-light" to project not just their likeness but also their "being" across the African diaspora. These media then function as means of archiving Black presence, not just within the subject's community but also far beyond its borders. In the absence of the resources or the eligibility needed to procure a visa to visit North America or London—and thus the ability to project the self and to make oneself visible to the world—a digital presence is far more valuable than its alternative: being (un)visible or unseen.

The playfulness of many of the outfits designed by these young boys reflects a new "normal" in dancehall popular culture. In her online essay, "Undressing Cheap and Clean: Notes from the Artist," Patterson reflects on how the minute aspects of fashion signify different social aspects about gender:

> The young adults, aged 19–21, did not have the same preoccupations as their younger counter parts. They had already been developing their own ideas about who they are, they concerned about fitting in [sic], but rather about projecting where they were heading, while being cautious about these projections. Pink? Yes miss, but isn't that a female colour? No Miss no one owns any colour. Would you wear this? I asked. No miss!!! Why? Because it's pink? I asked. "Yes miss but that is too much." It was pink floral in fact. The young man I was speaking with was a teenager. Sporting bright colours matching from head to toe, tattoos, a nice blackberry and just enough bling in his ear to say, "Yup mi tun up!" But his rejection also signaled that within a culture that is aesthetically camp, there **is** a boundary. The pink can become . . . too pink.[12]

Men's fashion's pastel and bright, even neon, colors and tight, fitted (curiously referred to as "distressed") clothing—particularly pants once referred to as "batty-man trousers"—which once raised questions about the wearer's masculinity, now project a masculine swagger that transcends the idea that "the clothes make the man." The poses of men and boys in the photographed stage of the project suggest a great deal about their understanding of the relationship between fashion, performance, and Black masculinity. One photograph in particular displays this trifecta. Darrion (figure 18) is outfitted in well-orchestrated red and black colors: black shorts, just above the knees but not too far above, and a black T-shirt with a stick figure drawing of a male and a female with a caption above the image that reads, "I Love My Girlfriend Very Much." This profession of love might seem unusually forthright when read against many of the representations of male–female relationships in dancehall culture.

However, there is a far more nuanced sense of masculinity being performed in the image, one that is couched between the "Jesus piece" on his necklace and just below his waist. The critical gesture in Darrion's photo is the crotch grab; it effectively refocuses any of the other *signs* at play in the photograph. So even though he may indeed be a God-fearing, girlfriend-loving young man, his masculinity and, indeed, his sexuality are central and not necessarily at odds with the other signs in the photograph.

For many of the younger boys like Chad (figure 19), the props (fake money or toy guns) do a similar kind of work to the physical gesture we see in Darrion's photograph. As such, we see the importance of play for younger boys in enabling them to arrive at their sense of what is male (gender) and what is man (biology), two of the themes discussed among the participants in the video documentary segment of this project. Money, power, and respect/ratings were three of the key terms used by the participants to describe how masculinity is determined, but they were also what they sought to portray in the clothes they designed.

In his book *Stuff*, Daniel Miller, an anthropologist who studies fashion and consumer culture around the world, spent several years living in Trinidad and Tobago to better understand why poor people consume what they do and what,

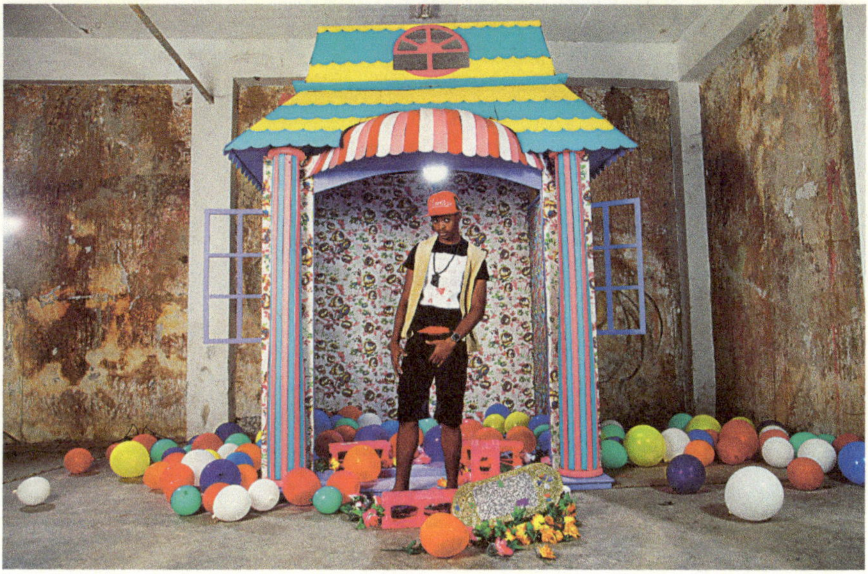

FIG. 18 Ebony G. Patterson. Darrion, from the *Cheap and Clean, Masculinities Interrogation Project*. Multimedia Interactive Project, 2012. Photo courtesy of Marvin Bartley.

if anything, it tells us about them. Even when resources are minimal, there are ways and means (usually borrowing an item from a friend or family member) to ensure they never wear the same outfit twice. Consumption, as Miller (1998, 15) reminds us, has never been about accumulation: "what is celebrated is the event, the moment." Outfits, shoes, hair and skin styling, and jewelry are procured weeks, if not months, in advance of a fete, and no cost is spared. Anthropologist M. Freilich, during his 1957–1958 ethnographic research in an impoverished village, reported that women he interviewed told him plainly that "every new function needs new clothes" (Freilich 1960, 15). The sociocultural function of dress and style in most communities is to convey a sense of wellness and to project that wellness to the world, regardless of one's circumstances. According to this same woman, "I would not wear the same dress to two functions in the same district" (73). This perspective is in no way unique to the working poor in pre-independence Trinidad and Tobago. Nearly sixty years later, while doing research on African diaspora aesthetics in Jamaica, Krista Thompson (2015, 148) also an anthropologist, is told by Ian Dice Charger, a dancer at Passa Passa, "There is no repeating in the video light." According to the practice of transience, "once they appeared on camera, the outfit had in essence been visually consumed and therefore could not be worn again" (148).

The intimate relationship between consumerism and citizenship is well established. The only surprising aspect of this relationship is the extent to which this path to citizenship now informs the foundation of the industries of pop culture.

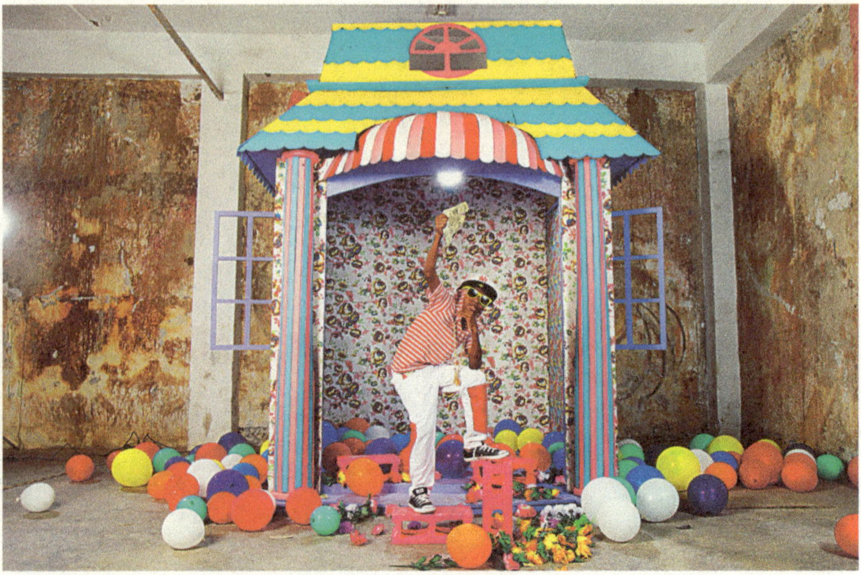

FIG. 19 Ebony G. Patterson. Chad, from the *Cheap and Clean, Masculinities Interrogation Project*, Multimedia Interactive Project, 2012. Photo courtesy of Marvin Bartley.

Recent developments highlight how consumption has stepped in to fill an ever-widening gap that separates Black subjects from the social and political institutions designed to ensure their rights and privileges under the badge of citizenship. Garcia Nestor Canclini (2001, 5), shines a light directly on the emergence of new pathways of access to citizenship:

> Especially [for] youth, the questions specific to citizenship, such as how we inform ourselves and who represents our interests, are answered more often than not through private consumption of commodities and media offerings than through the abstract rules of democracy or through participation in discredited political organizations. . . . We may also posit, as do James Holston and Arjun Appadurai, that the political notion of citizenship is expanded by including rights to housing, health, education, and the access to others good through consumption.

For the young people Patterson engages in her *Cheap and Clean* project, limited access to social and economic pathways means their families have had to "tun hand and make fashion" for them to stay alive in all the complex ways that day-to-day life entails. From images captured on cellphones and broadcast via the World Wide Web, to the shine or "bling" produced by the video lights, fashion, and adornment, there are a growing number of avenues to visibility. Yet the questions raised by these increased opportunities and media for visual accessibility are also numerous. Is all visibility valuable in the same way, particularly when subjects who are exposed to the glare of the "gaze" cannot participate in adjusting the filter, so to speak? Are viewers actually *seeing* the composition of the social and cultural portraits that are critical to the "larger" picture, or do the consumer goods and the status they represent effectively blur the connection between the image/individual and the viewer? In other words, under the barrage of visual images now available, how do we (as viewers) see the trees through the forest?

The *Cheap and Clean* project poses these questions specifically around young men's perceptions of masculinity in Jamaica; in so doing, it is a reflection on some of the complex considerations and negotiations that youth endure as they make their way toward adulthood, should they be fortunate enough to live that long. But there was another critical aspect of this project, poignantly dramatized in Nicholas Laughlin's (2015) comment on what he found most valuable about it, and that was the risk Patterson undertook: "What was most risky in *Cheap and Clean* was also what gave the project its potent charge: the unpredictability of the young men Patterson enlisted as collaborators, and the imperative for the artist to negotiate with their own desires and concerns. To allow them to project their ideal selves, to be seen as they wish to be seen: that respect for their agency is no small act in a society where the portrayal of young black men remains politically and ethically fraught." If this desire to be seen in their "ideal" light is felt by young acolytes of Jamaican popular culture, then it is all the more relevant for funeral preparations and processions, particularly for dons and dancehall stars. This practice has been celebrated in popular culture classics such as Michael Thelwell's *The Harder They Come*. We might remember well Miss Mando's lavish funeral that drew her Garveyite sisters and brothers from parishes near and far to celebrate her life and pay their respects. There is a clear sense that she has spared no effort in planning for her own funeral, leaving Mass Nettie with specific instructions, right down to who should be in attendance. In fact, when her grandson, Ivan, arrives in Kingston and informs his mother that Miss Mando, *her* mother, has died, she is as despondent about not having been able to attend the funeral as she is about the amount of money spent on it. Although Miss Mando is well known in her community, her funeral, as much as her life, will surely be one of the yardsticks for measuring her legacy.

The crocheted black rosez that adorn the three-panel installation, "Wilted Rosez, 2014" (figure 20), add an air of mourning to the exhibition space despite the presence of the bright colors—reflecting that in Jamaican dancehall culture these two aesthetic modes of expression have never been diametrically opposed. The formerly sacred space of mourning, after being introduced to the tradition of adornment popularized in dancehall culture, provides the kind of juxtaposition that unearths social inequities and injustices, putting them on display in the loudest, brashest, most unapologetic language and images imaginable. But once again, Patterson's work is not unique in portraying

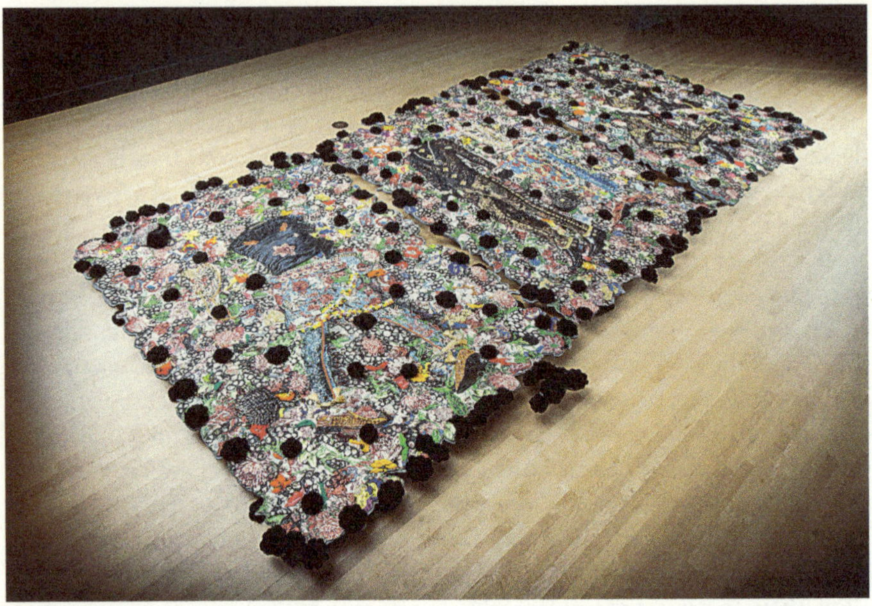

FIG. 20 Ebony G. Patterson, *Wilted Rosez*, 2014. Mixed media jacquard-weaved tapestry with jewelry, shoes, gold chains, tassels, and 100 crocheted flowers, 96 × 72 in. Installation view at the John Michael Kohler Arts Center, Sheboygan, WI. Image courtesy of the artist and Monique Meloche Gallery, Chicago.

this juxtaposition: Senior's poem "Brief Lives," in *Gardening in the Tropics* (2005, 85), also describes the razor-thin line between the secular and the sacred:

> Our cemeteries are thriving too.
> The newest addition was the drug baron
> wiped out in territorial competition
> who had this stunning funeral
> complete with twenty-one-gun salute
> and attended by everyone, especially
> the young girls famed for the vivacity
> of their dress, their short skirts and
> even briefer lives.

The irreverence of the "twenty-one-gun salute," an honor normally reserved for politicians, soldiers, and statesmen, to celebrate the "drug baron" makes "Wilted Rosez" a wonderful companion text to Senior's *Gardening in the Tropics*, with its fusion of funerary traditions and fashion (figure 20). One panel displays a body that is positioned face-down in a lush garden of flowers, jewelry, lace fringe, tassels, and other items of adornment. However, these cross-purposes of fashion also reflect the cross-gendered nature of Patterson's work. Viewing the tapestry requires viewers to extend their lens of vision to determine the relationship between the shiny satin shirt/blouse, the short skirt studded with pearls, the floral skinny jeans adorned with gold tassels, and the purposefully detailed men's shoes that punctuate this outfit. The center panel reflects a sartorial style reminiscent of African American "dandies," replete with the posture of "morally upright" male and female figures. The last panel features an equally well-dressed figure in an outfit that borrows the patterns and lace from the middle panel, but whose gesture reflects some of the more scandalous dance moves that have made dancehall culture so highly sought after by urban (and uptown) youth, to the horror of upper- and middle-class upholders of "respectability."

The presence of the "excess" adornments almost seems like an attempt to overload the circuits of interpretation we normally deploy around material trappings (or what Daniel Miller and Pimp C call "stuff"). These circuits inform so much of how we see and make (un)visible certain constituencies of citizens that one can appreciate on a deeper level how and why Thompson comes to use this term, excess, to explain these new technologies of visibility. But more importantly, we should also have a more astute appreciation for the magnificent shine of Ralph Ellison's protagonist in *Invisible Man* (1952) who,

> illuminated by siphoned electricity and 1,369 lightbulbs, has been seen as a precursor to and emblem of the ways visibility delineated a black political agenda in the mid-twentieth century. It may also be interpreted, for present purposes, as an early precursor to the contemporary emphasis on the technology and effect of light. The incessant focus on claiming visibility that is manifest in black popular culture practices captures a more long-standing emphasis on visibility as a mode as a mode of political representation. (Thompson 2015, 39)

For Patterson, fabric, crystals, pearls, and glitter function much in the same manner as the lightbulbs used by Ellison's protagonist—to shine brightly on the (un)visible in Caribbean society. But if we read Thompson's critique about contemporary popular cultural practices during the civil rights era as indicative of the failures of these modes of engagement, we are left to wonder what, if any, effect these efforts at illumination have on viewers.

If literal and metaphorical brightness is not enough to catch our attention, to make us *see* and acknowledge the presence, in the broadest sense of the term, of those disappeared by their social and economic circumstances, what other strategies could have that effect? I argue that performance is critically important as that vital link capable of reconnecting audiences to their shared humanity with (un)visible subjects/citizens. Patterson's recent appropriation of a tradition practiced by Africans in the New World and on the continent is such a strategy for achieving the desired level of visibility. During a two-week residency at Alice

Yard Trinidad in 2011, she undertook a project that through its performance accomplishes this effect in terms of vision, connection, and, ultimately, accountability that she seeks in her tapestry and installation art.

Patterson decided she wanted to make a work of art that reflected her experience of Trinidad: its pulse, its rhythm, its landscape. On day two of her residency, Patterson was taken by Christopher Cozier, codirector of Alice Yard, to Port of Spain to spend some time downtown near Frederick Street, the central artery of life in Trinidad. While there, she stopped at Samaroo's, a major supplier for Carnival materials in Trinidad:

> I was in Samaroo's looking at pearls and the glitter and, you know, the things that kind of entice me, hearing a woman lamenting about an announcement that had just come over the radio about somebody being killed. It's something that has stayed with me . . . and it's something that I felt that was repeated over and over during the course of my stay here. The sense of . . . genuine concern about the state of crime . . . in Trinidad. . . . Coming from a very similar experience in Jamaica where I've always felt that we've been desensitized for quite some time, so much so that when we hear about somebody being killed, it doesn't even register anymore. But I constantly go back to that moment in Samaroo's when I heard the lament of that woman, and this was somebody who she didn't even know. To hear her bellowing. It came from her stomach, and I felt compelled to respond to that and to all of what I was hearing. So, I decided that I was going to make a coffin for every murder that was committed within the roughly little bit more than a week of my two-week stay in Trinidad.[13]

To mark the nine murders committed in Trinidad and Tobago during her first week there, she had nine coffins constructed and fitted out according to dancehall "bling" tradition and "flam couture." Yet what gave even more power to this unique project was Patterson's approach to delivering it to the public. It was not solely or even primarily an exhibition in a museum or gallery setting. Rather, on July 25, 2011, a public call went out to supporters of Alice Yard, inviting them to come to a talk by the artist Ebony G. Patterson with a performance to follow. The audience, no doubt, did not anticipate being part of the performance.

The following extract is taken from a transcript of the talk given by Patterson that evening, in which she invited the audience, which numbered about forty to fifty people, to join a funeral procession through Woodbrook, on to Adam Smith Square, and then back to Alice Yard (roughly a thirty- to forty-minute walk). A crucial part of "bling funeral processions" in Jamaica is the sound system one finds on every other street corner in downtown Kingston and other urban centers. The sound system helps keep the procession and the "posse" of the deceased moving, giving them the energy and rhythm to carry the dead to the church or burial ground (figures 21–24). On this night, the sound system

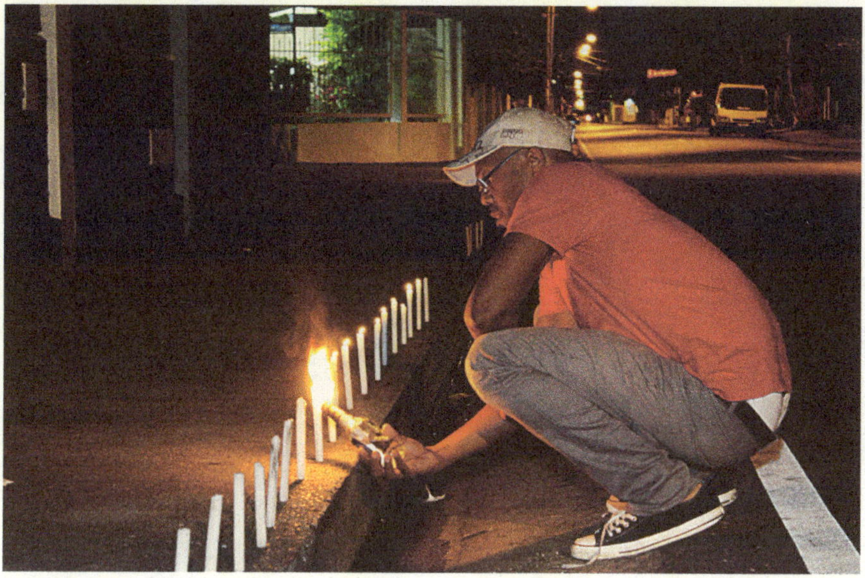

FIG. 21 Ebony G. Patterson, *9 of 219 Project* (Alice Yard, Act 5), 2011. Participant using a flambeau to light ritual candles for the deceased on the sidewalk outside Alice Yard, along Roberts Street, Port-of-Spain, Trinidad, July 25, 2011. Image courtesy of the artist and Alice Yard. Photo credit: Rodell Warner.

blared 3 Canal's rapso song "Piti Pata," which bemoans the gunshots raining in Trinidad and sends a clarion cry for listeners to wake up and realize that there are too many guns in the country. Equally critical to the sound system accompaniment, however, was the voice of one of the 3 Canal singers (Wendell Manwarren), who recited the names of the nine murdered people, the circumstances of their deaths, the areas they were from, and comments from their families about what they meant to them. His audio recounting of who they were, what they liked, and other things about them gave a sense of who these nine people were: it reminded others of their humanity. Presumably, these details were available in the daily newspapers, probably along with photographs similar to the one of Beverly Jones, killed by the military in a battle at Caura, that haunts Cozier's imagination forty years after seeing these images as a child. Thus, despite the visual nature of this project, the audio system (on two levels: song and narration) was a critical part of the "9 of 219" performance.

On their return to Alice Yard, Patterson took questions from the audience and thanked them for their participation in carrying the coffins and in the following discussion, as they listened and took the time to consider, in a meaningful way, what was going on around them and how artists and citizens could begin to respond to these tragic losses of life. One of the participants closed by thanking Patterson for having the vision to bring the project to fruition, sharing one

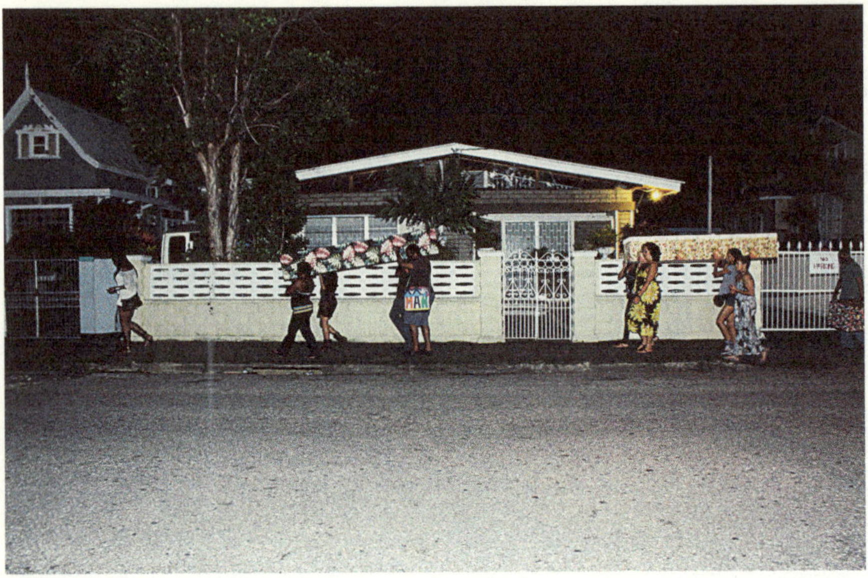

FIG. 22 Ebony G. Patterson, *9 of 219 Project* (Alice Yard, Act 5), 2011. Procession along Carlos toward Arapita Avenue, Port-of-Spain, Trinidad, July 25, 2011. Image courtesy of the artist and Alice Yard. Photo credit: Rodell Warner.

of the most profound insights I have heard about Patterson's work on the whole: "I think we ought to thank you as well because in a way, what you are asking for—that their memory remains alive—in carrying the coffin, you brought us into a personal relationship, I think . . . in bearing them. So that, by the time we put them down, I think we felt a sense of ownership, if you wish. A kind of responsibility, that I think matters. So . . . thank you."[14] Although my focus thus far has been on visibility, this comment evokes the other element of seeing, which moves beyond what the eyes take in, which extends the line of vision into the soul of the viewer. Arguably, this kind of engaged *vision* occurs out of the line of vision of the coffin, the body. In fact, it seems to occur in the absence of the iconic markers of death.

The art of funerary spectacle, then, is about this kind of visibility, but in life as much as in death (figure 25). Living is not merely about being seen, as Ellison reminds us; it is about the quality of visibility, the possibility of ascension into the eyes (and hearts?) of the audience. Paul Gilroy (2010, 25) may have put it best when he wrote, "In their own eyes, and perhaps also in the eyes of others, these subjected people become different in the light of their heavily branded visibility." The degradation of the dead and murdered is often chronicled by the absence of their names; they are recounted only by statistics, a practice that dates back to the slave books where slave owners referred to enslaved Africans as items, as property on a list. Patterson's "9 of 219" in Trinidad (like her "Of 72" installation in Jamaica) resonated with an interview I conducted with M. NourbeSe

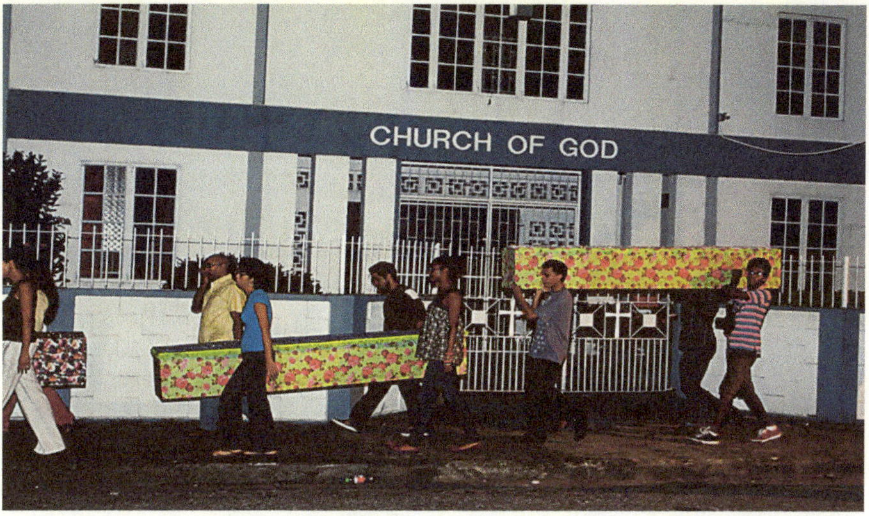

FIG. 23 Ebony G. Patterson, *9 of 219 Project* (Alice Yard, Act 5), 2011. Procession passing General Assembly of the Church of God on Carlos Street, Woodbrook, returning to Alice Yard, July 25, 2011. Image courtesy of the artist and Alice Yard. Photo credit: Rodell Warner.

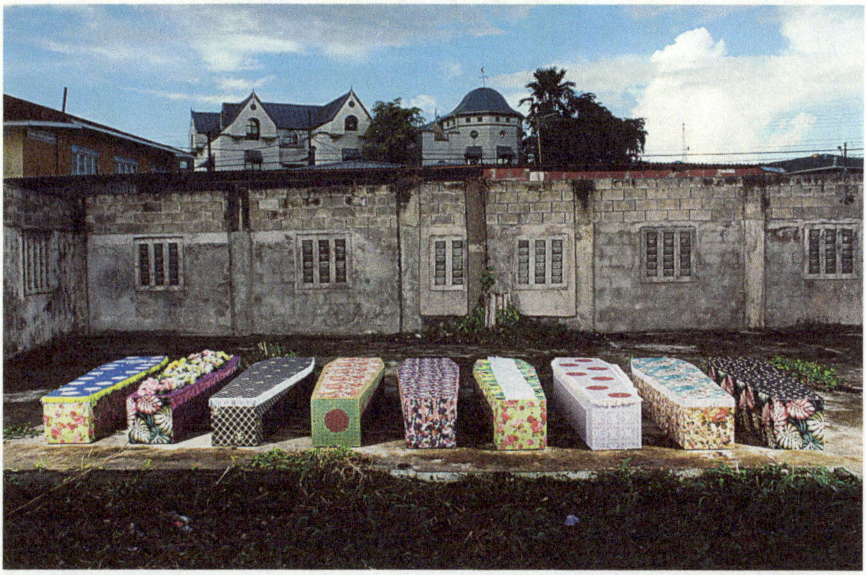

FIG. 24 Ebony G. Patterson, *9 of 219 Project* (Alice Yard, Act 5). Installed in Alice Yard, Port-of-Spain, Trinidad, 2011. Image courtesy of Alice Yard. Photo credit: Rodell Warner.

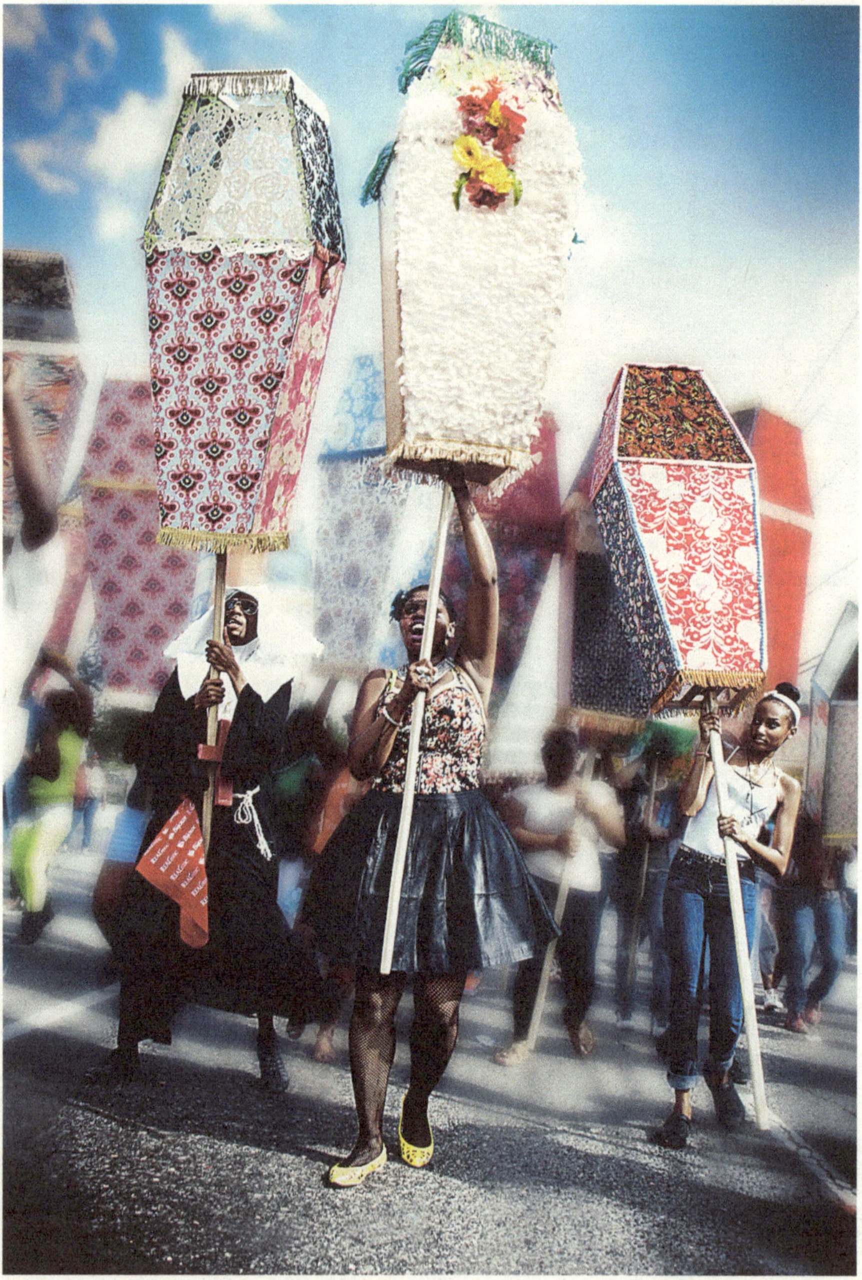

FIG. 25 Ebony G. Patterson, *Invisible Presence: Bling Memories*, 2014. Installation at UNTITLED Miami Beach, Monique Meloche Gallery booth. Image courtesy of the artist and Monique Meloche Gallery, Chicago. Photo credit: Gabriel Gaviria.

Philip about three years earlier, titled "Defending the Dead, Confronting the Archive," in which she says,

> I think it is totally subversive in the face of the kind of broad-brush brutalizing where people just get reduced to Negro man, Negro woman, and ditto, ditto, ditto. You pay attention to one, and it is such an amazing act—and one that spills over to all the other dittos—paying attention and taking care with just the one. Because that's all we can do is care one by one by one. And that's why it was so important for me to name these lost souls in the footnotes to the early poems. (Saunders 2008,78).

If we understand these funerary practices as such an act of subversion, similar to the #sayhername (or #saytheirnames) social campaigns that reject the inevitability of departing in the same manner in which one lived, as a statistical note, then adorning caskets and the grand processions of bling and finery is another way of naming, of leaving a mark on one's departure.

The most recent incarnation of the "9 of 219" project appeared in Jamaica, during the country's Carnival celebration. In keeping with the Carnival traditions of Trinidad, Patterson's coffins had been fitted with holders so that each individual could carry a coffin while participating in the Carnival procession (see figure 25). The Jamaican performance, astutely titled "Invisible Presence: Bling Memories," does precisely this *kind* of remembering and connecting to the individual. In an act of mourning, individuals who are cited statistically, like a Black body killed in a given year during the slave trade, are rejoined to their community through these small moments of recognition. There is no doubt that Patterson sees her role as an artist as one who is responsible for calling us to bear witness; to hold us (as viewers, audiences, participants) accountable for remembering not just through our eyes but also the soul, or the mind's eye, where the hard work of remembering and mourning begins.

Conclusion

"Puuulll Uuuuuuup": Dissident Dreams of Cultural Insurgency

Dany Laferrière reminds us that desire is a driving force that influences how and for what purposes the Black body is imagined. When framed by circumstances of inequity and colonization, desire can, and often does, produce unsavory results. But it is a two-way street, and both lanes are often occupied by people with significantly different means of acquiring what they desire. In an interview he notes,

> Physical desire and sex, as a political metaphor, seemed to me to be the fundamental element, something extraordinary, because, in a society where the relationships between social classes are so terrifying, where the gap between the rich and the poor is so huge, where humiliation, disdain, contempt for others is so intense, the only thing that can bring one particular person closer to another is physical desire. I'm not describing an innocent form of sexuality, but sexuality as an instrument of political, social, or economic power. We're dealing with a small group of very rich people who can buy anything, or who think they can buy anything, people or objects, and with others who are ready to sell the only thing they possess, their youth and their body. I wanted to find out if in this exchange, in this trade, where flesh meets flesh, there wasn't something more.[1]

This entirety of the short-story collection, *Heading South*, is framed by Laferrière's succinct evaluation of the ways in which desire and sexuality can become the uneasy bridge between producers and consumers on opposite sides of an ever-widening chasm of economic inequity. I have always been keen to know what lies on the other side of these kinds of exchanges and what, if anything, changes for either party in these exercises of "fair trade." What is "fair" for the tourist may well constitute a deadly scenario for local residents, as is the case for Legba and his ex-girlfriend. Many of the insurgent cultural representations discussed in the stories emerge out of the highly contested, yet to be determined, spaces of (often unequal) exchange and negotiation. This reality is no less true in the United States than it is in the Caribbean. One certainty remains: the gender politics of Black diaspora popular culture is changing, and women are leading the insurgency. The change has been undeniably incremental, with only a handful of female Caribbean artists able to sustain long, successful careers. What remains to be seen is how the male-dominated industries of music and television will respond and whether they shake free from the "men on top" model of policing women who are both producers and consumers of culture. Spice's breakthrough into the U.S. reality TV scene marks a critical shift in the power dynamics because only a handful of artists have successfully made that crossover. Both Spice and Ishawna have collaborated with Vybz Kartel, and like Kartel they realize the marketing potential of self-fashioning their Black subjectivity and their expression of it.

Ishawna's refusal to be shamed into silence in the face of her ex-fiancé's charges of "sexual deviance" and her willingness to share her personal experience of domestic abuse on the national airwaves are of a piece with the political action embodied in the Tambourine Army's slogan "nah mek dem win." This shift in the social narratives produced and consumed about women as sexual beings is indicative of an unapologetic turn toward women as primary, desiring consumers in Caribbean popular culture. But controlling the narrative represents only a portion of the work to be done: the crucial work still remains of enlisting public institutions to formulate proactive policies that address issues such as physical and sexual abuse, inequality in the workplace, and other social injustices described in so many of the songs by female deejays. According to the United Nations, "at least one in three [Caribbean] women have experienced sexual or physical violence at least once in their lives" (Chappell 2017): the region has one of the highest rates of sexual assault in the world. Of the three female deejays whose songs and performances I showcased here, Lady Saw and Ishawna have shared publicly that they experienced sexual or physical abuse. They have also used their songs and performances as improvised creative devices to address this crisis in their own lives and in the region. But theirs is not simply an effort to focus on their personal experiences: they have turned the lens squarely toward institutional structures that have been porous when recognizing, validating, and protecting girls and women from the all-too-common disappearance of women across the region and the subsequent discovery of their dismembered bodies: they are easily forgotten, quickly turning into mere statistics.

Lady Saw's abrupt departure from the dancehall industry in 2015 and her subsequent entry into the ranks of the Christian faithful surprised many listeners, but not more so than her sharing her experiences of being raped on several occasions as a child in Jamaica. She credits the death of her friend and rising dancehall deejay J Capri as the critical turning point in her decision to give her life to Christ.[2] In an online interview she discusses how, despite her experiences of sexual assault, she still saw sex as a way to empower herself and other women and, ultimately, to get her family out of the ghetto.[3] While acknowledging that "sex sells," Lady Saw's performances of what Daphne Brooks (2006, 5) calls "Afro-alienation acts" provide "a fruitful terrain for marginalized figures to experiment with culturally innovative ways to critique and to disassemble the condition of oppression." Her public performances of sexuality have brought discussions of sex and female sexuality out into the open, but not in the typical ways in which men characterized women's bodies and desires. For decades, the cloak of "man/woman business," shame and respectability, even in the dancehall, effectively served to concretize ubiquitous master narratives about how, where, and what Black women could desire and, more importantly, how they should express these desires. There are, however, new modes of insurgent resistance taking place in sectors of the society that have historically been opposed to one another. Rather than seeking to build bridges between these entrenched social sectors, these insurgent cultural movements force the dismantling of these spaces and insist on new social interventions that center sexuality and safety in their sexual selves that women have been told, by the church and the state, that they have no right to for centuries.

The line that separates sacred and secular modes of expression and resistance is finally being traversed and remixed through performances that are at once sonic, as is the case with dancehall music, and also silent as when fourteen women staged a peaceful protest at the Nazareth Moravian Church in the central parish of Manchester, rallying support for a fifteen-year-old schoolgirl allegedly abused by the pastor of the congregation.[4] The women gathered at the church laid claim to the "powerful stillness" that was once part of the dominant paradigms Black women were constantly scripted into; yet they turned this stillness, born from a literal silence within the church, into an embodied presence bearing the message, "We will not be silent anymore." The normalization of policing Black women's bodies—particularly through popular culture and the overwhelming power of the media and advertising to hyper-visualize Black men's bodies—is undermined when the bodies being scrutinized do not present themselves in the familiar or "authorized" roles that have been scripted for them. The tradition of shaming women and girls into silence and the expectation that sexual assault will encourage women to shrink away from their communities are both being rejected out of hand within Black diasporic communities. Women's movements that originate in the United States often take white women's experiences as their point of departure. Recently, however, rather than waiting for these movements to recognize the complex ways in which Black women and their bodies have been historically constructed as unrecognizable and even undifferentiated from Black men because of their "strength and resilience," women in communities of color have insisted on laying claim to their own experiences as sexual citizens.

Because many of these performances and interpretations of Blackness occur vis-à-vis cultural commodities that bind us together, we would do well to consider whether some moments of cultural dissidence might allow for a temporary disassemblage of the oppressive paradigms that have effectively imprisoned "Blackness" and how it has been allowed to signify (as human, valuable, free). Both Black men and women have had to fight continually for the freedom to express their selves politically and culturally, but Black men have had to do so against the backdrop of their subjectivity being understood largely through the lens of criminality and threat. The commonplace reality for Black men is that it is just a matter of time before they will have an encounter with the penal system in the United States, United Kingdom, or other parts of the diaspora.

Desiring Subjects and the Problem of Arrested Development

Since Buju Banton's release from prison and his "Long Walk to Freedom" tour, his revived career has served as a poignant example of the redemptive power of refashioning through insurgent modes of representation. On March 16, 2019, the National Stadium in Kingston, which has a stated capacity of 35,000, was overflowing with at least 40,000 patrons; they even occupied the green areas and outlying perimeter areas where seating is not available. His long-awaited return was not without its critics, however. Many in the Caribbean popular culture community felt that Buju should not be expected to account for his transgressions before being welcomed back home as a son of the soil, because he had been wrongfully imprisoned; many posts on social media referenced his incarceration and described it as "captivity." Most notably, while broadcasting from the concert, Winford Williams, host of the popular Jamaican entertainment program *Onstage*, titled his live segment, "Buju Banton Is still Buju Banton after 10 Years in Captivity, Unbroken Reggae Warrior."

Others felt that the name of the tour, "Long Walk to Freedom," that was so blatantly about social justice overlooked or hid the fact that Buju's conviction was on drug charges. Political historian Rupert Lewis, a prominent voice in the social and political landscape of Jamaica, remarked in *The Jamaica Gleaner* that "the appropriation of Mandela's 'Long Walk to Freedom' is unfortunate because what Mandela represented was collective struggle, the struggle of a people, the sacrifice. What Buju represents is more personal freedom, I take objection to people who confuse what that slogan meant and how it has been appropriated in this case" (Davis 2019). For Lewis, the issue was not simply the unacknowledged historical and political context of the tour title but it was also the fact that Biju had not publicly spoken out about his incarceration. Whether he and others believed he was wrongly convicted or not, some felt that before the journey to freedom and redemption could commence, there needed to be a public reckoning about the circumstances that had landed him in prison.

By most accounts, this was neither the time nor the place of this reckoning; this was a historical moment in Jamaica and, by extension, in the Caribbean diaspora. Buju was free, and this by itself was enough to vindicate his longstanding struggle against systemic oppression. The matter of why he was incarcerated was of little to no significance to many of his supporters. He was back home, and Jamaicans at home and in the diaspora wanted to celebrate his safe, unbowed return. Social media were flooded with responses to *The Gleaner* article, many asserting that Buju did not owe anything to anyone, least of all members of the middle class who were peddling the rhetoric of morality. In the same newspaper article, Jamaican cultural critic and retired UWI professor Carolyn Cooper protested Buju's condemnation: "Instead of pressuring Buju, the minister needs to focus on speeding up the decriminalization of ganja. There is so much hypocrisy about drug use in Jamaica. Alcohol and nicotine are potentially deadly drugs. Yet their use is perfectly legal. And it's not the small farmers who are going to profit from the eventual decriminalization of ganja. It's the same high-ups who run tings and don't give a damn about morality." The proverbial line in the sand, now drawn, was between the rhetorical and political force of respect versus respectability that frames so much of the Jamaican social and political landscape. Respectability, like respect, is intimately tied to Jamaican social and political institutions, the same ones that, as I have argued, working-class people have refashioned if for no other reason than the goalposts that mark the successful acquisition of both are constantly shifting. This refashioning is not a rejection out of hand but a reimagining of the terms of negotiation.

One concertgoer, dub poet Yasus Afari, had a very insightful perspective on what Buju's return performance symbolized for "enslaved people who were brought to Jamaica." In an extended postconcert interview with Winford Williams he asserted,

> In terms of the history of Jamaica and Jamaican music, I think it's a turning point, and me on record saying this: it's a pivot for a new paradigm. If you were to look back at the decades of the '70s and the decades of the '90s [sic], when even we the Christian soldiers had kinda ushered in this so-called reggae revival that Chronixx, Protoje, Jah 9, Kabaka Pyramid are helping to engineer and you think *this*, which come out of an unfortunate situation, however it had the potential to usher in something new to revive. . . . What him offer to the people in terms of the inspiration to the undertrodden, the have-nots, the dispossessed, the disenfranchised . . . he empower the people. You see that empowerment deh, what him invest in the people? We call that moral capital. The people say, yow, we nah forget Gargamel, you are our yute, and we ah

> embrace you, and you ah make a fresh start, and you will help lift we up. . . . What happen hereso tonight is a reassertion of the moral capital and dignity of the people, to show it is possible, irrespective of what else going on. ("Buju Brings Hope and Inspiration" 2019)

What Afari highlights here is of critical importance for understanding how and why Buju Banton has reemerged as a global cultural icon endowed with overwhelming power. In many ways he is the embodiment of the generational shift that Rupert Lewis refers to as a different interpretation of Mandela's "Long Road to Freedom." The period highlighted by Afari, "the decades of the '70s and the decades of the '90s," was not only a period of Black nationalism and of revolutionary changes in political systems in the Caribbean, but also of a mobilization that shut out Jamaicans who were not part of the brotherhood of "Christian soldiers." Large segments of the population—the "sufferers," who flocked to the gritty, hard-hitting, vulgar, and at times violent lyrics of Baby Cham, Bounty Killer, Ward 21, and other deejays mentioned earlier—had neither the desire nor the inclination to invest in this nationalist scheme. Their financial resources and social needs were such that they rejected out of hand the morality of the church, the state, and the burgeoning nation. Theirs was a need best met through a newly sanctified space, one that granted them license to "gwaan bad" for the sake of release and enjoyment, albeit in ways that often reproduced the same paradigms of respectability they wanted desperately to reject.

Although Buju's music has always been a voice for the dispossessed and disenfranchised, it also belonged to the shared national vision of "moral uprightness" that clung desperately to sociocultural values that were, by and large, unattainable. The dispute between Ishawna and many selectors who refused to play her song "Equal Rights" highlighted these long-held sociocultural values and the double standards that persist in dancehall music. How then might Buju's own revival after his "captivity" provide Black subjects in the Caribbean and the diaspora an opportunity to embrace the potential of what all the insurgent modes of representation discussed thus far seem to offer: a chance at rupturing, in a lasting, productive fashion, the system of signification affixed to Blackness (both male and female)? With the eyes of the world watching, via the internet, media coverage, and audiences live streaming to friends and family scattered across the diaspora, the opening of the "Long Walk to Freedom" concert in Jamaica provided a preamble to what Buju's journey might entail. A *Billboard* reporter described it like this:

> Minutes after 11 o'clock, Banton emerged on the darkened stage wearing a crisp white suit, his dreadlocks now reaching his waist. Patrons excitedly waved red, green and gold Rastafarian flags, blared air horns and illuminated the stadium with the blue glow of thousands of cell phones held aloft as they sought to capture his historic return. Backed by his superb Shiloh band, led by

> keyboardist Steven "Lenky" Marsden, Banton began his set by chanting a heartfelt prayer, "Oh Lamb of God have mercy on me." He then tore into the song that concisely described the rugged path he has traveled to reach this moment, "Not an Easy Road." As Banton continued, intently focused yet exuberant, the audience was clearly enthralled by his matured looks, agile moves and especially, the deep, coarse, ferocious voice that had been missing live for nearly a decade.[5]

Indeed, some would say Buju presented himself before his fans and his detractors as humbled: he fell to his knees singing, "I'm on bended knees, Jamaica I come." This opening prayer was quickly followed by this rhetorical question: "Are you ready, my people are you ready? Let me talk to you tonight!" This preface and the subsequent transitions throughout the concert were Buju's first effort to address his experience of incarceration. He then sang "Not an Easy Road" that described well his life and career as a performer. At the end of that song, he belted out an even more heartfelt greeting to his audience: "Greetings in the name of the Most High, Jaaah," before transitioning into "Had a Close One." He then sang "Give I Strength," a thoughtfully crafted narration in song of his journey up until his unfortunate encounter with the prison industrial complex in the United States, what sustained him during his incarceration/captivity, and then one bit of insight into his time in prison. The audience response to this segment of the performance spoke volumes about how social debt functions in the realm of the popular. These songs not only addressed his massive but also the proximity between the sacred and the secular that imbues Buju's career, Jamaican working-class people, and, indeed, the larger Black diaspora, who, like Buju, have had their brush with the prison industrial complex and returned to communities to seek redemption.

Returning to a conversational tone, he instructed the band to "low," a common command to the band and selectors when the performer has a message to deliver. The timing of such as digression is crucial, because it can either hype up the crowd or take the audience out of the moment.[6] In Buju's case, his performance was punctuated by few of these moments, but all were couched in a conversational tone, each sounding like there were things he had wanted to say to his audience after all these years he had been away. This particular "low" was of singular importance not just for him but, judging by their response, for his audience as well:

> Me come home, and some boy dem ah say, you know even though Buju Banton lock up, he still rough. Eight years, six months, twenty-seven days, thirteen hours, five minutes, and twenty-six seconds. Bring it down. I'm gonna say it. . . . This is a disclaimer, no disrespect to no one, I'm talking about me. Me don't care what in the media, me no business 'bout the news, me do 10 years of prison but no sexual abuse. No tear deh pon ah mi rectum, and mi anus no bruise. Mi see nuffa dem confuse![7]

As he reached the end of this freestyle, he lifted himself and the audience up with his rigorous crotch grab while jumping in the air. As the camera spanned the crowd, their approval was undeniable as, with hands raised in the shape of an imaginary double-barreled gun, they gave the simulated gun fyah salute. Buju clearly felt the need to address his audience about what he felt mattered most to them now that he was free and back in Jamaica. He was his own man, and he was "unbowed" sexually and spiritually.

With this matter settled, there seemed to be little else that people needed to see to prove that Buju had indeed returned to them whole: as a performer, as a Rastafarian, and as a Jamaican man. Buju's performance went a long way toward reaffirming his reputation for all to see. But as Michelle Stephens (2004, 194) reminds us, "There will always be something about embodied performance and black subjectivity that cultural history cannot capture by sight alone. Rather our cultural histories of blackness will have to mobilize other senses, other haptic and synesthetic optics, to represent a hint of the complexity of what gets performed when a racialized subject—accompanied by his double, his afterimage, his surrogate—steps onto a sociocultural stage." But for the time being, optics was the order of the day, as Buju continued his regionwide tour.

In the end, what people in Jamaica and across the Caribbean region were most interested to know on his return was whether Buju, the performer, still had the fire, the spirited delivery that had made him and uplifted them. The people understood that he did not have the ability to record new music while incarcerated: they were not expecting him to deliver new songs. Their response to his release and return to Jamaica tells as much about themselves at it does about Buju. He has always been a consummate lyricist and performer, and what was most evident in the physical dimensions of his performance was that "there is always a man, a perceptible embodiment, beneath or accompanying the image" (Stephens 2004, 195). This embodiment of Black subjectivity is what Jamaicans and Caribbean people in the diaspora came out to witness and embrace.

Move with Caution: Improvised Entertainment Development (IED) Underway

On the flipside of that popular culture coin is the overwhelming marketing machine that is Vybz Kartel and the Gaza Empire, which continues to roll on despite his conviction for murder. Seven years have elapsed since he was convicted, and yet his incarceration has not diminished his hold on the dancehall scene in Jamaica—quite the contrary. According to a *Rolling Stone* article,

> Musicians usually become enigmas by disappearing or holding back, but Vybz Kartel has become one by being impossibly present through his incarceration. He's released a book, *The Voice of the Jamaican Ghetto*, elaborating his views on topics ranging from parenting and abortion to third-world debt. He launched a

> clothing line, the Official VK Line; and created a literacy program which recently sponsored a robotics camp in his hometown of Portmore, Jamaica." (Serwer 2016).

If views on YouTube are any indicator, his staying power is undeniable, as songs like his 2011 hit "Summertime," which has garnered seventy million views since its release, continue to enjoy prominence. A few days after this *Rolling Stone* article was published, Kartel was transferred from the prison where he had spent the previous five years to the maximum-security Tower Street Adult Correctional Facility (Serwer 2016). His relocation to a maximum-security facility suggests that despite his incarceration, his ability to remain visible through music that had been digitally recorded from inside prison meant that a greater level of security was necessary. Yet in June 2020 Kartel released another album, *Dons and Divas*, while incarcerated in a facility where recording is prohibited, and his second book is scheduled to be published in 2021.

Kartel's stranglehold on the dancehall scene is buttressed by an army of fans who believe that the legal system is weighted against poor people who, even after achieving some success and mobility, need to be reminded of who controls the reins of power in Jamaica. Even his detractors highlight the numerous inconsistencies and legal infractions that characterized the trial that led to Kartel's conviction. One thing is certain: his ability to continue to expand his financial empire is a testament to the limitation of discourses and strictures of moral uprightness and respectability that inform consumer's palettes for cultural commodities. During one of the last recorded interviews before his own incarceration, Buju Banton had this to say about Vybz Kartel and the direction of dancehall music: "Right now I can say that Vybz Kartel is a man, him stimulate the heavens with the music. If only him coulda realize what him have and turn the spanner anti-clockwise, and then turn it inna the right direction." When asked by Winford Williams whether he felt Kartel was "misdirected," Buju answered that Kartel reminds him of Shabba, who said "things which were X-rated, that get the women excited, like a poem which is recited . . . and I find the similarities in this young man also. But him could still get some smooth down fi get the thing deh pon a level where him can . . . Because if the music can't be pon di radio, yuh missing yuh whole pension scheme, and yuh missing yuh initial revenue base, even though Jamaica don't adapt to that formality yet."[8] While Buju was incarcerated, Vybz Kartel was creating the blueprint that Buju would himself follow to relaunch his career after his release.

Radio and music executives who used to control distribution and airtime no longer hold the same power. This shift in the music power structures is similar to the transformation that West Indian cricket players brought to the British institution of cricket. They changed what the sport meant and how it was interpreted and consumed the world over—thereby altering the game forever. Although Kartel remains in the grasp of the prison industrial complex, he continues (somehow) to refashion himself and Jamaica's cultural landscape while keeping his music in demand and his profit scheme flourishing. Despite Buju's clear respect for Kartel, the generational chasm is notable—Buju's concern for music on rotation on radio stations speaks to a bygone era. In contrast, Vybz has mastered using the internet as a way to reach his audiences across the globe, ushering in a new era in dancehall music as a cultural commodity. In the process, he created of himself a unique product and a demand where none had previously existed—using his body, his flesh, as the canvas on which he would paint this new portrait of Jamaican dancehall culture.

People are still buying what Kartel is selling: tangible products like cake soap, rum, condoms, clothing, shoes, and music and an image of masculinity and Blackness that is at odds with the models previously visible on Jamaica's sociocultural stage. Spice recently released a song she allegedly recorded with Kartel in 2009, years before he was incarcerated and performed it with a Kartel doppelgänger much to the delight of fans; however, many believe that the song was recorded in prison and then mixed in the studio. Long before Vybz was incarcerated, he performed via satellite at the Best of the Best concert in Miami to an audience of more than ten thousand people because he had been denied a visa by the United States. Always the consummate trickster and businessman, his physical presence does not seem to be required, because his music and lyrics continue to fill the void his complex performance of Blackness has left behind. To the desiring subjects loyal to the "World Boss," his persistence in the cultural landscape is precisely part of the "afterimage, the surrogate, his double" that is, at least for now, manifest in the music he has produced (Stephens 2004, 194). But there is a palpable danger in the willingness of his supporters to place all of their hopes on his release from prison. The returns on their investments of loyalty and capital will fade out of necessity once reality sets in. Just as Laferrière wonders about what else lies beyond these circuits of consumption, so too do consumers, who have much more than just money caught up in these sociocultural dramas.

An insurgency is now taking root in Jamaican popular culture, one that has emerged quietly in the shadow of dancehall, borrowing some of the lessons learned but deploying them in ways that may provide another model for dissident artists in the Caribbean. A recent *Vogue* article, "Reggae Revival: Meet the Millennial Musicians behind Jamaica's New Movement," featured a number of artists who seem to be taking a new approach to consumerism and cultural commodification. When asked about this new movement in Jamaican music, Chronixx, one of the emerging stars of this "reggae revival," asserts confidently that it is not a new movement at all, that musicians have been making this music all along, but the commercialization of Jamaican dancehall music was such that no one was really paying attention to reggae music.

> "It was for commercial reasons," he says. "Commerce goes back and forth. Demand and supply go back and forth. So naturally there are going to be times

when people are not demanding reggae music as much." He goes on: "In economics, I learned something called ostentatious goods. I decided that if I was to ever be a good, if I was ever to be a product, I wanted to be an ostentatious product." I ask Chronixx what he means by an ostentatious product. "It's a kind of product that creates its own demand," he says. "Just by being there. Creates its own demand. It's not there because people want it. But people want it because it's there. See?"

"Society is becoming more in need of reality," he continues. "Some of them don't even know that they want it, but they do. They just want something real."[9]

This insightful gem cuts right to the heart of what Vybz Kartel must have realized, though not in the same register as this new generation of reggae artists. Before his arrival on the music scene, there was no context for anyone like him, certainly not lyrically in the dancehall and definitely not aesthetically. As I outlined earlier in the book, his violation of prevailing norms of masculinity and his irreverence toward other dancehall conventions related to female sexuality should have caused the public to reject him—yet he became one of the biggest icons of Jamaican music. Using his improvised creative devices, he transformed what consumers of dancehall wanted and how their practices of consumption were enacted. Yes, sexually charged lyrics had always been there, but not in the ways he fashioned them, and even when the establishment, in the form of radio deejays and record companies, tried to constrain his brand, they were unsuccessful. His mastery of internet resources assured his longevity and reach beyond the radio waves and into the World Wide Web, even while incarcerated.

This new generation of musicians and visual artists has set out on a similar journey, with their music and art still featuring the texture and some of the iconography of dancehall culture. However, lyrically and aesthetically they seem less invested in the policing of sexuality that has framed so much of Jamaican popular culture. If what Chronixx asserts is indeed the way forward, this new wave of insurgent art from Jamaica may well come to redefine what constitutes reality for consumers of the Caribbean abroad and in the region. So much of the Caribbean has been reified (as a product) through the visual and discursive lexicon of race and sexuality that people in the region have had to trade in these signs just to be recognized within the systems of exchange. The development of new currencies and forms of capital routed/rooted in social and spiritual revival is an encouraging response to the question of what lies beyond desire, commerce, and consumption.

Us *Verzuz* Ourselves: Toward a Soulful Reimagining of Community in the Wake

As I neared the completion of this book nine months after news of the novel coronavirus, COVID-19 first reached the United States, the virus had already laid waste to nearly two million lives globally. I raise the pandemic here as an opportunity to reflect, yet again, on the need for us to, as Christina Sharpe implores us, see *care* and *concern* as problems for thought in the midst of this crisis. As she reminds us, "thinking needs care . . . and thinking and care need to stay in the wake" (Sharpe 2016, 5). In March 2020, the closure of borders throughout the Caribbean region, North and South America, Europe, Africa, and Asia seemed unimaginable. Not since 9/11 had a single crisis so thoroughly disrupted global commerce and the movement of citizens. If the national response to 9/11 was for then-president George W. Bush to encourage Americans to go shopping and take their families to Disneyworld, the national response to the pandemic, despite initial hesitation, was to shelter in place and not venture out. In bringing most of the world to a literal standstill, the pandemic opened possibilities of answering the rhetorical question of what lies beyond desire, commerce, and consumption. What would this literal immobility mean for the world of artistic production, particularly for musicians in developing countries whose livelihood relies on touring Europe and the United States? How would Black people survive an ongoing social justice crisis and a public health crisis that put them at greater risk for dying from the COVID-19 virus because of the double-edged sword of limited access to health care and over-representation in frontline jobs that put them at heightened risk? The cruelty of Black citizens being shut off from the social and cultural communities that have fed their souls and applied the salve during times of suffering by itself would suffice as a particularly unbearable form of suffering. However, when we add the reality of being overexposed to the harm and hatred that, even before COVID-19, made life a form of barely living, the advent of "social isolation" was more than most Black citizens, regardless of their station, could bear.

How then could Black diaspora subjects, struggling to stay alive and connected to their loved ones in a pandemic, begin to fashion forms of social survival when churches, concerts, clubs, schools, and restaurants were all closed? This was not just a hypothetical consideration; I wondered this aloud for members of my own family. We turned to WhatsApp, Zoom, and Google Chat to stay connected to family and friends in Trinidad, London, and Kenya. Scouring social media to find out where and how people were creating spaces of respite from the catastrophe that was all around us, I stumbled onto a beacon of light in a period of darkness. Cultural critic Nadia Ellis (2015, 4) refers to these spaces as "territories of the soul" or "a set of cultural and political practices that exemplifies a structure of belonging and a metaphorical space of multiplicity and suspension." Her description of Ebony G. Patterson's "Of 72 Project" (2012) is worthy of note here because it highlights a shared concern about community as both a location and a practice within the African diaspora:

> Patterson's visual elegies articulate a future diasporic belonging in which local performance practices, however, unwittingly and usually in situations of dire extremity, call out to the diaspora, carving a black space out of materials that, at first glance, should never allow it. Even in regions and experiences of the

> most violent circumspection, the call of the diasporic elsewhere can be heard . . . Territories of the soul have long been taking up residence in black subjects, through art, culture, and music. (Ellis 2015, 17)

What Ellis describes as "black spaces" constructed out of materials that seem incongruent with the aims of gathering and being in community with others is a most apt description of how *Verzuz* emerged in the social and cultural crossroads of the pandemic. Cocreated by Timbaland and Swizz Beats, the webcast series became a critical cultural space for Black subjects to find community and belonging during the pandemic. Its DJ-curated "battles" featured artists (usually from the same genre), competing with one another while drawing only from their own catalogs, each taking turns in an effort to outdo the other. The inaugural battle on *Verzuz* on Instagram was between its cocreators, Timbaland and Swizz Beats. Once they opened their catalogs and launched into a five-hour showdown, no one could doubt the depth of talent possessed by each of these two giants of hip-hop and R&B music as songwriters, producers, and vocalists. Timbaland's lineup featured songs he had produced for Jay Z, Missy Elliot, Justin Timberlake, Nelly Furtado, and many other famous singers. Swizz Beats had an equally strong catalog that boasted songs performed by DMX, Beyoncé, Eve, T.I., and Jay Z. The range of artists participating in the series has been staggering, reaching across genres and generations to include Teddy Riley vz. Babyface (R&B); Erykah Badu vz. Jill Scott (soul/neo-soul, R&B, spoken word); Kirk Franklin vs. Fred Hammond (gospel); Ryan Tedder vz. Benny Blanco (pop, alternative rock); Snoop Dogg vz. DMX (hip-hop); Gladys Knight vz. Patti LaBelle (soul, R&B); and the only international musicians to participate thus far, Bounty Killer verzuz Beenie Man (dancehall). Some of the artists also collaborated with each other to produce live streamed shows for online consumption.

In addition to the competitive aspect of this new mode of entertainment, the live- streamed commentary by listeners that transcends generations, genres, and geographies has made *Verzuz* battles the closest thing to the legendary house parties for a generation who came of age in the 1980s and 1990s and are now in their fifties and sixties: they have gleefully learned how to use Instagram to get in on the *Verzuz* battle craze. The attraction of reliving the soundtracks of their youth, together with their children and nieces and nephews, is felt also by the list of VIPs (across generations) who attend the battles. Movie stars, politicians, news media personalities, and sports stars in attendance often post in the comments section while enjoying the music; for example, Michelle Obama was in the house for both Gladys Knight and Patti LaBelle's and Brandy and Monica's *Verzuz* battles. The stars offer their commentaries on the music, the memories evoked by certain songs, and make endless on- and off-stage jokes, sometimes at the expense of the artists, at other times at the expense of other commenters on the live feed.

Thus, *Verzuz* TV emerged as another way of imagining and participating in community at a time when the general public was prohibited from gathering in large groups and artists were locked in their homes. It was a predominantly Black space that drew together people from the places they all retreated to out of necessity to survive the pandemic. With real-time audiences that ranged from 250,000 (for April's Scott Storch vz. Mannie Fresh matchup) to 710,000 (May's Jill Scott vz. Erykah Badu),[10] young audiences were being educated about the music of their parents' generation and gaining a whole new appreciation for the deep and abiding talent that fuels contemporary music in the Americas. In turn, they were downloading Instagram for their aunties and uncles whose exposure to social media began and ended with Facebook, so that they too could have the pleasure of these community gatherings. NBC correspondent Blayne Alexander tweeted, "I called and gave my mom a 10-minute crash course on Instagram *just* so she could log into this #Verzuz."[11] *Verzuz* battles, far from pitting artists against one another, became a celebration of Black music and culture at a time when there was little in the world to celebrate. On May 9, 2020, CNN news journalist and reporter Yamiche Alcindor tweeted, "#Verzuz is literally saving the week. We needed this ya'll."[12] It is important to note that Alcindor's tweet appeared just two days after Gregory and Travis McMichael were finally arrested and charged in the killing of Ahmaud Arbery, whom McMichael had shot to death on February 23, 2020. This was indeed a particularly trying time for Black Americans because by May the world witnessed the horror of police officers murdering George Floyd in Minneapolis. When Alcindor says "we needed this," she is signifying on a space, in this case digital, and a "set of cultural practices that exemplifies a structure of belonging and a metaphorical space of multiplicity and suspension" similar to what Nadia Ellis (2015, 11) calls "territories of the soul." In this particular instance, the threat of the pandemic was increasing at the same time the deadly virus of racism was also reaching a crescendo. If ever there had been a need for collective acts of belonging, particularly by Black subjects, the events of 2020 made it starkly visible.

The *Verzuz* battles also resulted in commercial payoffs: artists soon came to recognize the value of the "*Verzuz* Effect," noting that within days of their battles the number of streams of their music increased exponentially. In an article discussing the #Verzuz phenomenon, *Rolling Stone* reported,

> Verzus [sic] started as a celebration of the past, but it has also started to shape listening habits in the present. Artists who participated saw their streams jump by 88 percent on average in the three days following the show compared to the previous three days, according to Alpha Data. By comparison, artists who performed on *The Late Show with Stephen Colbert,* television's highest-rated late-night network talk show, in the six months before the pandemic started saw their streams go up by an average of five percent.[13]

Verzuz certainly seems to be an excellent example of an "ostentatious good" capable, as Chronixx describes, of creating its own demand. To be sure, it did not emerge in response to consumer demands: people responded to it because it was available at a time when more traditional forms of entertainment were no longer accessible. We have to wonder how long it will be before major brands realize the potential of #Verzuz as a marketing tool. Thus far, the only two brands associated with *Verzuz* are Ciroc Vodka (in which Sean Combs/P Diddy holds a 50 percent profit-share stake[14]) and Apple Music, which began a partnership with the *Verzuz* series when it became increasingly clear that the demand for these events was far too large for Instagram to handle. Apple Music provides free streaming for users, while at the same time increasing its market share of consumers by creating advertisements for many of the *Verzuz* battles. It is already very clear that proximity to the *Verzuz* brand is worth its weight in gold.[15]

There are other signs that suggest the cultural landscape is changing for Black diaspora arts and culture, just as it has done with professional athletes. There is now a kind of *freed* agency,[16] quite different from the concept of "free agency" in professional sports. Culturally this freed agency is routed/rooted in independent labels and brands, collaborative ventures, and, in many instances, a turning away from traditional modes of producing culture. We have not come full circle, but I want to conclude with a meditation prompted by Steve McQueen's short acceptance speech when receiving the 2020 MOBO (Music of Black Origin) Inspiration Award. In his acceptance speech he commented that his series of short films, *Small Axe*, chronicling West Indian immigrant life in London from 1960–1980, was born out of a moment of critical acknowledgment that "when people didn't want to recognize us, we recognized ourselves."[17] Now, in the United States, we stand at a moment of self-recognition socially and culturally or at least what *should* be self-recognition initiated by the two coterminal disasters of 2020: the COVID-19 pandemic and continued waves of anti-Black racism. There is an increasing insistence on focusing on the reckoning that the public health and social justice crises forced into the global consciousness.

This reckoning cannot succeed if it does not begin with a recognition of the ways in which America has always trafficked in hatred, while clinging to the opiate of whiteness to satisfy the country's need to hold onto its innocence while holding on to the instruments of power that have ensured the continuation of this narrative. I emphasize recognition not because it is more important than reckoning, but rather because it is a constitutive element of reckoning. There can be no real redress and no movement forward unless the work begins with acknowledging the unwillingness to recognize what communities of color have always experienced and warned was taking place across the Black diaspora. What McQueen's observation makes visible to all who will listen and look is that the cleavages that shook the four corners of the globe in 2020 have been in the making for generations. The institutional forces that made citizens dissidents in their homelands are also the locations out of which cultural insurgencies necessarily continue to emerge.

Acknowledgments

This project has been a very long time in the making, and so there are many people to thank. For well over a decade, this book has been a part of my life and the lives of so many people in my community of family, friends, collaborators and, when necessary, co-conspirators. But as is usually the case, when one stops to take stock of the time it takes to complete a book manuscript, you realize that just as there have been people who supported your work, the same is also true about the various places that were also integral to this project seeing the light of day. Although I cannot recall all the people I met in many of these places, this much was certain: whenever I showed up, they welcomed me and gave me a place to think, write, and. most certainly, nourish my mind and body. I ended up in some of the most unlikely places all over the world, and no matter where my travels took me, there were so many gracious people who made me and my thoughts feel at home.

Before I ever visited Jamaica, there were friends who brought Jamaica and my ideas about Jamaican culture into a more nuanced, textured engagement over long, rigorous reasonings. I am forever thankful to Glyne Griffith, Annie Paul, Val and Barbara Carnegie, and Dennis Brown. For their generosity of spirit and skill, I would like to thank Mikey Bennett, Grafton Studio and all the musicians, sound techs, and Auntie Jelly, whose steam fish made a long day in the studio seem like just a short moment in time, flavored with levity. Bless up to all of you! I am so grateful to all my newfound family in Jamaica who housed me, nourished me, introduced me to the world of Jamaican radio programming, and treated me like their own: special thanks to Mr. and Mrs. Ashley and Winnifred Smith and Mr. and Mrs. John and Freddi Page. Thank you, Faith and Kezia for looking out for a Trini in Jamaica and gifting me the joy and company of your families while I worked.

Although this book was the kind of wayward citizen of the world I had always wished to be, there were useful institutional spaces that gave this unabashedly errant project the shelter and sustenance it needed to reach fruition. A book completion grant from the Office of the Dean at the University of Miami moved this project forward at a critical moment. Likewise, the manuscript workshop grant from the University of Miami Institute for Advanced Study of the Americas afforded me the opportunity to engage with interlocutors who gave of their time and intellect in a most generous fashion. A debt of gratitude is owed to Jafari Allen, Nadia Ellis, Kaiama Glover, and Laurie Lambert, as well as the graduate students who participated in the workshop: Laura Bass, Marta Gierczyk, Benjamin Moats, and Barry Williams. A special thanks to the Office of the Senior Associate Dean for Research and Graduate Education for its support in acquiring the copyrights for several of the images that appear in this book. I would also like to thank each of the artists—Chris Cozier, Leasho Johnson, and Ebony G. Patterson—for their generosity of time and talent and their willingness to trust me with their work. My sincerest thanks to the Monique Meloche Gallery for granting me the permission and support with captions and the cover of the book. Several public institutions in Miami have also been affirming of my work and the ideas articulated in this book while also providing me with opportunities to collaborate and to expand my thinking and intellectual practice. Special thanks are due to Diaspora Vibe Cultural Arts Incubator and its founder, Rosie Gordon Wallace, as well as the director of the Perez Art Museum of Miami (PAMM), Franklin Sirmans, and its former chief curator, Tobias Ostrander.

I am grateful to a large group of friends and interlocutors whom I have known and collaborated with for more than two decades. They read my work and challenged my thinking; their engagement and insightful questions pushed this book into places I could not have imagined. They are a band of wonderfully ungovernable intellectuals if ever there was: Roseanne Adderly, Simone Alexander, Rafe Dalleo, Nadia Ellis, Donette Francis, Rhonda Frederick, Linden Lewis, Elena Machado, Harvey Neptune, Kezia Page, Traci Robinson, Michelle Rowley, Faith Smith, Deborah Thomas, and Hilbourne Watson. When I arrived in Miami more than a decade and a half ago, there was a very small but tremendously generous core of people that made the city feel like home. Many years and conversations at their dinner tables or poolside, Sandra and Basil Paquet continue to be my steadfast calm in every storm. I also found a new community of scholars and artists from so many different walks of life. These friends became a traveling writing group that met up at local coffeehouses—often scouted out by Ingrid Carter, who knew how picky I was about the ambience of cafés and my coffee. We spent long days writing, talking, reading, studying for medical exams and flight exams, grading papers, plotting next moves, and driving ridiculous distances just to work and write in each other's company. Much love to the baristas at Panther Coffee (Miami Beach, Coconut Grove, and Little Haiti), big up Dany Muela and Steve Price. Many years, marriages, and kids later, my deepest appreciation goes out to Ingrid Carter, Sika Dagbovie, Chris Mullens, and Hilary Jones, and Bahia Ramos.

Large segments of this book were written during the summer while in London where my dear friend in chocolate, curry, and Carnival fetes, Roanna Gopaul, gave me a quiet place to think, read, and write. I promised I would come visit, but I am sure you did not think that meant every single summer! But a promise is a promise!

My Miami massive continues to grow in the most unexpectedly enriching ways. During the long periods of the pandemic quarantine, a small group of friends formed the Pandemic Writing Group, mostly to provide a space for us to think, talk, and share our work—whatever we managed to get done in this unprecedented time in all our lives. As the pandemic wore on, the convening of the group gave me a chance to stay connected to the ideas I had been pursuing before life as we knew it had ceased: it gave some structure to the hours that became days that became weeks and months, which felt like years. I am grateful to Erica James, Kate Ramsey, and Yolanda Martinez San Miguel for being present and conscious of our need to be connected not only to our work but also to each other at a time when everything around us was about maintaining distance. It felt good to be present intellectually, though distanced physically.

Editors and their staff are a special kind of people. They often fight for the life of the book even when authors are near giving up. Kimberly Guinta has stood by me, and this book manuscript, through thick and impossibly thin times in the face of all the vagaries of life that manage to emerge the closer you are to finishing. Remaining steadfast and committed to this project in the way that you have, for as long as you have, is truly a testament to your dogged persistence and faith in the projects you have signed onto. There are so many people who read manuscripts each year, putting their own work aside momentarily to give generative feedback to others. Without my readers, this work would not be possible. To those who read my manuscript, thank you for your time and selflessness. To the Critical Caribbean Studies series editors at Rutgers University Press, your enthusiasm and critical insights about this book far exceeded mine in the beginning, to be honest. Your enthusiastic engagement challenged me to embrace its waywardness as a reflection of my own methodology and way of thinking about Caribbean culture. Thank you.

Finally, none of this would have been possible without my family. I embarked on the journey to becoming a parent while writing this book, a journey that had more twists and turns than seemed humanly possible. And yet, at every single step of the journey there were friends who are now family members that guided me through the process: those who stood next to me when necessary, in front when I did not know it was necessary and behind me when I was sure I would fall. Deepest thanks to Paula Morgan, Hazel Ann Addiah, Miss Helen La Pompe, Lynette Joseph Brown, Barbara Lodge Johnson, and Sandra and Basil Paquet. As I figured out the vagaries of parenting while maintaining a career in academia, there was a small community of women in Miami who looked after my daughter, advised me in the ways of thriving throughout the experience of wanting to do more but sometimes needing to do just what I could in the moment (and know that was enough). Thank you, Miss Jenny and Amaldiris Gomez, the teachers at Upper Room Academy: Madelyn Napolis, Bertie Payne, Donna Barnes, and Gail Roberts. Then, there is this amazing generation of young folks coming up who are so solidly family oriented and committed to ensuring that my little girl has everything within her that she needs for this world. Josiah, Chinyere, Jabari, "Big Imani," Charlotte, and Noelia, you all give me hope for the future. These are the people Imani affectionately refers to as her "one hundred thousand million aunties and uncles." When the pandemic took hold of the world, I felt the physical distance between my family and me for the very first time in a long while—but children have a way of reminding us of the immediacy of love and its capacity to fill up time, space, and distance, no matter where you are. Physical distances are real, but so too are the love, care, and concern that occupy these spaces until we gather again to renew and remember what binds us, one to another. Imani Saunders, you are a real treasure. Your arrival encouraged so many of us to summon our best selves, and in so doing, we are all the better for it, and we will be here, as always, for you. We all believe this is not your first journey in this world, and we know you will make this one even better than the last.

There are the little bits of yourself that you guard, sometimes selfishly, sometimes out of an abundance of caution, and share only with those closest to you because they truly know your heart. If you leave yourself open to it, the universe has a way of sending you people who encourage you to be the person you would like but are afraid to be. That is when you realize there is a carelessness about love that is both joyous and dangerous because it encourages you to completely let go of your cautiousness. It is a joy to have experienced the tumult that this kind of love can bring; it teaches that there is comfort in caution and in letting go too. G., what we shared was adventurous, intense, and most certainly memorable. The thing I miss most is you reading me stories, feeding me words in the mornings. I still cannot believe you are gone. Keep smiling.

When you work on a book for as long as I have worked on this one, the seasons of life shift, and elders and loved ones cross to the ancestral side. My uncles Derek Benjamin and Lawrence LaCroix were among the men who married into the Blackman family from Belmont—I miss them, all of them. I miss my mom, Shirley Blackman, most of all: she became a quiet presence in my life, and I grew to appreciate this aspect of our relationship as I got older. We spoke about food often, and through our love of cooking, we grew to appreciate our differences. She was a "slight peppa" person, and I preferred fire in my mouth but joy in my belly. Yet curry was the undeniable bond between us and always created a space to start the other conversations that were needed. She loved it, and she loved us, fiercely. I also remember her sister (my auntie) Marva Benjamin, whose unapologetic love of every aspect of Carnival was contagious. I spent many years in her company while she judged the king and queen competition on Dimanche Gras in the Savanah and the old-time masquerade competitions in Adam Smith

Square, from late in the night into well into the next day. There are times when the sudden, unexpected loss of a loved one just leaves a huge hole in your world, and it's difficult to even fill that hole with memories because a part of you believes they are not really gone. Whenever I go to the beach I remember my uncle, Richard Saunders, whose smile when he was in or near the sea was simply radiant. I will never forget that. I only wish you were here longer to share that joy with your niece who seems to share your deep affinity for the water. Family, whether biological or logical, has always been a presence in my waking and resting moments, whether in my homes away from home or in the place that will always be home, Trinidad. Long before I knew myself, I knew each of you, and that knowledge has buoyed me in the most turbulent of seas.

An earlier draft of portions from chapter 1, "Is Not Everything Good to Eat, Good to Talk: Sexual Economy and Dancehall Music in the Global Marketplace," was published in *Small Axe* 7.1 (2003): 95–115; and an earlier draft of parts of chapter 2 was published as "Buyers Beware, Hoodwinking on the Rise: Epistemologies of Consumption in Terry McMillan's Caribbean," in *Sex and the Citizen: Interrogating the Caribbean*, ed. Faith L. Smith, 21–36 (Charlottesville: University Press of Virginia, 2011). Chapter 6 was previously published as "Gardening in the Garrisons, You Never Know What You Will Find: (Un)Visibility in the Works of Ebony G. Patterson" in *Feminist Studies*, vol. 42, no. 1 (2016): 98–138.

Notes

Introduction

1 Several people, responding to a post regarding the "real" cost of Carnival in 2019 commented that the cost of Carnival depended on "which Carnival experience" you wanted. Jamaican author Kei Miller, a regular participant in Trinidad and Tobago Carnival, commented that he can only catch a few of the remaining fetes for the season because he arrives during the week leading up to Carnival. He noted that "there are the fetes that begin on Boxing Day" (like Army fete, UWI fete, Bishops fete) and there are those that occur in the week prior to Carnival (D'Original Vale Breakfast Party, Beach House Fete, Brian Lara Carnival Sunday Party). These fetes range in price from US $200–400 and are not included in any of the band costume prices. The "experience" of Carnival isn't simply about playing mas on Monday and Tuesday, which is what the costume affords revelers. The full Carnival experience also must include a few fetes as well.

2 According to the Alice Yard blog, "Alice Yard is the backyard space of the house at 80 Roberts Street, Woodbrook, Port of Spain. This was once the house of Sean Leonard's great-grandmother. Four generations of children played and imagined in this yard, and now we continue this tradition. Alice Yard is a space for creative experiment, collaboration, and improvisation" (http://aliceyard.blogspot.com). The extension of the vision that began with Alice Yard and expanded to Granderson Lab in Belmont is the reclamation of Port of Spain as a locale for experimentation in the arts on a more local, independent, organic scale. Their model of artistic collaboration insists on remaining free of the constraints imposed by depending on support from corporations and international funding agencies. Their model relies on a system of collaborative bartering and creative exchange.

3 From V. S. Naipaul's now (in)famous statement, in *The Middle Passage* ([1962] 2001) that "history is built around achievement and creation; and nothing was created in the West Indies" to Derek Walcott's adroit response in "The Caribbean: Culture or Mimicry (1974)," this debate has bled into the fabric of postcolonial literary criticism. When Homi Bhabha entered the fray in his essay, "Of Mimicry and Man" (1997), the debate had already begun to dissolve as Caribbean cultural studies critics began to challenge these notions of cultural ambivalence by asserting that cultural

hybridization had its place in social and political landscapes in the Caribbean. Some of the texts that most effectively moved this debate into more critically generative grounds include Shalini Puri's seminal essay, "Canonized Hybridities, Resistant Hybridities: Chutney Soca, Carnival, and the Politics of Nationalism" (1999); Gerard Aching's *Masking and Power: Carnival and Popular Culture in the Caribbean* (2002); and, a few years later, Shalini Puri's *The Caribbean Postcolonial: Social Equality, Post/Nationalism, and Cultural Hybridity* (2004).

4 The dietary pyramid reminds us of the inequitable relationship between consumers of foods, particularly fruits imported from the Caribbean region and those who grow them. Caribbean countries have been forced, through structural adjustment policies, to import crops grown locally.

5 Anansi is a trickster figure in West African folklore, more specifically Ghanaian folklore from the Ashanti-Akan people. The Anansi stories made their way into Caribbean culture through the trans-Atlantic slave trade.

6 Lowe and Halberstam are the editors of this Duke University series. The body of scholarly work included in this series is a unique departure from traditional epistemological and disciplinary boundaries that have compartmentalized critical studies on race, sexuality, and nationalism: it is aimed at highlighting the constitutive nature of these interventions. According to the series editors, "Books in the series have elaborated such perversities in the challenge to modern assumptions about historical narrative and the nation-state, the epistemology of the human sciences, the continuities of the citizen-subject and civil society, the distinction between health and morbidity, and the rational organization of that society into separate spheres. The project also highlights intellectual 'perversities,' from disciplinary infidelities and epistemological promiscuity, to theoretical irreverence and heterotopic imaginings." Titles in this series include M. Jacqui Alexander's *Pedagogies of Crossing: Meditations on Feminism, Sexual Politics, Memory, and the Sacred* (2006) Kara Keeling's *The Witch's Flight: The Cinematic, the Black Femme, and the Image of Common Sense* (2007); Christina Sharpe's *Monstrous Intimacies: Making Post-Slavery Subjects* (2010); and Jafari Allen's *¡Venceremos?:The Erotics of Black Self-Making in Cuba* (2011).

1. Is Not Everything Good to Eat, Good to Talk

Epigraph: Buju Banton, "Untold Stories," *Til Shiloh*, PolyGram Records, 1995

1 Arturo Escobar uses this term in *Encountering Development: The Making and Unmaking of the Third World* (1995) to describe the unavoidable intersections between "local" and "global" cultures in the global marketplace.

2 The term *batty* in Jamaican English means bottom, backside, or anus. In this context, *batty-bwoy* refers to men who participate in anal sexual intercourse.

3 This debate was taken up in the pages of the *Massachusetts Review*, *Vibe Magazine*, and the *Village Voice*, where the cover of the January 12, 1993, issue features the headline, "Batty Boys in Babylon: West Indian Gay Culture Comes out in Brooklyn. And So Does Violence."

4 For a more detailed discussion of Jamaican political violence, which reached its peak in the 1980s, and the subsequent migration of several Jamaican dons and drug lords to New York City, read Laurie Gunst's *Born fi' Dead: A Journey through the Jamaican Posse Underworld* (1995). Her book traces the emergence of Jamaican posses in New York during the height of Reaganomics and crack cocaine, focusing

on the interconnections between these two phenomena and the culture of political violence in Jamaica.

5 A popular term used to describe the hidden agendas often present in governmental practices and legislation that are offered as relief for Jamaica's economic crises.

6 The first trial ended in a mistrial after the jury was unable to reach a verdict after three days of deliberation. Howard Campbell, *Jamaica Gleaner*, September 28, 2010, http://jamaica-gleaner.com/gleaner/20100928/lead/lead2.html.

7 Alternative interpretations of the acronym IMF include "Is Manley's Fault," the "International Mother F**kers," and "International Misery Foundation."

8 The saying "plain talk, bad manners" is a Trinidadian expression that highlights the extent to which truth and honesty, when put in the plainest terms, can be considered bad manners, particularly to those whom the truth exposes.

9 Changes to swear words and sexually explicit language throughout the manuscript are the prerogative of the publisher and not the author. My critical practice assumes that profanity is first and foremost performative and always political in popular culture. In Jamaica, in particular, the ongoing transformation of profane language from insults to embodied discourses of resistance is aimed at breaking down the façades of respectability and laying bare the exploitative violence that often lurks behind polite conversation. Innovations in the use of Jamaican English began in the roots and reggae tradition (with system/sh*tstem, television/tell lie vision, understanding/overstanding, and many more) and has heavily influenced how dancehall artists utilize profanity in their songs (as is evidenced throughout this book).

10 *Kriss* means to "look fine." The term usually applies to clothing, cars, home furnishings, and other material goods. The fact of its association with weapons, however, is worth noting because it marks guns as a hot commodity item that is also fashionable.

11 The term "shottah" (shooter) is used to describe hired gunmen or men whose reputations are derived from murdering people with guns.

12 I am using the terms "work" and "wuk" to represent the simultaneous connections and intimacies among labor, gender, sexuality, and commodification in Jamaican culture. Throughout the chapter the terms should be understood as interchangeable in their sexual and economic contexts.

13 The double entendre is intended to highlight the multiple ways that discourses on sexuality and politics often overlap in very rich and thought-provoking ways in dancehall music. This tradition is also most apparent in calypso and soca music.

14 The phrases "gi di gyal wuk," "tekin di wuk," and "stead out inna bed" all describe various renderings of the sex act that have commonly appeared in dancehall songs over the last thirty years. The responses to said sexual acts are usually described through discourses of pain and suffering as women "bawl fi mercy" and "wince under agony."

15 The songs I focus on in this chapter are by no means anomalous. Other songs in this genre include "Pum Pum" (Elephant Man), "Don't" (Prof. Nuts), and "Nuh Play Chess" (Madd Anju).

16 Despite Capleton's designation as the "fyah man" (because fire is his weapon of choice for fighting corruption, homosexuality, and Roman Catholicism), his sentiments about homosexuality are not unique. The most notable song in this tradition is Anthony B's "Fyah pon Rome," which was banned in Jamaica. Other songs that express similar antigay sentiments include "Anything a Anything" (Elephant Man and Ward 21), "Roll Deep" (Beenie Man), "Chi Chi Man" (TOK), "Chi Chi Kru" (Alozade), "Chuckie Poo" (Mr. Vegas), and several songs by Scare Dem Crew, Bounty Killer, and others.

17 I am reading the linguistic play on the word *foreign*, commonly pronounced as "farin" in Jamaican English, and this signification on the proximity or distance from an imagined cultural (and quite possibly economic) home. The distance is also measured in relation to the autonomy, or the lack thereof, of the Jamaican state's exercise of nationalist politics and its ability to regulate its own terms of citizenship and belonging.

18 Examples of the proliferations of these "riddims" include the "Bellyas" riddim, the "Y2K Bug" riddim, and the "Busta" riddim. Each of these beats has been recorded by at least six artists, who add their own lyrics to the mix. This practice forces the listener (foreign or otherwise) to focus on the lyrics of each artist, and not so much the music itself, because the music for any given artist is uniform and comes from a handful of popular rhythms released each year.

19 I am indebted to Michelle Rowley, at the University of Maryland, College Park, for pointing out this important similarity between calypso music and dancehall music: it highlights another way of imagining the insider/outsider politics of location.

20 The term "boogah" is slang for the word *bugger*, which is the legal term for the crime of buggery as defined in the legislation of several Caribbean countries.

21 A phrase used to describe men who, though not homosexuals, lack the "ratings" of stallions (flashy cars, money, sexual talent, power). They are often described as men who lust after women and spread false rumors about their sexual escapades and prowess. Moreover, the phrase, as deployed by TOK, implies an absence of agency when some men encounter punanny. Hence, the title "watchman" effectively manifests the con/fusion between work and "wuk."

22 The use of the term "seeding" in dancehall lyrics offers a fruitful opportunity to consider how women's bodies, specifically their wombs, become conduits for nationalist landscapes, such as through the common use of the term "breeding." The discursive power of these terms, when read through Jamaica's colonial slave plantation economies, suggests a return to global market systems that measure productivity through "units" produced, with little regard for the dehumanizing and exploitive processes that make "production" possible and profitable.

2. Buyers Beware, Hoodwinking on the Rise

1 For a more detailed analysis of the emergence of chick lit in contemporary women's fiction, see Caroline Smith's *Cosmopolitan Culture and Consumerism in Chick Lit* (2008). For a more detailed analysis of the social complexities that distinguish chick lit from sistah lit, see Lisa Guerrero's "Sistahs Are Doin' It for Themselves: Chick Lit in Black and White" (2006).

2 The recent film *Something New*, starring Sanaa Lathan and Simon Baker, is based on a similar theme but with a notable twist: the African American woman's love interest is a white, working-class man. The adventure is doubly intriguing—not simply because of the interracial coupling but also because her love interest (Brian Kelly) is a landscaper, while she (Kenya McQueen) is a corporate lawyer. Both films share the motif/dilemma of successful Black women who find themselves with great careers and financial stability but no romance or love interests.

3 In his 1987 film *Eddie Murphy Raw*, Eddie Murphy performs a scene in which a wronged wife or girlfriend gets even with her partner by taking off on a vacation to the Bahamas, where she links up with a reggae-loving, dreadlocked ladies' man. When the woman encounters Dexter St. Jacques, he asks why a pretty woman like her is on the beach alone. The crucial part of the scene occurs when Murphy,

swinging the microphone, a stage double for Dexter's penis, throws it over his shoulder and listens while the young woman recounts her misfortune. In the novel, Stella is repeatedly asked whether "the rumor" is true about Caribbean men. The novel thus leads us to believe that the rumor has to do with penis size, rather than with Caribbean men being good listeners. However, in McMillan's novel, Winston seems to be gifted in both respects.

4 Jamaica Kincaid's *A Small Place* (1988) focuses on this aspect of the tourist industry in Antigua. However, her critique of tourism assumes that the visitor is white, not Black. As such, McMillan's novel offers an interesting companion text that complicates some of the assumptions made about the attitudes of white British and American tourists.

5 In this respect, Colin Channer's 2010 novel *Waiting in Vain* might qualify as a more transnational, gender-conscious envisioning of the same cultural and political project.

6 For another article that addresses these dynamics, see Deborah Pruitt and Suzanne LaFont's "For Love and Money: Romance Tourism in Jamaica," *Annals of Tourism Research* 22, no. 2 (1995): 422–440, 195.

7 The divorce papers filed in Contra County Court were posted on the website *The Smoking Gun*, which focuses on celebrity scandals and run-ins with the law. The court documents are now archived at "'Stella' Exhales in Nasty Divorce," *The Smoking Gun,* June 30, 2005, http://www.thesmokinggun.com/documents/celebrity/stella-exhales-nasty-divorce.

8 My use of the term "(mis)recognition" is an adaptation of Krista Thompson's definition of "recognition." According to Thompson (2012, 34), "The choice of the term *recognition,* meaning to know again or to perceive to be identical with something previously known, echoes the meaning of the picturesque, a landscape re-cognized through a preexisting model."

9 For a full transcript of the numerous phone calls allegedly made by McMillan to Plummer, visit *The Smoking Gun* website. http://www.thesmokinggun.com/file/terry-mcmillan-sues-her-little-fag-ex. In many of these conversations, she repeatedly calls Plummer a faggot.

3. "Who's on Top?"

Epigraph: Letter from a planter to the Cuban governor after the Haitian Revolution (Franco 1954, 131)

1 Santo Domingo was the name given to the island of Hispanola which was completely under the control of Spain from the 1494 until the early seventeenth century, when the French took over the western half of the island in 1659.

2 Stephen Morton, *Gayatri Spivak: Ethics, Subalternity and the Critique of Postcolonial Reason* (Cambridge, UK: Polity, 2007), 28–340.

3 C. Auguste and M. Auguste, *L'Expédition Leclerc 1801–1803* (Port-au-Prince: Impremerie Henri Deschamps), quoted in Paul Farmer's *Aids and Accusation: Haiti and the Geography of Blame* (2006, 162).

4 The Treaty of Ryswick, signed in 1697 between France and Spain, formally granted control of the western portion of Hispanola to the French, who had already begun to establish control of this portion of the country as early as 1657.

5 David Geggus, *The Haitian Revolution: A Documentary History* (2014, 47).

6 Peter Moses and John Moses, "Haiti and the Acquired Immune Deficiency Syndrome," *Annals of Internal Medicine* 99, no. 4 (1983): 565, quoted in Paul Farmer's *Aids and Accusation* (2006, 2).

7 The conflation of the popular and the scientific produced a number of problematic quasi-scientific findings about Haiti, vodoun, and the spread of the HIV/AIDS epidemic in the 1980s. One example, expressed by Paul Farmer in *Infections and Inequalities: The Modern Plague* (1999, 3) shows us how these conflations affected even the most reputable journals in the medical field:

> Although further acquaintance with the syndrome made it difficult to posit a Haitian origin for AIDS, armchair theorists were reluctant to let go of voodoo altogether. The *Journal of the American Medical Association* published a consideration of these theories under the fey title, "Night of the Living Dead." Its author asks, "So necromantic zombiists transmit HTLV-III/LAV during voodooistic rituals?" Tellingly, he cites as his source not the by then substantial scientific literature on AIDS in Haiti, but the U.S. daily press.

8 For a more detailed analysis of the production of Haiti as a site of social and medical disease, see Paul Farmer's *Infections and Inequalities* (1999).

9 Paul Farmer's *Aids and Accusation: Haiti and the Geography of Blame* (2006) takes great care to locate the impending health crisis of the AIDS epidemic to larger, systemic destabilization of rural communities in Haiti. The first chapter, "Misery Without Number," gives an exhaustive, detailed chronicle of the deforestation of Do and Ba Kay, the flooding and subsequent destruction of the rice farms there, and the mandatory slaughter of Haitian pigs by officials who believed the pigs were the cause of an infection spreading across the island. Farmer is intentional in insisting that understanding the AIDS epidemic and its arrival in Haiti must be understood in the context of the concurrent destabilization of rural communities which, without means of sustenance, were in no way able to guard themselves against the impending disaster of disease and death that was awaiting their small community.

10 There are several scenes in Cantet's *Heading South* where Legba's dialogue reflects exchanges between Fanfan, Chico, and the band of other young boys who populate Laferrière's stories.

11 I describe Brenda's act as a sexual assault to draw attention to the unequal power relationship between a minor and an adult. What Brenda describes is an act of statutory rape, though *sexual assault* is the phrase most often used in legal statutes today. A key premise in statutory rape laws to protect minors is the fact that minors are "economically, socially, and legally unequal to adults" and therefore need to be protected by adults (U.S. Department of Justice). R. Eidson, "Constitutionality and Statutory Rape Laws," *UCLA Law Review* 27, no. 3 (February 1980): 757–815.

4. "Fashion ova Style"

Epigraph: Monica Miller, *Black Dandyism and the Styling of Black Diasporic Identity* (Durham, NC: Duke University Press, 2009), introduction. Michelle Stephens. *Skin Acts: Race, Psychoanalysis, and the Black Male Performer* (Durham, NC: Duke University Press, 2014), 81.

1 See https://www.npr.org/templates/story/story.php?storyId=88478467, accessed March 12, 2010. This address is now commonly referred to as Obama's "A More Perfect Union" speech.

2 The world of the "Black dandy" is not simply a world of high fashion and haute couture, it also leans heavily on a broad appreciation for Black culture. While there has long been a tradition of Black academics investing in Black Diaspora culture and art, in large part because of their work as cultural critics engaging the social and

political impact of culture in the way we understand the world around us, the emergence of sports and entertainment figures in the world of art, culture, and high fashion is more recent. Much has been made of the prominent list of NBA players and hip-hop artists who have begun building formidable collections of African American art. Some of the most notable collectors include Amar'e Stoudemir, Dwayne Wade, Kanye West, Pharrell Williams, and Kasseem "Swizz Beatz" Dean, who started the now famous No Commission Art Fair, which draws thousands of visitors and collectors annually at December's Art Basel in Miami Beach. See, for example, https://www.artsy.net/article/artsy-editorial-nba-all-star-amar-e-stoudemire-is-turning-athletes-into-emerging-art-collectors; https://www.blackartinamerica.com/index.php/2021/05/04/how-the-hip-hop-generation-is-disrupting-the-art-world/; https://www.nytimes.com/2019/02/13/t-magazine/swizz-beatz-art.html, accessed October 27, 2021.

3 See https://www.youtube.com/watch?v=RAXMRiyUx_Q, accessed October 23, 2021.

4 See https://ballislife.com/remembering-when-the-nba-created-a-dress-code-in-2005-was-it-racist, accessed November 27, 2020.

5 ESPN Radio. http://www.espn.com/espnradio, accessed June 3, 2014.

6 See https://www.standardmedia.co.ke/article/1144022031/ragga-beef-gully-vs-gaza, accessed August 5, 2013. "Division inside the Gully over War with Alliance." https://urbanislandz.com/2011/08/31/division-inside-the-gully-over-war-with-alliance, accessed November 10, 2013.

7 See https://dancehallmusic.fandom.com/wiki/Gaza/_Portmore_Empire, accessed December 2013.

8 See https://dancehallmusic.fandom.com/wiki/Gully/_Alliance, accessed June 10, 2014.

9 See https://www.youtube.com/watch?v=-8gdAnOPf1Q, accessed May 23, 2017.

10 See https://twitter.com/e60/status/1012779261009235971?lang=en, accessed May 7, 2019.

11 See https://www.youtube.com/watch?v=8OaTMkpgmkQ, accessed May 7, 2019.

12 See https://www.youtube.com/watch?v=NUhW6wlMQsw, accessed June 5, 2016.

13 See https://www.youtube.com/watch?v=d93u5IZ1u-4&list=RDd93u5IZ1u-4&index=1, accessed October 24, 2021.

14 The THUG LIFE tattoo was brought to prominence by Tupac Shakur, who famously explained that the expression had little to do with criminality per se. Rather, the letters in the tattoo inscribed on his body are an acronym for "The Hate U Gave Little Infants Fucks Everybody." https://www.youtube.com/watch?v=0TfEr_BLW30, accessed August 4, 2009.

15 I am utilizing the term "accessorizing" in the way in which it is implied in Pertrine Archer's essay "Accessories/Accessaries; or, What's in Your Closet." She introduces this term as a way to explain the way in which skin color, and the phenomenon of skin bleaching, was an explicit effort to gain access to certain cultural spaces (like clubs, video shoots, commercials). Where skin color and bleaching once provided economic opportunities, the emergence of bleaching as an accessory that could be deployed for cultural events like parties, dance sessions, and concerts has shifted the emphasis away from minimizing Blackness to maximizing fashion and style.

16 See https://www.leashojohnson.com/copy-of-cocktales-and-pumpum, accessed November 2, 2021.

5. "Outta Order" or "Outta Door?"

Epigraph: Daphne Brooks. *Bodies in Dissent: Spectacular Performances of Race and Freedom, 1850–1910.* (Durham, NC: Duke University Press, 2006): 4–5.

1 A mixed tape is best described as a compilation of songs or raps featuring songs by an artist, sometimes in collaboration with other rappers, produced and distributed to listeners free of charge to build a fan base and get recognized. Mixed tapes were originally released on cassettes; eventually cassettes gave way to the CD; and now mixed tapes are released digitally on the web. Many Chance the Rapper's *Acid Rap* (2013), which was released as a free download, is one of most successful mixed tapes ever. Mixed tapes also have another critical social function. For more details, see https://www.urbandictionary.com/define.php?term=Mixtapes, accessed October 27, 2021.

2 "Spice explains her fake skin bleaching photo: "I wanted to create awareness to 'colorism.'" https://www.thefader.com/2018/11/02/spice-explains-skin-bleaching-photo, accessed =January 9, 2019

3 See "Survivors of Sexual Abuse Stage Protest at Nazareth Moravian Church." *Jamaica Gleaner*, January 9, 2017. http://jamaica-gleaner.com/article/lead-stories/20170109/survivors-sexual-abuse-stage-protest-nazareth-moravian-church.

4 In a corresponding footnote, Thomas notes that "the other source of power she identified was spirituality (as distinct from formal religion)."

5 See https://www.youtube.com/watch?v=EhAkkF-8-oA&t=745s, accessed June 5, 2018.

6 In her response to Foota's assertion that they had "physical encounters," Ishawna says pointedly to Winford Williams that for him to claim they had "physical encounters" downplays the abuse she had to endure. She refutes Foota's claim of minor physical encounters, saying, "I can't fight Foota . . . he is almost 300 pounds, you understand? I was being abused, you understand. I was being cheated on, and I cannot speak. I am hearing how much you do for me every day, so I cannot leave you?"

7 See https://www.youtube.com/watch?v=-QhpmnbtmYs&t=219s, accessed May 12, 2018.

8 See https://www.youtube.com/watch?v=8ZJYlRAX418, accessed January 20, 2018.

9 See https://www.youtube.com/watch?v=pFItaKcCHmM, accessed June 1, 2019.

10 See https://www.youtube.com/watch?v=pFItaKcCHmM.

11 See https://www.youtube.com/watch?v=pFItaKcCHmM.

6. Gardening in the Garrisons

Epigraph: Olive Senior, "Meditation on Yellow," in *Gardening in the Tropics* (Toronto: McClelland & Stewart, 1994), 11.

1 The use of the term "un-visibility" in the title derives from Ralph Ellison's introduction to the 1981 edition of his book *Invisible Man* (1952). As Krista Thompson (2105, 40) explains in *Shine: The Visual Economy of Light in African Diasporic Aesthetic Practice*, Ellison "describes blacks in US society as so hypervisible that they have been rendered *un*-visible. . . . Un-visibility describes the state of not being seen or not being recognized, as well as the 'moral blindness' toward the 'predicament of blacks.'"

2 A few examples are Alejo Carpentier, *El reino de este mundo* (1949); Jean Rhys, *Wide Sargasso Sea* (1966); Wilfredo Lam, *The Jungle* (1943); and, most famously,

Michel-Jean Cazabon's nineteenth-century paintings of Trinidadian landscapes. For a more thorough account, see Thompson (2007).

3 The small, 9 by 7-inch drawings and inscriptions, which at the time numbered 250, all include hues of brown. These muted colors create a filter that is particularly effective as a means of frustrating our eye's expectation for an aesthetic of "bright" (sunlit) landscapes made all the more vivid by decades of paintings, photos, and commercial representations.

4 Like "Afro-Ophelia," "see through body" is also inspired by an image on the front page of the newspaper. For a detailed explanation of the inspiration for this image see https://www.flickr.com/photos/56271618@N00/492617108/in/album-72157600176542058/.

5 Tivoli Gardens is a housing community initiated by Prime Minister Edward Seaga's Jamaica Labour Party (JLP) government in the 1960s. On its completion, properties were distributed to JLP supporters, solidifying its current standing as a political garrison for the JLP.

6 Although the statistics indicate that a total of seventy-three people went missing, Patterson's project focuses on the lives of the seventy-two residents who went missing. Most of the figures in the installation appear to be men. However, because many have bandanas covering most of their faces, there are instances where it is difficult to discern, based on the eyes, whether the subject in question is male or female.

7 See http://www.theof72project.com/project-text.php.

8 See https://anniepaul.net/2012/03/17/who-were-the-tivoli-73-a-preview-of-ebony-g-pattersons-of-72/, accessed on October 26, 2021.

9 Comment made by Damien King, head of the Economics Department at the University of the West Indies. http://anniepaul.net/2012/03/17/who-were-the-tivoli-73-a-preview-of-ebony-g-pattersons-of-72, accessed July 19, 2015.

10 Unpublished interview with Ebony Patterson by Karen Patterson, associate curator at the John Michael Kohler Arts Center in Sheboygan, Wisconsin, for the *Dead Treez* installation exhibited January 18 to September 13, 2015.

11 Ebony G. Patterson, http://www.cheapandcleanproject.com, accessed July 19, 2015.

12 Ebony G. Patterson, "Undressing Cheap and Clean: Notes from the Artist http://www.cheapandcleanproject.com, accessed July 25, 2015.

13 Transcribed from the ARTZPUB film, *Alice Yard, "act 5"*. Ebony Patterson, "9 of 219 Project." Artist, Ebony G. Patterson; Photography Darren Cheewah. Made in Trinidad and Tobago. https://vimeo.com/28884230. Accessed on July 20, 2015.

14 Transcribed from the ARTZPUB film, *Alice Yard, "act 5"*.

Conclusion

1 Quoted in the press kit for *Ver le Sud*, http://www.shadowdistribution.com/headingsouth/downloads/HeadingSouthPresskit.pdf, accessed June 1, 2019).

2 In an interview with Winford Williams, Lady Saw describes the impact of the sudden death of her close friend and sister. Just a few days after her death, on December 14, 2015, Lady Saw (who now goes by Minister Marion Hall) accepted God into her life and walked away from dancehall music, but not the life of performing. https://www.youtube.com/watch?v=LOHrsJMO9sU, accessed April 5, 2018.

3 See https://www.youtube.com/watch?v=39buYW-CPyo, accessed January 12, 2018.

4 See https://www.eurasiareview.com/29032017-jamaicas-tambourine-army-on-the-gender-violence-warpath, accessed March 12, 2019.

5 See https://www.billboard.com/articles/news/8503607/buju-banton-long-walk-freedom-concert-jamaica-10-years-prison, accessed May 10, 2019.

6 During his B.F.F. performance Bounty Killer was guilty of overusing this strategy, in large part because he was so preoccupied with driving home his displeasure about Ishawna's song.

7 See https://www.youtube.com/watch?v=w9hBjr-Swb8, accessed March 20, 2020.

8 See https://www.facebook.com/watch/?v=326280181360193, accessed June 10, 2019.

9 See https://www.youtube.com/watch?v=QrnUevg, accessed October 22, 2021.

10 See https://variety.com/2020/digital/news/verzuz-dj-battles-swizz-beatz-timbaland-jill-scott-1234614586, accessed January 8, 2021.

11 See https://www.cnn.com/2020/05/23/us/verzuz-instagram-battles-popularity-explained-trnd/index.html, accessed on January 14, 2021.

12 See https://www.cnn.com/2020/05/23/us/verzuz-instagram-battles-popularity-explained-trnd/index.html, accessed January 10, 2021.

13 See https://www.rollingstone.com/pro/features/verzuz-timbaland-swizz-beatz-future-25-1079682, accessed January 14, 2021.

14 See https://www.billboard.com/articles/news/1047716/diddy-inks-deal-to-develop-vodka-brand; https://www.washingtonpost.com/news/wonk/wp/2015/10/02/sean-p-diddy-combs-donald-trump-is-not-the-only-person-who-is-a-model-mogul, accessed, August 13, 2019.

15 Popular music media outlets began keeping scorecards to report to listeners and readers who, according to their experts, had emerged victorious after each *Verzuz* battle. *Billboard Magazine* began this trend during the battle between DJ Premiere and RZA of the Wu-Tang Clan, and *Vibe Magazine* and *Revolt TV News* followed in close succession. While there has been continuous debate about winners and losers, there have also been numerous draws, particularly in a situation in which the "battle" format was not invoked because the event was billed as "A Healing" in response to police brutality and escalating racial tensions. One such event opened with a prayer by T. D. Jakes and featured Kirk Franklin and Fred Hammond, along with guest appearances by other gospel notables such as Grammy Award winners Marvin Sapp and Tamela Mann. But thus far, the pinnacle of the *Verzuz* series was the Master Class offered by Patti Labelle and Gladys Knight (with a guest appearance by Dionne Warwick). To date, theirs is the only draw/tie, with many agreeing that the winner that night was music lovers the world over.

16 I am expanding on the concept of free agency in the National Football League where an athlete is no longer under a contract with a specific team and can therefore sign with another club or franchise. The term also applies to a player who is still under contract but is permitted to solicit offers from other teams.

17 See https://www.youtube.com/watch?v=DL1agM7YYUc, accessed January 11, 2020.

Bibliography

Aching, Gerard. *Masking and Power: Carnival and Popular Culture in the Caribbean*. Minneapolis: University of Minnesota Press, 2002.

Aguirre, Abby. "Reggae Revival: Meet the Millennial Musicians behind Jamaica's New Movement." *Vogue*. October 28, 2015. https://www.vogue.com/projects/13362670/reggae-revival-jamaica-chronixx-protoje-root s-music?fbclid=IwARoopNyGjsxi2SbvO4um8jrTeP8bMUZ1fUcvYthnH5t7Pbtdz8Ecoo QMZs8, accessed July 10, 2020.

Alexander, M. Jacqui. "Not just (Any) Body Can Be a Citizen: The Politics of Law, Sexuality and Postcoloniality in Trinidad and Tobago and the Bahamas." *Feminist Review*, no. 48 (1994): 5–23.

Allsopp, Jeannette, and Richard Allsopp. *Dictionary of Caribbean English Usage*. Kingston: University of the West Indies Press, 2003.

Almond, Steve. "How I Became a Dick Lit Author without Even Trying." *MobyLives* (blog). June 17, 2003. http://www.mobylives.com/Almond_lit.html.

Archer, Petrine. "Accessories/Accessaries; or, What's in Your Closet," *Small Axe* 14, no. 2 (July 2010): 97–110.

Astramskas, David. "The NBA Dress Code of 2005: Why It Was Created & How Players Reacted to It." Ball Is Life. October 17, 2018. https://ballislife.com/remembering-when-the-nba-created-a-dress-code-in-2005-was-it-racist/.

Baby Cham, and Bounty Killer. "Another Level." Track #9 on *WOW: The Story*, Vols. 1 & 2, Artists Only! Records, 2000.

Bakare-Yusuf, Bibi. "Clashing Interpretations in Jamaican Dancehall Culture." *Small Axe* 10, no. 3 (2006): 161–173.

———. "Fabricating Identities: Survival and the Imagination in Jamaican Dancehall Culture." *Fashion Theory: The Journal of Dress, Body & Culture* 10, no. 4 (2006): 461–483.

Barnes, Natasha. *Cultural Conundrums: Gender, Race, Nation, and the Making of Caribbean Cultural Politics*. Ann Arbor: University of Michigan Press, 2006.

Bhabha, Homi. "Of Mimicry and Man: The Ambivalence of Colonial Discourse." *Discipleship: A Special Issue on Psychoanalysis* 28 (1997): 125–133.

Bounty Killer. *Fifth Element*. TVT Records, 1999.

Bounty Killer, and Baby Cham. "Ghetto Pledge." Mad House Records. 1999.

Bourdieu, Pierre. *Distinction: A Social Critique of the Judgement of Taste*. Cambridge, MA: Harvard University Press, 1984.
Bradshaw, A., and A. Shankar. "The Production and Consumption of Music." *Consumption, Markets and Culture* 11, no. 4: (2008): 225–227.
Brooks, Daphne A. *Bodies in Dissent: Spectacular Performances of Race and Freedom, 1850–1910*. Durham, NC: Duke University Press, 2006.
Brown, August. "Buju Banton's Grammy Nomination Angers Gay Rights Groups." January 29, 2010. *Los Angeles Times Music* (blog). https://latimesblogs.latimes.com/music_blog/2010/01/buju-bantons-grammy-nomination-angers-gay-rights-groups.html#sthash.xDkd8p8t.dpuf.
Brown, Desmond. "Jamaica's 'Tambourine Army' on the Gender Violence Warpath." *Eurasia Review*. March 29, 2017. https://www.eurasiareview.com/29032017-jamaicas-tambourine-army-on-the-gender-violence-warpath, accessed March 12, 2019.
Brown, Huntley. "Dancehall Music Can Empower the Young." *Jamaica Gleaner*, February 8, 2009. http://jamaica-gleaner.com/gleaner/20090208/ent/ent1.html.
Buju Banton. "Boom Bye Bye." Track #1 on *Strictly the Best*: *Volume 9*, 1993.
———. "Untold Stories," Track #5 on *Til Shiloh*. PolyGram Records, 1995.
———. *Before the Dawn*. Gargamel Records, 2010. CD. "Buju Brings Hope and Inspiration: Dub Poet Yasus Afari talks with Winford Williams." Majesty Media, Facebook. March 17, 2019. https://m.facebook.com/watch/?v=1048887718631448&_rdr.
Byrd, Cathy. "Is There a 'Post-Black' Art? Investigating the Legacy of the 'Freestyle' Show." *Art Papers* 26, no. 6 (2002): 34–39.
Campbell, Curtis. "Dancehall Breaks New Ground." *Jamaica Gleaner*, November 5, 2012. http://jamaica-gleaner.com/gleaner/20121105/ent/ent1.html.
———. "Lock Off Foreign Music!" *Jamaica Gleaner*. June 23, 2013. http://jamaica-gleaner.com/gleaner/20130623/ent/ent1.html.
———. "'Woman Time' again in Dancehall." *Jamaica Gleaner*. June 28, 2013. http://jamaica-gleaner.com/gleaner/20130618/ent/ent2.html.
———. "Is Dancehall Killing Itself?" *Jamaica Gleaner*. July 7, 2013. http://jamaica-gleaner.com/gleaner/20130707/ent/ent1.html.
Campbell, Howard. "Artistes See Upside in Buju Hung Jury." *Jamaica Gleaner*. September 28, 2010. http://jamaica-gleaner.com/gleaner/20100928/lead/lead2.html.
Cantet, Laurent, Charlotte Rampling, Karen Young, Louise Portal, and Dany Laferrière. 2005. *Vers le sud /Heading South*. [Canada]: Séville Pictures. DVD.
Channer, Colin. *Waiting in Vain: A Novel*. New York: Random House, 2010.
Chappell, Kate. "Tambourine Army Hits back against Sexual Violence in Jamaica." *The Guardian*. March 10, 2017. https://www.theguardian.com/world/2017/mar/10/jamaica-caribbean-tambourine-army-sexual-violence.
Chude-Sokei, Louis. "Post-Nationalist Geographies: Rasta, Ragga, and Reinventing Africa." *African Arts* 27, no. 4 (1994): 80–96.
Cooper, Carolyn. *Sound Clash: Jamaican Dancehall from Lady Saw to Dancehall Queen*. New York: Palgrave Macmillan, 2004.
———. *Sweet & Sour Sauce: Sexual Politics in Jamaican Dancehall Culture*. York, UK: York University/Centre for Research on Latin America and the Caribbean, 2005.
———. "At the Crossroad—Looking for Meaning in Jamaican Dancehall Culture: A Reply." *Small Axe* 10, no. 3 (2006): 193–204.
———. "Sound Clash: Jamaican Dancehall Culture at Large." *Journal of Latin American Anthropology* 11, no. 2 (2006): 501–502.
Cozier, Christopher. *Afro-Ophelia*. 2007. https://www.flickr.com/photos/56271618@N00/492693555.

Craven, Wes, dir. *The Serpent and the Rainbow*. Hollywood: Universal Pictures. 1988.
Cutteridge, J. O. *Nelson's West Indian Readers First Primer*. Oxford: Oxford University Press, 2014.
"Dancehall, The Genesis of Hip Hop?" *Jamaica Gleaner*. December 2, 2012. http://jamaica-gleaner.com/gleaner/20121202/ent/ent3.html.
Davis, Carlene. "Buju no Mandela—Lewis, Tufton Criticize Singer for Silence on Drug Conviction." *Jamaica Gleaner*. January 23, 2019. http://jamaica-gleaner.com/article/lead-stories/20190123/buju-no-mandela-lewis-tufton-criticise-singer-silence-drug-conviction, accessed December 28, 2020).
"Diddy Inks Deal to Develop Vodka Brand." *Billboard*. October 24, 2007. https://www.billboard.com/articles/news/1047716/diddy-inks-deal-to-develop-vodka-brand, accessed January 14, 2021.
"Division inside the Gully over War with Alliance." *Urban Islandz*. August 31, 2011. https://urbanislandz.com/2011/08/31/division-inside-the-gully-over-war-with-alliance/.
Dreisinger, Baz. "Reggae's Civil War." *Village Voice*. March 2, 2010. https://www.villagevoice.com/2010/03/02/reggaes-civil-war/.
Dyson, Michael Eric. "Tour(é)ing Blackness." Foreword to Tour(é), *Who's Afraid of Post-Blackness? What It Means to Be Black Now*. New York: Simon & Schuster, 2012.
Edmondson, Belinda. *Caribbean Middlebrow: Leisure Culture and the Middle Class*. Ithaca: Cornell University Press, 2009.
Elam, Harry. "The Device of Race." In *African American Performance and Theater History*, edited by Harry Elam and David Krasner, 3–16. New York: Oxford University Press, 2000.
Ellis, Nadia. *Territories of the Soul: Queered Belonging in the Black Diaspora*. Durham, NC: Duke University Press, 2015.
Ellison, Ralph. "Change the Joke and Slip the Yoke." *Partisan Review* (1958): 212–222.
———. *Invisible Man*. New York: Knopf Doubleday, 2010.
E60. "Sammy Sosa Discusses the Social Reaction to His Appearance Twitter, June 29, 2018, 3:26 P.M.. https://twitter.com/E60/status/1012779261009235971.
Escobar, Arturo. *Encountering Development: The Making and Unmaking of the Third World*. Princeton: Princeton University Press, 1995.
Farmer, Paul. *Infections and Inequalities: The Modern Plagues*. Berkeley: University of California Press, 1999.
———. *AIDS and Accusation: Haiti and the Geography of Blame*, 2nd ed. Berkeley: University of California Press, 2006.
Ferriss, Suzanne, and Mallory Young. *Chick Lit: The New Woman's Fiction*. New York: Routledge, 2006.
Fischer, Sibylle. *Modernity Disavowed: Haiti and the Cultures of Slavery in the Age of Revolution*. Durham, NC: Duke University Press, 2004.
Francis, Donette. *Fictions of Feminine Citizenship: Sexuality and the Nation in Contemporary Caribbean Literature*. New York: Palgrave Macmillan, 2010.
Franco, José Luciano. *Documentos para la historia de Haití en el Archivo Nacional*. Havana: Archivo Nacional de Cuba, 1954.
Frater, A. "Dancehall Night Exudes Class- I-Octane; Bounty Killer and Lady Saw Were the Stars." *Jamaica Gleaner*. July 13, 2013. http://jamaica-gleaner.com/gleaner/20130727/ent/ent1.html.
Freilich, M. "Cultural Diversity among Trinidadian Peasants." PhD diss., Columbia University, New York, 1960.
García Canclini, Néstor, and Yúdice, George. *Consumers and Citizens: Globalization and Multicultural Conflicts*. Minneapolis: University of Minnesota Press, 2001.

"Gaza/Portmore Empire." *Fandom*. Wikipedia, dancehall wiki. https://dancehallmusic.fandom.com/wiki/Gaza/_Portmore_Empire.

Geggus, David. *The Haitian Revolution: A Documentary History*. Indianapolis: Hackett Publishing Company, 2014.

Gerhart, Ann. "Terry McMillan's Epilogue to 'Groove' Affair: Author Files for Divorce, Claiming Husband is Gay," *Washington Post*. June 29, 2005. https://www.washingtonpost.com/archive/lifestyle/2005/06/29/terry-mcmillans-epilogue-to-groove-affair/27a46abc-bdc3-4f49-8438-e756a4c35c73/.

Gilroy, Paul. *Darker than Blue: On the Moral Economies of Black Atlantic Culture*. Cambridge, MA: Harvard University Press, 2010.

"Girl Power Drives Reggae Sumfest's Dancehall Night." *Jamaica Gleaner*. July 6, 2013. http://jamaica-gleaner.com/gleaner/20130707/ent/ent2.html

Goett, Jennifer. A. "Diasporic Identities, Autochthonous Rights: Race, Gender, and the Cultural Politics of Creole Land Rights in Nicaragua." PhD diss., University of Texas, Austin, 2006.

"Grammys Reward 'Kill LGBT' Performer Buju Banton Again." my.firedoglake.com. February 6, 2011. http://my.firedoglake.com/heathen07/tag/buju-banton-mark-myrie-grammy-murder-musi
c-dancehall-rasta-rastafari-rastafarian-jamaica-homophobia/.

Green, Sharon L. "On a Knife Edge: Sistren Theatre Collective, Grassroots Theatre, and Globalization." *Small Axe* 10, no. 3 (2006): 111–124.

Guererro, Lisa. "'Sistahs Are Doin' It for Themselves": Chick Lit in Black and White." In *Chick Lit: The New Woman's Fiction*, edited by Suzanne Ferriss and Mallory Young, 87–102. New York: Routledge. 2006.

Gunst, Laurie. *Born fi' Dead: A Journey through the Jamaican Posse Underworld*. New York: Henry Holt & Co.

Hall, Stuart. "What Is this "Black" in Black Popular Culture?" *Social Justice* 20, no. 1/2 (51–52) (1993): 104–114.

Hall, Stuart, and Robert Taylor, dir. *Representation and the Media: Featuring Stuart Hall*. 1997; Media Education Foundation, Open University.

Hamri, Sanaa, dir., *Something New*. 2006; Universal Pictures Home Entertainment, DVD.

Hartman, Saidiya. *Scenes of Subjection: Terror, Slavery, and Self-Making in. Nineteenth-Century America*. New York: Oxford University Press, 1997.

Henriques, Julian. "The Vibrations of Affect and their Propagation on a Night out on Kingston's Dancehall Scene." *Body & Society* 16, no. 1 (March 2010): 57–89.

Henry, Davina. "Still the King of the Dancehall." *Jamaica Gleaner*. July 18, 2013. http://jamaica-gleaner.com/gleaner/20130718/ent/ent4.html.

Higman, Barry W. *Jamaican Place Names*. Kingston: University of the West Indies Press, 2009.

Hippolyte, Idara. "Collapsing the 'Oral-Literary'Continuum: Jamaican Dancehall and Anglophone Caribbean Literary Culture." *Interventions* 6, no. 1 (2004): 82–100.

Hope, Donna. P. "The British Link-Up Crew: Consumption Masquerading as Masculinity in the Dancehall." *Interventions* 6, no. 1 (2004): 101–117.

———. "Passa Passa: Interrogating Cultural Hybridities in Jamaican Dancehall." *Small Axe* 10, no. 3 (2006): 125–139.

———. "Fashion ova Style: Contemporary Notions of Skin Bleaching in Jamaican Dancehall Culture." *JENdA: A Journal of Culture and African Women Studies* 4, no. 4 (2010): 165.

———. "From Browning to Cake Soap: Popular Debates on Skin Bleaching in the Jamaican Dancehall." *Journal of Pan African Studies* 4 (2011): 165–194.

Howard, David. *Kingston: A Cultural and Literary History*. Kingston: Signal, 2005.
Hunter, Karen, and Jonathan Plummer. *Balancing Act*. London: Pocket Books, 2013.
Hurston, Zora Neale. *Their Eyes Were Watching God*. New York: Amistad, 2006. (Originally published in 1937).
Huxley, Aldous. *Eyeless in Gaza*. London: Random House, 2010.
Ishawna. "Equal Rights." Legendary Records, 2017.
James, C. L. R. "What Is Art?" In *Beyond a Boundary: 50th Anniversary Edition*. Durham, NC: Duke University Press, 2013.
Johnson, Leasho. "Of Cocktails and Pum Pum." 2017. https://www.leashojohnson.com/copy-of-cocktales-and-pumpum.
Kenner, Rob. "V Opinion: Spragga Benz's 'Shotta Culture' Is the 'Detox' of Dancehall." *Vibe*. September 7, 2010. http://www.vibe.com/article/v-opinion-spragga-benzs-shotta-culture-detox-dancehall.
———. "BOOMSHOTS Heavy Rotation: Cham feat. Mykal Rose & Rodney Price 'Stronger' Remix." *Vibe*. October 22, 2010. https://www.vibe.com/music/music-news/boomshots-heavy-rotation-cham-feat-mykal-ro se-rodney-price-stronger-remix-39575/.
Kincaid, Jamaica. *A Small Place*. New York: Farrar, Straus, & Giroux, 1988.
King, J. L., and Karen Hunter. *On the Down Low: A Journey into the Lives of "Straight" Black Men Who Sleep with Men*. New York: Broadway Books. 2004.
Krampelhube, Sandra, dir. *Queens of Sound: A Herstory of Reggae and Dancehall*. Vienna: Very Vary Film Productions, 2005.
Lady Saw. "Heels on Feat. Flo Rida." *Alter Ego*. Divas Records, 2014.
Laferrière, Dany. *Dining with the Dictator*. Toronto: Coach House Press, 1994.
———. Interview quoted in "Director's Note." *Heading South* Press Kit. 2005.
———. *Heading South*. Toronto: Douglas & McIntyre. 2010.
Laughlin, Nicholas. "Working Notes: On Christopher Cozier's Tropical Night Drawings." In *Little Gestures: From the Tropical Night Series, An Exhibition at the Jaffe-Friede Gallery*. Catalog. http://nicholaslaughlin.net/tropical-night-working-notes.html.
———. "Body Counts." http://www.cheapandcleanproject.com/essays.php, accessed July 20, 2015.
Leight, Elias. "Verzuz's Founders Timbaland and Swizz Beatz—Future 25." *Rolling Stone*. October 29, 2020. https://www.rollingstone.com/pro/features/verzuz-timbaland-swizz-beatz-future-25-1079 682, accessed January 14, 2021.
Lewis, R. Anthony., and Robert Carr. "Gender, Sexuality and Exclusion: Sketching the Outlines of the Jamaican Popular Nationalist Project." *Caribbean Review of Gender Studies* 3 (2009): 1–22.
Lovelace, Earl. *The Dragon Can't Dance: A Novel*. New York: Persea Books: 1998. (Originally published 1979)
Mad Cobra. "Not Dis Face." Springvale Music, 2000.
Manuel, Peter, and Wayne Marshall. "The Riddim Method: Aesthetics, Practice, and Ownership in Jamaican Dancehall." *Popular Music* 25, no. 3 (2006): 447–470.
Massumi, Brian. *Parables for the Virtual: Movement, Affect, Sensation (Post-Contemporary Interventions)*. Durham, NC: Duke University Press, 2002.
Mbembé, J.-A., and Libby Meintjes. "Necropolitics." *Public Culture* 15, no. 1 (2003): 11–40.
McClintock, Anne. *Imperial Leather: Race, Gender, and Sexuality in the Colonial Contest*. New York: Routledge, 1995.
McMillan, Terry. *Waiting to Exhale*. New York: Viking. 1992.

———. *How Stella Got Her Groove Back*. New York: Viking, 1996.

McMillan, Uri. *Embodied Avatars: Genealogies of Black Feminist Art and Performance*. New York: NYU Press, 2015.

Meschino, Patricia. "After 10 Years in Prison, Jamaican Star Buju Banton Reclaims Musical Destiny with Historic Long Walk to Freedom Concert." *Billboard*. March 21, 2019. https://www.billboard.com/articles/news/8503607/buju-banton-long-walk-freedom-concert-jamaica-10-years-prison, accessed May 10, 2019.

Miller, Daniel. *Stuff*. London: Wiley, 2010.

Miller, Monica L. *Slaves to Fashion: Black Dandyism and the Styling of Black Diasporic Identity*. Durham, NC: Duke University Press, 2009.

MOBO Awards. "Steve McQueen | MOBO Inspiration Award Presentation." YouTube Video, 1:04. December 10, 2020. https://www.youtube.com/watch?v=DL1agM7YYUc, accessed January 11, 2020.

Morton, Stephen Morton. *Gayatri Spivak: Ethics, Subalternity and the Critique of Postcolonial Reason*. Cambridge, UK: Polity, 2007.

Mühleisen, S., and B. Migge, eds. *Politeness and Face in Caribbean Creoles*. Amsterdam: John Benjamins, 2005.

Mullings, Beverley. "Globalization, Tourism and the International Sex Trade," In *Sun, Sex and Gold: Tourism and Sex Work in the Caribbean*, edited by Kamala Kempadoo, 55–81. Oxford: Rowman & Littlefield, 1999.

Murray, Robin. "Reggae and Dancehall #12: The Months Goings On." *Clash*. September 19, 2012. http://www.clashmusic.com/feature/reggae-dancehall-12.

"Music Made Sean 'Diddy' Combs Famous, but Here's What Made Him Rich." *Washington Post*. October 2, 2015. https://www.washingtonpost.com/news/wonk/wp/2015/10/02/sean-p-diddy-combs-donal d-trump-is-not-the-only-person-who-is-a-model-mogul/?variant=116ae929826d1fd3, accessed January 14, 2021.

Naipaul, V. S. *The Middle Passage: Impressions of Five Colonial Societies*. London: Macmillan-Picador, 2001. (Originally published 1962)

Niaah, Sonia. S. "Making Space: Kingston's Dancehall Culture and Its Philosophy of 'Boundarylessness.'" *African Identities* 2, no. 2 (2004): 117–132.

Noel, Peter. "Batty Boys in Babylon: West Indian Gay Culture Comes out in Brooklyn, and so Does Violence." *Village Voice*. January 12, 1993, 29–36.

Obama, Barack. "A More Perfect Union." Speech delivered at the National Constitution Center, Philadelphia, March 18, 2008.

O'Callaghan, Evelyn. *Woman Version: Theoretical Approaches to West Indian Fiction by Women*. London: St. Martin's Press, 1993.

Olsen, Barbara, and Stephen Gould. "Revelations of Cultural Consumer Lovemaps in Jamaican Dancehall Lyrics: An Ethnomusicological Ethnography." *Consumption, Markets and Culture* 11, no. 4 (2008): 229–257.

OnStage TV. "FOOTA HYPE: "ISHAWNA GIMMI BUN WITH SCATTA."" YouTube Video, 18:31. September 20, 2014. https://www.youtube.com/watch?v=EhAkkF-8-oA.

———. "ISHAWNA: "FOOTA BEAT ME IN FRONT OF MY CHILD."" YouTube Video, 21:09. September 27, 2014. https://www.youtube.com/watch?v=-QhpmnbtmYs.

———. "Marion Hall, Formerly Lady Saw, back in School, Opens up on New Life." YouTube Video, 25:17. January 3, 2017. https://www.youtube.com/watch?v=LOHrsJMO9sU, accessed April 5, 2018.

———. "Buju Banton Is Still Buju Banton after 10 Years in Captivity, Unbroken Reggae Warrior." YouTube Video, 12:43. March 17, 2019. https://www.youtube.com/watch?v=w9hBjr-Swb8, accessed March 20, 2020.

Patterson, Ebony. "The Of 72 Project." *Small Axe* 16, no. 2 (2012): 119–138.
———. *Ebony G. Patterson: Dead Treez. Invisible Presence: Bling Memories*. Atlanta Contemporary Art Center. 2014.
———. "Excerpts from an Interview with Ebony Patterson." Interview by Karen
Patterson. November 30, 2015. https://issuu.com/moniquemelochegallery/docs/ep15-_dead_treez_publication_for_is./
Patton, Stacey. "Black Dandies Fashion New Academic Identities." *Chronicle of Higher Education.* May 1, 2013. https://www.chronicle.com/article/black-dandies-fashion-new-academic-identities/?cid2=gen_login_refresh&cid=gen_sign_in.
Paul, Annie, "Hung out to Dry . . . Who were the Tivoli 73? A Preview of Ebony G. Patterson's Of 72." *Active Voice* (blog). March 17, 2012. http://anniepaul.net/2012/03/17/who-were-the-tivoli-73-a-preview-of-ebony-g-pattersons-of-72, accessed July 16, 2015.
"Peep This: White Dancehall Queen Goes In." *Vibe*. 2011. http://www.vibe.com/article/peep-white-dancehall-queen-goes.
Pierre, Brittny. "Dancehall Star Vibz Kartel Charged with Murder." *Vibe*. October 4, 2011. http://www.vibe.com/article/dancehall-star-vybz-kartel-charged-murder.
Pinnock, Agostinho. M. "'A Ghetto Education Is Basic': (Jamaican) Dancehall Masculinities as Counter-Culture." *Journal of Pan African Studies* 1, no. 9 (2007): 47.
Plummer, Jonathan, and Terry McMillan. *Oprah Winfrey Show*. Interview by Oprah Winfrey, November 9, 2005. https://www.youtube.com/watch?v=5F8ol4bLurE&t=105s/.
"Popcaan Speak out against Kidnappers—Lady Saw Talk about Being Rape!!"
Rawpa Crawpa Vlog2.YouTube Video, 10:01. February 19, 2017. https://www.youtube.com/watch?v=39buYW-CPyo, accessed January 12, 2018.
Pruitt, Deborah, and Suzanne LaFont. "For Love and Money Romance Tourism in Jamaica." *Annals of Tourism Research* 22, no. 2 (1999): 422–440.
Puri, Shalini. "Canonized Hybridities, Resistant Hybridities: Chutney Soca, Carnival, and the Politics of Nationalism." In *Caribbean Romances: The Politics of Regional Representation*, edited by Belinda Edmondson, 12–38. Charlottesville: University Press of Virginia, 1999.
———. *The Caribbean Postcolonial: Social Equality, Post/Nationalism, and Cultural Hybridity*. 2004. New York: Palgrave Macmillan.
Reddock, Rhoda. *Women, Labour & Politics in Trinidad & Tobago: A History*. Kingston: Ian Randle, 1994.
Rhys, Jean, Judith L. Raiskin, and Charlotte Brontë. 1999. *Wide Sargasso Sea*. New York: W. W. Norton.
Roach, Joseph R. *Cities of the Dead: Circum-Atlantic Performance*. New York: Columbia University Press, 1996.
Roslan, Chris. "Statement Regarding Pat Robertson's Comments on Haiti." *CBN*. January 12, 2010. http://www.cbn.com/about/pressrelease_patrobertson_haiti.aspx.
Ross, Andrew. "Mr. Reggae DJ, Meet the International Monetary Fund." *Black Renaissance* 1, no. 3 (July 1998): 208.
Rowley, Michelle V. *Feminist Advocacy and Gender Equity in the Anglophone Caribbean: Envisioning a Politics of Coalition*. London: Routledge, 2011.
Saunders, Patricia. "Defending the Dead, Confronting the Archive: An Interview with M. NourbeSe Philip." *Small Axe* 26 (June 2008): 63–79.
———"Gardening in the Garrisons, You Never Know What You Will Find: (Un)Visibility in the Works of Ebony G. Patterson." *Feminist Studies* vol. 42, no. 1 (2016): 98–137.

Semaj-Hall, Isis. "Dub Versioning Ishawna's 'Equal Rights': From Chanting down to Louding Up." *Jamaica Journal* 37, no 1–2 (2018).

Senior, Olive. *Gardening in the Tropics*. Toronto: Insomniac Press, 2005.

Serwer, Jesse. "Vybz Kartel: Still Ruling Dancehall after Years in Prison." *Rolling Stone*. November 16, 2016. https://www.rollingstone.com/music/music-features/vybz-kartel-speaks-after-five-years-in-prison-he-still-rules-dancehall-122188/.

Shabba Ranks. "Wicked in Bed." VP Records, 1990.

Sharpe, Christina. *In the Wake: On Blackness and Being*. Durham, NC: Duke University Press, 2016.

Shaw-Nevins, Andrea. E. "Tuck in Yuh Belly": Imperatives of Female Slenderness in Jamaican Dancehall Music." *Fat Studies* 1, no. 2 (2012): 40–152.

Sheller, Mimi. *Consuming the Caribbean: From Arawaks to Aombies*. London: Routledge. 2003.

———. *Citizenship from Below: Erotic Agency and Caribbean Freedom*. Durham, NC: Duke University Press, 2012.

Smith, Caroline J. *Cosmopolitan Culture and Consumerism in Chick Lit*. New York: Routledge, 2008.

Smith, Faith. "Waiting in Vain." *Small Axe* 5, no. 2 (2001): 41–59.

———. "'You Know You're West Indian if . . .': Codes of Authenticity in Colin Channer's 'Crosses/Crossroads/Crossings.'" *Small Axe* 11, no. 3 (2007): 130–138.

Spivak, Gayatri Chakravorty. *Can the Subaltern Speak?* Basingstoke: Macmillan, 1988.

Spragga Benz. "Cyan Get No Gyal." *Platinum Jam 2000: The Bug and The Clone Riddims*. Madhouse Records, 2000.

Stanley-Niaah, Sonia. "Kingston's Dancehall A Story of Space and Celebration." *Space and Culture* 7, no. 1 (2004): 102–118.

———. "'Dis Slackness Ting': A Dichotomizing Master Narrative in Jamaican Dancehall." *Caribbean Quarterly* (2005): 55–76.

"'Stella' Exhales in Nasty Divorce." *The Smoking Gun*. June 30, 2005. http://www.thesmokinggun.com/documents/celebrity/stella-exhales-nasty-divorce.

Stephens, Michelle. *Skin Acts: Race, Psychoanalysis, and the Black Male Performer*. Durham, NC: Duke University Press, 2014.

Thelwell, Michael. *The Harder They Come: A Novel*. United States: Grove Press, 1988. (Originally published 1980)

Thomas, Deborah A. *Modern Blackness: Nationalism, Globalization, and the Politics of Culture in Jamaica*. Durham, NC: Duke University Press, 2004.

———. *Exceptional Violence: Embodied Citizenship in Transnational Jamaica*. Durham, NC: Duke University Press, 2011.

Thompson, Krista A. *An Eye for the Tropics: Tourism, Photography, and Framing the Caribbean Picturesque*. Durham, NC: Duke University Press, 2006.

———. *Shine: The Visual Economy of Light in African Diasporic Aesthetic Practice*. Durham, NC: Duke University Press, 2015.

"T.I. Says Sammy Sosa's Alleged Skin Bleaching Is 'Self-Hate.'" TMZ Sports. November 13, 2017. https://www.tmz.com/2017/11/13/t-i-sammy-sosa-t-i-mlb-skin-bleaching/.

Tosh, Peter. "Equal Rights." Track #5, side 2, *Equal Rights*. Columbia Records, 1999.

Touré. *Who's Afraid of Post-Blackness? What It Means to Be Black Now*. New York: Free Press, 2011.

Townsend, Robert, dir., *Eddie Murphy Raw—Dexter St. Jacques Scene*. Hollywood: TM & Paramount, 1987. DVD.

Ulysse, Gina. *Downtown Ladies: Informal Commercial Importers, a Haitian Anthropologist and Self-Making in Jamaica*. Chicago: University of Chicago Press. 2008.

"Vybz Kartel Lectures at UWI." YouTube Video, 17:10. March 11, 2011. https://www.youtube.com/watch?v=-8gdAnOPf1Q.
Walcott, Derek. "The Caribbean: Culture or Mimicry?" *Journal of Interamerican Studies and World Affairs* 16, no. 1 (1974): 3–13.
Walcott-Hackshaw, Elizabeth. "The Anthropologist. http://caribbeanreviewofbooks.com/crb-archive/24-november-2010/the-anthropologist/, accessed October 20, 2021.
Wandera, Hussein. "Spice Explains Her Fake Skin Bleaching Photo: 'I Wanted to Create Awareness to "Colorism.'" The Fader. November 2, 2018. https://www.thefader.com/2018/11/02/spice-explains-skin-bleaching-photo, accessed January 9, 2019.
White, Annika. Y. "A Content Analysis of Popular Themes and Sexuality in Rap and Reggae Music." PhD diss., Washington State University, Seattle, 2010.
Williams, Eric Eustace. *From Columbus to Castro: The History of the Caribbean, 1492–1969*. New York: Vintage Books, 1984.

Index

Note: Page numbers followed by "f" indicate figures.

3 Canal, 169

Aching, Gerard, 10
aesthetics
  African diaspora, 163
  of concealment, 21, 64, 107
  dancehall, 113, 114–123, 133–135, 165–166, 184
  post-Black aesthetics, 97–99
  of taste, 77–78
Afari, Yasus, 178–179
Afro-alienation acts, 124, 176
agency
  dancehall culture and, 18
  erotic agency, 14
  free agency, 188
  masculinity and, 165
  political and social agency, 15
  sexual agency, 70–71, 79, 82, 88–89, 91, 92, 128
  "strategic withholding" and, 70–71, 79
  zombies and, 68
Aidonia, 103
Alcindor, Yamiche, 187
Alexander, Blayne, 187
Alexander, M. Jacqui, 40, 44
Alice Yard, 2–3, 168–171, 195n2
Allsopp, Jeannette, 68
Allsopp, Richard, 68
Almond, Steve, 48–49
anancyism, 12, 13, 59, 68, 126–129
Anansi, 196n5. *See also* anancyism
antigay sentiment, 24–25, 29–32, 43–44, 59–60, 103, 109–110. *See also* homophobia
Arbery, Ahmaud, 187
Archer, Petrine, 101, 112, 113, 201n15
Art Basel (Miami), 1
Ash Wednesday, 3
aspiration, 2, 6, 8–9, 157
austerity, 28, 32
"authenticating culture," 9
authentic food, 52–56, 79
authenticity, 5–6, 9–10, 12, 25, 52, 68, 79

Baby Doll, 103
Baby Cham, 179
  "Another Level" (with Bounty Killer), 41–43
  "Ghetto Pledge" (with Bounty Killer), 43–44
Baker, Lorenzo Dow, 51
Balancing Act (Hunter and Plummer), 12, 48, 60–69, 85
bananas, 8, 51, 145–146
Barnes, Natasha, 10–11, 30–32
"barrel children," 35
Bataille, George, 74

Beenie Man, 131, 132, 151, 186, 197n16
Bembe Thursday, 113, 159
Beyoncé, 111, 186
biopower, 74
Black academics, 99–100, 200–201n2
Black dandies, 99–102, 113–114, 167
Black diaspora, 22, 99–100, 102, 104, 107–108, 125, 146–147, 160–161, 175, 178–181, 185–188
#blacklivesmatter, 158
Black nationalism, 72, 78, 136–137, 179
Black self-fashioning, 4, 15–17, 93–123
  commodity fetishism and, 95–96, 107
  continuity as mode of performance, 160
  cricket and, 4
  marketing of, 175
  origins of, 160–161
  skin bleaching and skin lightening, 15–16, 94–95, 102–113
  See also fashion
Black subjectivity, 105, 112, 125, 160, 175, 177, 181
Black transnationalism, 28, 33, 94
Blak Rhyno, 103
bling
  NBA players and, 16, 101
  Patterson on, 161
  Patterson's multimedia installations and, 21, 165, 168–173
Bling Dawg, 103
Bodies in Dissent: Spectacular Performances of Race and Freedom (Brooks), 124, 135
body modification, 15–16, 94–95, 104–108, 111. *See also* Black self-fashioning; skin bleaching and skin lightening; tattoos
Bolt, Usain, 6
"Boops" (Super Cat), 36
Born fi' Dead (Gunst), 35–36, 196–197n4
Bounty Killer, 179, 186
  "Another Level" (with Baby Cham), 41–43
  "Anytime," 33–35
  B.F.F. Labor Day performance, 141–142, 204n6
  collaborations, 132
  The Fifth Element, 33–34
  founder of Gully Alliance, 103
  "Ghetto Pledge" (with Baby Cham), 43–44
  "Look into My Eyes," 141–142
  "Me Cyaan Believe Mi Eyes," 141
  "No Cream in Mi Face," 142
  "the poor people's governor," 28
Bourdieau, Pierre, 54
Brooks, Daphne, 125, 126, 135, 176
Buju Banton, 23–25, 28–31, 33
  absence from Grammy Awards, 29–30
  "Boom Bye-Bye," 24, 25–26, 31
  Before the Dawn, 28–30
  career and success of, 24
  drug trafficking charges, 29–30
  "Give I Strength," 181
  on Kartel, 182
  "Long Walk to Freedom" tour, 177–181
  "Not an Easy Road," 180
  Rastafarianism and, 28, 33, 179, 181
  release from prison, 177
  Til Shiloh, 25
  "Untold Stories," 23, 25, 26
Bush, George W., 185
Busy Signal, 103

Cantet, Laurent, 14, 56, 60, 79–88
capitalism, 16–17, 24, 26, 51, 55
Capleton (aka The Fireman), 24–25, 41, 197n16
Cappo, 109
"Caribbean middlebrow," 6, 8–9
Carnival
  costs of, 2–3
  cross-cultural trade of, 26–27
  as subculture in United States, 26–27
  in Trinidad and Tobago, 2–4, 20, 168, 173
Carnival Tuesday, 3
Carpentier, Alejo, 74
Catholic Church, 24, 37–38, 41, 197n16
Ce'Cile, 127, 128
Channer, Colin, 199n5
chick lit, definition of, 48
Christian Broadcasting Network, 76–77
Chronixx, 186–188
Chude-Sokei, Louis, 45
circuits of consumption, 12, 14–15, 17, 71, 79, 80, 92, 123, 183. *See also* consumption
Cobra, 36–38
commodity fetishism, 10, 16, 55–56, 80, 95–96, 107
conscious vibes music and artists, 24–25, 41
consuming Blackness, 85–86, 94–98. *See also* consumption

Consuming the Caribbean: From Arawaks to Zombies (Sheller), 29
consumption
of Blackness, 85–86, 94–98
Carnival and, 2–4
circuits of, 12, 14–15, 17, 71, 79, 80, 92, 123, 183
conspicuous, 2, 3, 53
ethics of, 54
of fashion, 101–113
of female sexuality, 15
globalization and, 17, 26, 35, 52, 55, 58, 62, 64, 69, 80
ironies of, 51
mobilities of, 29
palates of, 52
patterns of, 82
of representations of Black youth culture, 15
rituals of, 3
technologies of, 80
of women's bodies, 143
See also food
Cooper, Carolyn, 127, 178
COVID-19 pandemic, 184–188
Cozier, Christopher, 2–3, 20, 146–150
Afro-Ophelia, 147–148, 149f
see-through body, 148, 150f
Tropical Night, 20, 146–150
Craven, Wes, 50, 77–78
cricket, 4, 125, 182
Crop Over, 2
"Cyan Get No Gyal" (Spragga Benz), 38–39

dancehall aesthetics and culture, 15–19, 113, 114–123, 126–127, 133–135, 165–166, 184
antigay sentiment and homophobia, 24–25, 29–32, 43–44, 59–60, 103, 109–110, 112
anxieties expressed in dancehall songs, 10–11, 28–29, 45, 67–68, 94
Bembe Thursday, 113, 159
"class-coded cultural practices," 33
dancehall music as insurgent mode of mobility, 10, 27–29
female genitalia and, 115, 117–118, 123
foreign appeal of, 24
informative function of dancehall music, 27–28
masculinity and, 31, 32, 37, 104, 112, 131, 132
modes of consumption in dancehall lyrics, 32–36
Passa Passa, 112, 113, 159, 163
respect/respectability and, 32–33
slackness and, 10, 18, 24, 44
visibility and, 108
Weddi Weddi, 113
See also Bounty Killer; Buju Banton; deejays; Ishawna; Kartel, Vybz; Lady Saw; Spice
de Certeau, Michel, 111
deejays, 27–28, 31
female, 18, 44–45, 127–128, 143, 175
See also Bounty Killer; Buju Banton; Ishawna; Lady Saw; Spice
dehumanization, 17, 124, 198n22
Dennis, Craig, 103, 109
desire
beyond desire, 184, 185
consuming fashion and, 101–113
economies of, 48, 53–54, 56–57
Lady Saw and, 126–131, 143, 176
Laferrière on, 174
in works of Laferrière, 13, 14, 70–72, 79, 174–175
Dessalines, Jean-Jacques, 72, 73
dick lit, definition of, 48–49
Diggs, Taye, 12, 53
Dining with the Dictator (Laferrière), 14, 79, 92
Le gout des jeunes filles (French title), 70–71
title change from *Le gout des jeunes filles*, 70–71
Dominican Republic, 76, 77, 105–106
The Dragon Can't Dance (Lovelace), 4
Dreisinger, Baz, 103–104
DuBois, W. E. B., 114
Duke, Winston, 6
Duke University, 99
Dyson, Michael Eric, 97–99

economies of desire, 48, 53–54, 56–57. *See also* desire
Eddie Murphy Raw (Townsend; 1987), 198n3
Edmondson, Belinda, 6, 8–9
Elephant Man, 103, 197nn15–16
Ellis, Nadia, 17–18, 94, 185–186, 187
Ellison, Ralph, 131, 167, 170, 202n1 (chap. 6)
Encountering Development: The Making and Unmaking (Escobar), 26, 196n1

"Equal Rights" (Ishawna), 19, 135–137, 140–142, 179
Escobar, Arturo, 26, 41, 196n1
Exceptional Violence (Thomas), 11
exoticism, 5, 8, 12, 17, 24, 27, 50–52, 69, 82, 145
An Eye for the Tropics: Tourism, Photography, and Framing the Caribbean Picturesque (Thompson), 7, 51

Fanon, Frantz, 106
Farmer, Paul, 77, 200n7, 200n9
fashion, 15–17, 93–99
  Black academics and, 99–100, 200–201n2
  Black dandies, 99–102, 113–114, 167
  Carnival and, 2–3
  commodity fetishism and, 95–96, 107
  "fashioning" of Blackness, 99–114
  knockoffs and counterfeits, 2, 5, 13, 68
  as mode of gendered and racial performance, 107
  NBA and, 16, 100–102, 200–201n2
  "post-Black" era and, 95–97
  "touring" Blackness and, 98–99
  See also Black self-fashioning
Fashion Week, 1
femininity, 18, 31, 40
feminism, 126–130, 135–139
  ghetto feminism, 126–130, 137, 139
  global feminism, 89
  sexual pleasure and, 88–89, 92
  "tun-up" pum-pum and, 117
  Western liberal feminism, 45
Ferriss, Suzanna, 48
"First World," 14, 54, 62
Fischer, Sybille, 72, 73, 75
Floyd, George, 187
folk culture, 12, 16, 113
folklore, 196n5
food
  "authentic," 52–56, 79
  in Laferrière's novels, 13, 79–80, 83–84, 89–92
  sex, power, pleasure, and, 13, 79–80, 83–84, 89–90, 92
  United Fruit Company, 51–52
Foota Hype, 19, 137–139, 202n6
"foreign," use of the term, 198n17
"foreign" consumers, 128–129
"foreign" influence, 38–44
"foreign" tastes, 80, 126, 129
Foucault, Michel, 74

Gardening in the Tropics (Senior), 21, 145–147, 166
gay culture, 43–44. *See also* LGBTQ people and issues
Gaza Empire, 103–104, 109–110, 132, 181–182
gaze, 7, 62, 84, 96, 107, 112, 127, 133, 165
ghetto feminism, 126–130, 137, 139
globalization, 17, 26, 35, 52, 55, 58, 62, 64, 69, 80
glocal communities and consumption, 24, 27
Golden, Thelma, 98–99
Golding, Bruce, 104, 113
Granderson Lab, 2–3, 195n2
Guerrero, Lisa, 49–50
Gully Alliance, 103–104
"Gully Queens," 110
Gunst, Laurie, 35–36, 196–197n4

Haiti
  "darkness" and, 72
  history of, 72–75, 77–78, 80, 90
    HIV/AIDS and, 77, 200n7, 200n9
    Jamaica compared with, 71–72
    necro-politics and necro-romance in popular representations of, 73–78
  in popular imagination, 71–72, 73–78
  religion and, 75, 76–77, 78
  sovereignty and, 73–75, 87
  voudoun culture, 72–78, 87
  See also Laferrière, Dany
Haitian Revolution, 72–75, 77–78, 80, 90
Halberstam, Jack, 12, 196n6
Hall, Marion. *See* Lady Saw
Hall, Stuart, 96, 104, 106, 108, 112
Hamilton, Grace Latoya. *See* Spice
Hammond, Beres, 151
The Harder They Come (Thelwell), 117, 128, 136, 142, 165
Harlem Renaissance, 114
Harney, Stefano, 10
Hartman, Saidiya, 111–112
Heading South (Cantet; 2005), 14, 56, 79–88
Heading South (Laferrière), 14, 174–175
  "Beach Bar," 90
  Caribbean pop culture and, 14
  dining and consumption in, 78–92

"Heading South," 79–80, 84–85
"A Mortal Blow," 90
"The Network," 89
strategic withholding in, 70–71, 79
Hegel, Georg Wilhelm Friedrich, 74–75
"High Mas'" (Rudder), 115
hip-hop, 16, 30, 33, 53, 93–94, 100–102, 112, 133–134, 200–201n2
HIV/AIDS, 30, 77, 114, 200n7, 200n9
Holland, Sharon, 99
homophobia, 11, 24, 25, 30–32, 113. *See also* antigay sentiment
homosexuality. *See* LGBTQ people and issues; queer
Hope, Donna, 108, 109
How Stella Got Her Groove Back (McMillan), 12, 48–61, 64, 68–69, 71, 198–199n3
commodity fetishism and, 55–56, 64
food in, 52–56
oral sex and sexual positions in, 64–65
sexuality in, 55–59
How Stella Got Her Groove Back (Sullivan; 1998), 12, 50, 57–58
Hunter, Karen
Balancing Act (with Plummer), 48, 60–69, 85
On the Down Low: A Journey into the Lives of 'Straight' Black Men Who Sleep with Men (with King), 60
Hurston, Zora Neale, 49
Hype, Lisa, 103

Imperial Leather (McClintock), 55–56
informal commercial importers (ICIs), 2, 35–36
International Monetary Fund (IMF), 32, 41, 197n7
Ishawna, 135–143
B.F.F. Labor Day performance, 140–141
collaborations, 175
"Equal Rights and Justice," 19, 135–140–142, 179
"Everybody Needs Someone," 140
Foota Hype and, 19, 137–139, 175, 202n6
"Mi Belly," 140
"Slippery When Wet," 140
Iverson, Allen, 16, 101

Jamaica
All Angles (television talk show), 108
antigay sentiment and homophobia in, 24–25, 29–32, 43–44, 59–60, 103, 109–110, 113
austerity measures, 28, 31
Economic Protection Zones (EPZs), 35
"fashan ova style," 94, 104
foreign influences on, 38–44
Haiti compared with, 71–72
labor riots in, 136
poverty in, 33–34, 35, 36, 39
See also Bounty Killer; Buju Banton; conscious vibes music and artists; dancehall aesthetics and culture; Ishawna; Lady Saw; Patterson, Ebony G.; Spice
James, C. L. R., 125
James, LeBron, 111
Jay-Z, 111, 112, 186
J Capri, 176
Jeffries, Hasan Kwame, 99
Johnson, James Weldon, 114
Johnson, Leasho, 16–17, 115, 116–123
6:30, 122f
Back-fi-a-bend, 123f
Di Good Hole, 120f
Gumtion, 119f
Pum-Pum Tun-Up East and West, 117f
Pum-Pum Tun-Up Heaven Bound, 121f
Pum-Pum Tun-Up North and South, 118f
Stab-up the Meat, 116f
Johnson, Rashid, 98

Kartel, Vybz, 181–184
"Benz Punaany," 115
bleaching crème line, 16
collaborations, 175
"Coloring Book," 108–109
Dons and Divas, 182
"Ever Blessed," 114, 115, 117
"Eye of Providence" tattoo, 111
feud with Mavado, 103–104
"The Good Hole," 115
"Gumtion," 115
"Happy Pum-Pum," 117
incarceration, 181–182
lyrical turn of, 15, 94–95
murder conviction, 181–182

Kartel (cont.)
"pum-pum laureate" of Jamaican dancehall music, 15, 94, 115
"Pum-pum Paradise," 117
Shebada (stage character), 110
skin bleaching controversy, 15–16, 94–95, 102–105
speech at University of the West Indies, 104
"Summertime," 182
tattoos, 109–111
THUG tattoo, 109, 201n14
Kincaid, Jamaica, 60, 199n4
knockoffs, 2, 5

Lady Saw, 44–45
anancyism and, 126–129
candidness of, 131
childhood sexual abuse, 175–176
collaborations, 131–132
departure from dancehall music, 175–176, 203n2
featured in "Bossman," 131, 132
featured in "Healing," 131
ghetto feminism and, 128–130
"Heels on Feat. Flo Rida," 132
lyrics of, 126, 127–132
"No Less than a Woman (Infertility)," 128
performance of, 17–18, 127–132, 143
queer performance and, 17–18
Sting performance, 129–131, 137
"Summer Love," 132
Laferrière, Dany
colonialism and imperialism in works of, 71, 80, 88–89, 92
"cultures of taste" in works of, 13–14
on desire as political metaphor, 174
desire in works of, 13, 14, 70–72, 79, 174–175
"fair trade" practices in works of, 15, 71, 79
food, sex, power, and pleasure pyramid in works of, 13, 79–80, 83–84, 89–90, 92
How to Make Love to a Negro without Getting Tired, 71, 90
mechanism of survival in works of, 13–15
pleasure in works of, 13, 14–15, 78, 79, 84, 88–90, 92
politics of positionality in works of, 92
power negotiations and politics in works of, 14–15, 71, 78–82, 84–86, 87–92
sexuality in works of, 13–15, 70–71, 78–92, 174–175
social hierarchies in works of, 80, 82, 87, 89, 92
visual literacy in works of, 82
Why Must a Black Writer always Write about Sex, 71
women as sociosexual beings in works of, 91–92
See also Dining with the Dictator (Laferrière); *Heading South* (Cantet; 2005); *Heading South* (Laferrière)
Laughlin, Nicholas, 2–3
Le gout des jeunes filles (Laferrière). *See Dining with the Dictator* (Laferrière)
Leonard, Sean, 2–3
Lewis, Rupert, 177, 179
LGBTQ people and issues
activist Latoya Nugent, 135
antigay sentiment in Jamaica, 24–25, 29–32, 43–44, 59–60, 103, 109–110
in *Balancing Act* (Hunter and Plummer), 65, 66
Buju Banton controversy, 24–25, 28–31
in dancehall lyrics, 24–25, 28–31, 40–41, 43, 44, 197n16
gay tourists, 44
homophobia, 11, 24, 25, 30–32, 112
Kartel's Shebada stage performance and, 109–110
masculinity and, 110
McMillan-Plummer marriage and divorce, 52, 58–60, 69
"nonproductive" sexuality and, 32, 43
religion and, 37, 38
Sodom and Gomorrah, 40, 41
state-administered codes of conduct and, 39
use of the term "queer," 17–18
"local" communities, 26–27
"local" tastes, 126, 129
Locke, Hew, 146
Lovelace, Earl, 4
lowbrow culture, 6–7, 8–9
Lowe, Lisa, 12, 196n6
"lower regions," 8, 12, 15, 94–95, 113

magazines, fashion and self-help, 48
Major League Baseball (MLB), 101, 105–107
Mandela, Nelson, 177, 179

"market goods," definition of, 47–48
Marley, Bob, 6, 51
Marshall, Wayne, 103
Martin, Trayvon, 102
Marx, Karl, 55
masculinity
dancehall culture and, 31, 32, 37, 104, 112, 131, 132
Kartel and, 183, 184
masking and, 131
in Patterson's multimedia installations, 16ver163, 165
performance of Black masculinity, 92, 95,
power structures and, 126
racism and, 95
sexuality and, 13, 28–29, 109
in sistah/chick/dick lit, 49, 60
social mobility and, 92
Masicka, 109
masking, 101, 112, 131
Mavado, 103–104
Mbembe, Achille, 74–75, 77
McAlister, Elizabeth, 126
McClintock, Anne, 55–56
McMillan, Terry
Disappearing Acts, 49
divorce from Plummer, 12, 52–53, 57, 58–60, 68–69
marriage to Plummer, 52–53, 58–69
as progenitor of sistah lit genre, 49
Waiting to Exhale, 49, 50, 52–53
See also How Stella Got Her Groove Back (McMillan)
McMillan, Uri, 125
Meintjes, Libby, 74–75, 77
"middlebrow, Caribbean," 6, 8–9
middle class, 8–9, 31–33, 50, 52–53, 62–63, 79, 82, 112–113, 126, 167, 178
Miller, Daniel, 162, 167
Miller, Dionne Jackson, 108
Miller, Kei, 195n1
Miller, Monica, 94, 99, 113–114, 160–161
Minaj, Nicki, 6
mobilities of consumption, 29
mobility, 8–9, 10, 13, 27, 28, 92, 104, 113, 125, 126, 182, 185
Montego Bay, Jamaica, 5
Mullings, Beverly, 52, 57
Myrie, Mark. *See* Buju Banton

National Basketball Association (NBA), 16, 100–102, 200–201n2
nationalism, 2, 10–11, 14, 28, 40, 43, 45, 113, 196n6, 198n17, 198n22. *See also* Black nationalism
Nazareth Moravian Church protest, 176
Negril, Jamaica, 5
New Orleans, 3, 4, 153–154
Noel, Peter, 38, 44
"Not Dis Face" (Cobra), 36–38
Nuclear, 103

Obama, Barack, 95–96–97
Obama, Michelle, 186
O'Callaghan, Evelyn, 128
Ocho Rios, Jamaica, 5
oral sex, 16, 37–44, 64–65, 138
cunnilingus, 24, 38, 40, 130
fellatio, 24, 38, 40, 63, 65
outernational communities, 27
"outing," 17, 18

Palmer, Adidja. *See* Kartel, Vybz
"paradise", Caribbean, 5, 14–15, 20, 49–50, 62, 86
Passa Passa, 112, 113, 159, 163
patronage, 62
Patterson, Ebony G., 20
9 of 219 Project, 169–173, 169f, 170f, 171f
in di grass-beyond the bladez, 21, 153, 155–156, 156f
Invisible Presence: Bling Memories, 21–22, 172f, 173
New Orleans Prospect 3: Notes for Now, 153–154
"Of, 72 Project," 21–22, 148–153, 151f, 152f, 185–186
shrubz, 153, 157, 157f, 158f
two birds-beyond the bladez, 153–154, 154f, 155f
Paul, Annie, 110, 152
Paul, Sean, 131–132
perverse modernities, 12, 114
piercings, 130
Pimp C, 160, 161, 167
pimp/prostitute paradigm, 61, 67
Plummer, Jonathan
Balancing Act (with Hunter), 48, 60–69, 85
divorce from McMillan, 12, 52–53, 57, 58–60, 68–69

Plummer, Jonathan (cont.)
interview on *Oprah Winfrey Show*, 59–60
marriage to McMillan, 52–53, 58–69
restraining order filed against McMillan, 58–59, 60, 66
Poitier, Sidney, 6
police
in "Anytime" (Bounty Killer), 34, 35
attitudes toward LGBTQ people, 109, 110
in Ghetto Pledge" (Bounty Killer and Baby Cham), 44
in *Heading South* (Cantet; 2005), 84, 87
rape victims and, 66
police brutality and violence, 95, 158, 187, 204n15
policing
moral policing, 37, 43
self-policing in the public sphere, 125–126
of sexuality and bodies, 11, 19, 28, 31, 32, 176, 184
of women as cultural producers and consumers, 175
Popcaan, 103
Portal, Louise, 80
poverty
in "Another Level" (Baby Cham and Bounty Killer), 41–42
in "Anytime" (Bounty Killer), 33–34, 35
body modification and, 108, 112
dancehall aesthetics and, 113
desire and, 174
fashion and, 159, 162, 164
freedom of sexual expression and, 89
in "Ghetto Pledge" (Baby Cham and Bounty Killer), 43–44
globalization and, 35
in Haiti, 76, 87, 89
in Jamaica, 33–34, 35, 36, 39
middlebrow literature and, 8–9
in *The Serpent and the Rainbow* (Craven; 1998), 50
sexuality and, 41–42, 59
stereotypes of, 50, 62–63, 72
praise songs, 114, 115, 117, 137
Prince Pin, 142
productivity, 28, 32, 39–45, 60, 61
Prospect 3: Notes for Now (New Orleans), 153–154
"pum-pum," 15, 45, 94, 114, 115, 117, 137, 138
"pum-pum tun up," 115, 117, 160
Puri, Shalini, 10

queer
queering aesthetic practices in dancehall culture, 114–123
racial queering, 15–16
use of the term, 17–18, 94

racism
COVID-19 pandemic and, 187–188
fashion and, 95
institutional, 125
liberalism and, 85
"post-Blackness" and, 95, 97
Rampling, Charlotte, 80, 86
rape, 66, 135, 136, 176, 200n11
Rastafarianism
Buju Banton and, 28, 33, 179, 181
Capleton and, 24, 41
conscious vibes music, 24–25, 41
flag, 41, 155, 179
Rebel, Tony, 24–25
reggae, 25, 27, 29, 30, 33, 38, 50, 61, 102, 103, 177–178, 183–184, 197n9
religion
antigay sentiment and, 25, 37, 43
"Black progress" narratives and, 111, 112
Christian Broadcasting Network, 76–77
dancehall culture and, 25, 28, 30, 32–33, 37
Haiti and, 75, 76–77, 78
Rastafarianism, 24–25, 28, 33, 41, 155, 179, 181
Roman Catholic Church, 24, 37–38, 41, 197n16
voudoun culture, 72–78, 87, 200n7
remixes, 20, 21, 137, 140, 142, 176
respect, 11, 32–33, 44, 63, 141, 162, 165, 178, 183
respectability, 32–33, 44, 61–63, 104, 113, 117–118, 125, 126, 167, 178–179
Rhys, Jean, 144–145
Rihanna, 6, 111
rituals of consumption, 3. *See also* consumption
Roach, Joseph, 3
Robertson, Pat, 76–77, 112
Roman Catholic Church, 24, 37–38, 41, 197n16

Roslan, Chris, 76
Ross, Andrew, 27
Rudder, David, 115

Safhya, 103
Savage, 103
Schaap, Jeremy, 105–106
"Second World," 62. *See also* worlding
Segal, Lynne, 88, 92
self-fashioning. *See* Black self-fashioning
Semaj-Hall, Isis, 135–137
Senior, Olive, 153, 156
  "Brief Lives," 166–167
  Gardening in the Tropics, 21, 145–147, 166
  "Meditation on Yellow," 145
The Serpent and the Rainbow (Craven; 1998), 50, 77–78
sexual assault, 84, 175, 176, 200n11
sexual deviance, 19, 41–42, 138–139, 175
sexuality
  consumption of, 15
  feminism and, 88–89, 92
  poverty and, 42, 59, 89
  tropes of, 68
  in works of Laferrière, 13–15, 70–71, 78–92, 174–175
  in works of McMillan, 55–59, 64–65
sexual pleasure, 88–89, 92
sexual positions, 64–65
Shabba Ranks, 182
Shakur, Tupac, 103, 109, 201n14
Sheller, Mimi, 51
  on commodified Black bodies, 68
  Consuming the Caribbean: From Arawaks to Zombies, 29
  on everyday politics of "inter-embodiments," 14
  on impact of mobility on Black bodies, 104
  on metropolitan culture, 69
Shine: The Visual Economy of Light in African Diasporic Aesthetic Practice (Thompson), 107, 160, 202n1 (chap. 6)
sistah lit
  definition of, 11, 48
  How Stella Got Her Groove Back as, 49–50
  romance narrative in, 58, 60
  See also How Stella Got Her Groove Back (McMillan)
Sizzla, 24–25
skin bleaching and skin lightening, 15–16, 94–95, 102–113, 134, 159–160, 201n15
slackness, 10, 18, 24, 44, 113
slavery, 3–4, 8, 72–76, 86, 97, 99, 111–113, 145, 160–161, 173
Slaves to Fashion (Miller), 99, 113, 160–161
Slimmaz, 103
Small Axe (McQueen; 2020), 188
A Small Place (Kincaid), 60, 199n4
Smith, Faith, 50
Smith, Ishawna Natalia. *See* Ishawna
Smith, Stephen A., 106
social justice, 107, 138, 158, 177, 185, 188
social media, 1, 134–135, 156–158, 177–178, 185, 187
social welfare programs, 28, 38
Something New (Hamri; 2006), 198n2
Sosa, Sammy, 105–107
sovereignty, 20, 29–30, 55, 73–75, 87
Sparta, Tommy Lee, 103
Spice, 18–19, 44–45, 128, 132–134, 175, 183
  "Black Hypocrisy," 18, 134
  collaborations, 175
  explanation of fake skin bleaching photo, 202n2 (chap. 5)
  featured in "Conjugal Visit," 132
  featured in "Romping Shop," 132
  "Like a Man," 132–133
  in *Love and Hip Hop: Atlanta*, 133–134
Spillers, Hortense, 124
Spivak, Gayatri, 62, 67, 70–71
Spragga Benz, 10, 39, 40–41, 44, 130
  "Cyan Get No Gyal," 38, 212
Stacious, 103
Stephens, Michelle, 22, 95–96, 181, 183
Stephens, Tanya, 127, 128, 137
stereotypes
  of African poverty, 63
  of Black men, 49, 85, 98, 99
  of Caribbean culture, 5, 141
  as counternarratives, 49
  fashion, Black academics, and, 99
  in film, 85
  imperialist, 62–63
  of Jamaican culture, 141
  of poverty, 50, 62–63, 72
  racism and, 85
  in sistah/chick/dick lit, 49, 62–63
  of sistah/chick/dick lit, 49

Straight Sex: Rethinking the Politics of Pleasure (Segal), 88, 92
strategic withholding, 61, 66–67, 70–71, 79
structural adjustment programs (SAPs), 11, 27
subaltern, 67, 101, 112
Sullivan, Kevin Rodney, 12
Super Cat, 36

Tambourine Army, 19, 135–137, 143, 175
tattoos, 109–111, 201n14
Thelwell, Michael, 117, 128, 136, 142, 165
"Third World," 14, 26, 33, 54, 61, 62
Thomas, Deborah, 130, 131, 143
  on dancehall culture, 126–127
  Exceptional Violence, 11
  on ghetto feminism, 126–127, 128, 137, 139
  on racial hierarchies, 31–32
  on respect and respectability, 11, 31–33
Thompson, Krista
  on "aesthetics of concealment," 21, 64, 107
  on "alternate image worlds," 7
  on "circuits of consumption," 17
  on excess, 167
  An Eye for the Tropics: Tourism, Photography, and Framing the Caribbean Picturesque, 7, 51
  on *Invisible Man* (Ellison), 167, 202n1 (chap. 6)
  on photography, 7
  on recognition, 199n8
  Shine: The Visual Economy of Light in African Diasporic Aesthetic Practice, 107, 160, 202n1 (chap. 6)
  on skin bleaching and media visibility, 107
  on transience in dress and style, 163
  on "visual economies," 51, 81
Thurman, Wallace, 114
Tinsley, Omise'eke Natasha, 94
Tosh, Peter, 19, 135–137, 141, 142
Touré, Kwame, 98–100
tourism and tourists, 4–7, 14–15, 17–18, 21, 35–36, 48, 51–53, 45–57, 60, 64, 70, 79–88, 115, 146, 175
translation
  cultural, 14, 34
  language, 14, 24, 25, 71
  mistranslation, 25, 34
transnationalism, 28, 33, 94, 199n5
trickster figures, 59, 87, 183, 196n5. *See also* anancyism
Trinidad and Tobago, 162–163, 168–173, 195n1, 197n8
  Alice Yard, 2–3, 168–171, 195n2
  Black Power movement in, 148
  Carnival, 2–4, 20, 168, 173
  education and print media in, 147
  history of, 20 136, 147–148
  humor and, 127
  Jamaat al Muslimeen coup attempt, 20
  labor riots in, 136
  "playing dead to catch corbeau (vulture) alive," 20
  patterns of consumption in, 163–164
  poverty in, 163–164
  sexual offense legislation in, 39–40
  See also Cozier, Christopher
tropes
  American exceptionalism, 114
  Caribbean Blackness, 6
  Caribbean paradise, 50, 62, 147
  Jamaica as signifier for Caribbean, 50–51
  neocolonial, 145
  New Negro movement, 114
  sex/sexuality as negotiation, 68
Tropical Night (Cozier), 20, 146–150
  Afro-Ophelia, 147–148, 149f
  see-through body, 148, 150f
"tun up," 104, 115, 117, 160, 162
Tweety Bird, 109
Tyrical, 103

Ulysse, Gina, 2, 31
United Fruit Company, 51–52

Verzuz (webcast series), 186–188
#Verzuz, 187–188
Victorianism, 4, 8, 55
visibility, 50, 96, 99, 106–108, 156–161, 164–170, 172–173
visual economies, 48, 51, 81. *See also* economies of desire
voudoun culture, 72–78, 87, 200n7
Vulgar Fraction, 2–3
vulgarity, 4, 9, 123, 179

Waiting in Vain (Channer), 199n5
Waiting to Exhale (Whitaker; 1995), 53

Walcott-Hackshaw, Elizabeth, 80
Wallace, Michelle, 96
West, Jerry, 100
West, Kanye, 112
whitelash, 95–96
Wide Sargasso Sea (Rhys), 144–145
Williams, Winford, 138, 177, 178–179, 182, 202n6, 203n2
withholding, strategic, 61, 66–67, 70–71, 79
womanhood, 48
Woman Version (O'Callaghan), 128
World Bank, 32
worlding, 61–62
  "First World," 14, 54, 62
  "Third World," 14, 26, 33, 54, 61, 62
world literature, 25–26
world music, 25–26

Young, Karen, 80
Young, Mallory, 48

zombies and zombification, 68, 78, 200n7

About the Author

PATRICIA JOAN SAUNDERS is associate professor of English at the University of Miami and senior co-editor of *Anthurium: A Caribbean Studies Journal*, an open-access, peer-reviewed journal. She is the author of *Alienation* and *Repatriation: Translating Identity in Anglophone Caribbean Literature* and coeditor of *Music. Memory. Resistance: Calypso and the Literary Imagination.*

Her work has appeared in the *Journal of West Indian Literature, Small Axe, Bucknell Review, Contemporary French and Francophone Studies,* and *Feminist Studies.*

Available titles in the Critical Caribbean Studies series:

Giselle Anatol, *The Things That Fly in the Night: Female Vampires in Literature of the Circum-Caribbean and African Diaspora*
Alaí Reyes-Santos, *Our Caribbean Kin: Race and Nation in the Neoliberal Antilles*
Milagros Ricourt, *The Dominican Racial Imaginary: Surveying the Landscape of Race and Nation in Hispaniola*
Katherine A. Zien, *Sovereign Acts: Performing Race, Space, and Belonging in Panama and the Canal Zone*
Frances R. Botkin, *Thieving Three-Fingered Jack: Transatlantic Tales of a Jamaican Outlaw, 1780–2015*
Melissa A. Johnson, *Becoming Creole: Nature and Race in Belize*
Carlos Garrido Castellano, *Beyond Representation in Contemporary Caribbean Art: Space, Politics, and the Public Sphere*
Njelle W. Hamilton, *Phonographic Memories: Popular Music and the Contemporary Caribbean Novel*
Lia T. Bascomb, *In Plenty and in Time of Need: Popular Culture and the Remapping of Barbadian Identity*
Aliyah Khan, *Far from Mecca: Globalizing the Muslim Caribbean*
Rafael Ocasio, *Race and Nation in Puerto Rican Folklore: Franz Boas and John Alden Mason in Porto Rico*
Ana-Maurine Lara, *Streetwalking: LGBTQ Lives and Protest in the Dominican Republic*
Anke Birkenmaier, ed., *Caribbean Migrations: The Legacies of Colonialism*
Sherina Feliciano-Santos, *A Contested Caribbean Indigeneity: Language, Social Practice, and Identity within Puerto Rican Taíno Activism*
H. Adlai Murdoch, ed., *The Struggle of Non-Sovereign Caribbean Territories: Neoliberalism since the French Antillean Uprisings of 2009*
Robert Fatton Jr., *The Guise of Exceptionalism: Unmasking the National Narratives of Haiti and the United States*
Rafael Ocasio, *Folk Stories from the Hills of Puerto Rico/Cuentos folklóricos de las montañas de Puerto Rico*
Yveline Alexis, *Haiti Fights Back: The Life and Legacy of Charlemagne Péralte*
Katerina Gonzalez Seligmann, *Writing the Caribbean in Magazine Time*
Jocelyn Fenton Stitt, *Dreams of Archives Unfolded: Absence and Caribbean Life Writing*
Alison Donnell, *Creolized Sexualities: Undoing Heteronormativity in the Literary Imagination of the Anglo-Caribbean*

Vincent Joos, *Urban Dwellings, Haitian Citizenships: Housing, Memory, and Daily Life in Haiti*
Krystal Nandini Ghisyawan, *Erotic Cartographies: Decolonization and the Queer Caribbean Imagination*
Yvon van der Pijl and Francio Guadeloupe, eds., *Equaliberty in the Dutch Caribbean: Ways of Being Non/Sovereign*
Patricia Joan Saunders, *Buyers Beware: Insurgency and Consumption in Caribbean Popular Culture*